SELF-MANAGEMENT: ECONOMIC THEORY AND YUGOSLAV PRACTICE

SOVIET AND EAST EUROPEAN STUDIES

Editorial Board

JULIAN COOPER, RON HILL,
MICHAEL KASER, PAUL LEWIS, ALASTAIR MCAULEY,
MARTIN MCCAULEY, FRED SINGLETON

The National Association for Soviet and East European Studies exists for the purpose of promoting study and research on the social sciences as they relate to the Soviet Union and the countries of Eastern Europe. The Monograph Series is intended to promote the publication of works presenting substantial and original research in the economics, politics, sociology and modern history of the USSR and Eastern Europe.

SELF-MANAGEMENT: ECONOMIC THEORY AND YUGOSLAV PRACTICE

SAUL ESTRIN

CAMBRIDGE UNIVERSITY PRESS

CAMBRIDGE

LONDON NEW YORK NEW ROCHELLE

MELBOURNE SYDNEY

Harriet Irving Library
JAN 9 1986
University of New Brunswick

Published by the Press Syndicate of the University of Cambridge
The Pitt Building, Trumpington Street, Cambridge CB2 1RP
32 East 57th Street, New York, NY 10022, USA
296 Beaconsfield Parade, Middle Park, Melbourne 3206, Australia

© Cambridge University Press 1983

First published 1983

Printed in Great Britain at
the Pitman Press, Bath

Library of Congress catalogue card number: 83–5239

British Library Cataloguing in Publication Data

Estrin, Saul
Self-management: economic theory and Yugoslav
practice. – (Soviet and East European studies)
1. Employees representation in management – Yugoslavia
I. Title II. Series
658.3′152′09497 HD5660.Y8

ISBN 0 521 24497 8

Contents

PART 2 YUGOSLAV PRACTICE

Tables

Preface

In this book, I hope to outline some of the ways in which the Yugoslav economy has been influenced by the unique system of workers' self-management. Many radical thinkers have discussed such a system, normally in response to the perceived dehumanising and undemocratic aspects of industrial work. However, their ideas were for the most part abstract and impractical. The Yugoslavs have shown that democratic control of the workplace is feasible, and the next topic for research is to examine how the system has influenced peoples' behaviour. This could be approached in many ways and the emphasis here is economic. Even so, no prior knowledge of either self-management theory or the Yugoslav economy is assumed. Chapters 2 and 3 provide self-contained introductions to each area respectively. Hence, the study will hopefully be of interest to general students of workers' self-management as well as of Yugoslavia.

This book was developed out of my 1979 doctoral dissertation at Sussex University. I was motivated ultimately to write a book on the topic, even though some of the arguments had already appeared in academic journals, by the particular nature of the subject matter. Of course, descriptive material, however interesting, is generally ill-suited for publication in journals. More seriously, the subject matter is linked by common themes which would necessarily be lost in a series of shorter articles. The analytic and the applied work are both pointed in the same direction: to deduce and test hypotheses about the economic effects of self-management. Moreover, in a long piece of work one can bring out more clearly the crucial relationship between technical and institutional points. Though some elements of the study can stand alone, it is hoped that the book as a whole is stronger than the sum of its separate parts.

The work was finally written in the spring and summer of 1982, while I was visiting the Department of Economics at Cornell University. Since, for better or worse, it reflects the culmination to date of my thinking about Yugoslav self-management, the potential list of acknowledgements is voluminous. However, I shall limit myself here to thanking by name only a few of the most important contributors to my thinking. My intellectual debts for certain points are made clear in text. Moreover, I should stress at this point that although many people have helped me to develop those ideas, responsibility for the final outcome is entirely my own.

First and foremost, I would like to thank Geoff Heal who, as my DPhil. supervisor, helped me to draw what became the basic outlines of this book. Important comments and advice at that stage were also received from Hugh Wills, Peter Holmes and Peter Wagstaff. My understanding of self-management models has benefited significantly from discussions with John Bonin, Norman Ireland and Jan Svejnar, as well as members of the Program on Participation and Labor-Managed Systems at Cornell University. Turning to Yugoslavia, I have relied enormously on colleagues for explanation, interpretation and even translation of the more obtruse points. My thanks go particularly to David Dyker of Sussex University, who gave me access to all his records and notes and ironed out my most glaring misinterpretations of recent economic history. Also critical for my understanding were discussions with Will Bartlett, Branko Horvat, Miro Labus, Christopher Prout and Peter Wiles. The material was first outlined in this format for a course taught on the Economics of Participation and Labor Management at Cornell, and the critical input of those students is gratefully acknowledged. Especial thanks are also due to Cornell University for facilities, and to Stephen Smith for his invaluable comments on the manuscript. Finally, the initial reaction of the typists, Fiona Savory, Diana Horgan, Pat Paucke and Linda Majeroni, to my scrawl makes me suspect that this book could never have been produced in a system of genuine worker's self-management. My debt to them for anyway producing a neat final text is therefore enormous.

SAUL ESTRIN
Southampton University

1

Introduction

In this book we examine Yugoslav industrial organisation and allocative efficiency from the perspective of self-management theory. A large literature has grown up in recent years to analyse how firms will behave when the labour force plays the role of entrepreneur. However, few of the resulting hypotheses have been tested empirically. On the other hand, Yugoslavia has based its entire economic system on enterprise self-management, but there have been few empirical studies based on the relevant theory. This study is intended to fill this gap in the literature, analysing the Yugoslav economy with reference to the distinctive propositions of self-management theory.

The book has two parts, devoted respectively to deducing and testing hypotheses about the Yugoslav economy. In the first part, an abstract theoretical literature and a mass of institutional material is steered in the direction of empirical application. The relevant aspects of self-management theory are outlined in Chapter 2, and the Yugoslav economy is introduced in Chapter 3. Both chapters draw heavily on the existing literature, but the presentation in each is self-contained. Various issues in Yugoslav industrial organisation and resource allocation are explored in the second part of the book. Chapter 4 is concerned with changing market structure and Chapter 5 with income differentials and the pattern of industrial development. The general consistency between the empirical findings and our predictions is confirmed by estimating a formal model of income determination on Yugoslav data, with the results being reported in Chapter 6. Overall, our findings broadly confirm that self-management was affecting Yugoslav resource allocation in the predicted way between 1965 and 1974. Even so, we point out in Chapter 7 that our results can only be one element in an overall assessment of the system since the beneficial aspects of self-management have not been considered in the study.

Economic theory has shown that a competitive economy can sustain a Pareto efficient equilibrium under capitalism or self-management (Vanek, 1970; Drèze, 1976). Thus, self-management could only affect resource allocation in a competitive system by changing the shape of technology or of preference sets. In fact, it has been suggested that differences in internal organisation and incentives under self-management could alter production possibilities (see Vanek, 1970), and this view has motivated some empirical studies (see Balassa and Bertrand, 1970; Cable and Fitzroy, 1980). However, both the models and the empirical work are largely ad hoc at this stage, and the topic may anyway be of secondary interest in a relatively less developed economy such as Yugoslavia. On the other hand, much of the social and political work favouring the adoption of self-management (e.g. Vanek, 1971; Hunnius, Garson and Case, 1973; Zwerdling, 1979) has assumed that the satisfaction derived from a given allocation varies according to the allocative mechanism. Thus, state dependent utility functions are invoked to show that individuals would be happier under self-management for non-economic reasons. This approach also yields few empirically testable propositions about Yugoslavia at this stage. Therefore, we move outside the framework of competitive equilibrium in this study to consider whether the disequilibrium allocation will display any peculiar characteristics under self-management. In fact, the theory shows that labour market forces are weak in a self-managed system, which affects the course of adjustment to competitive equilibrium. Our empirical work comprises a search for these particular allocative inefficiencies on Yugoslav data.

To be more specific, self-management theory distinguishes co-operatives by their maximand; average earnings per worker. Such firms are assumed to pay out pure profits, the surplus of revenue over costs, to their worker-members as current income. In contrast to capitalist firms, which are normally modelled as choosing desired employment on the basis of market wages, self-managed firms are therefore seen as determining their own incomes as well as membership. In principle, the movement of workers between alternative uses ensures common wages for particular skill groups in other competitive systems. However, these labour market forces are inoperative under self-management because each firm has already chosen its own optimal labour demand point according to the enterprise specific demand and cost conditions, and is insensitive to further labour market pressures. It is the entry and exit of firms changing relative prices in product markets, or 'general equilibrium effects', which ultimately drive the system to an efficient allocation. Producers enter markets where earnings include an element of pure profit and depart from those where they include pure losses until an equilibrium price vector emerges which sustains equal incomes in different uses. In the interim, resource allocation will be distinguished by inter-firm income differentials and inefficiency in the choice of production techniques. More generally, allocative inefficiencies from whatever source, including for example product market imperfections, will always be reflected in a misallocation of labour under self-management. These issues are addressed more formally in Chapter 2, with the exposition being primarily geometric, and mathematical reasoning being largely confined to the appendix to the chapter.

The Yugoslav economy and the operation of the various allocative systems are described in Chapter 3. Our intention is to summarise the historical and institutional material relevant for our study, as well as to specify estimation periods. The complexity of the Yugoslav economy cautions against an excessively strict interpretation of our equilibrium propositions from the theory, and the information provided in this chapter is used throughout the second part of the book to help explain our empirical findings. We also divide post-war Yugoslav economic history into a number of periods, each representing the duration of a particular formalised allocative mechanism. Market self-management, to which our models apply, is argued to have only been operational between 1965 and 1974. Thus, much of the empirical work is devoted to analysing resource allocation in this period, and testing whether various Yugoslav indicators altered in the predicted manner around 1965.

Chapter 4 is about the Yugoslav industrial structure, and provides something of a link between the two parts of the book, offering further descriptive material as well as some preliminary evidence on the relevance of the theory. We establish that Yugoslav product markets were severely non-competitive, which leads us to stress market structure in the remainder of the study. We also specify the changing industrial structure from 1956 to 1974, and examine what determines enterprise entry and exit. Self-management theory attaches considerable significance to these findings since they determine the extent and effectiveness of general equilibrium pressures in the system. Finally, we investigate whether one can observe the predicted associations between changing firm numbers, industrial concentration and average earnings. One would like to use our information to investigate the relationship between self-management and industrial structure as well,[1] but Chapter 3 indicates that one could not adequately abstract from the effects of underdevelopment and planning.

Chapter 5 describes our empirical work on the allocative consequences of self-management in Yugoslavia. We examine various facets of labour market misallocation including income differentials, the choice of technique, wage and employment patterns and the changing structure of industrial growth. Our general method is to examine the Yugoslav allocation of labour from as many angles as possible to strengthen any conclusions drawn. The findings are broadly consistent with predictions, with the most striking results concerning income differentials in the self-management era and the choice of more capital-intensive techniques after 1965. However, it is important to note that consistency with predictions cannot be interpreted as 'proof' of the theory. There could be other explanations of the findings, some of which are discussed in Chapters 2 and 3. The descriptive statistics of Chapter 5 only indicate the scale of allocative problems which one might attribute to self-management if the relevance of the theory had already been accepted.

The desire to establish something firmer than this leads us to test the explanatory power of the models in Chapter 6. On the basis of the discussion in Chapter 2, earnings equations are derived as the reduced form of the cooperative optimisation problem. The formulation nests various hypotheses from the theory and is estimated on cross-section data for each year of the self-management era as well as over the whole period. Numerous estimation procedures establish a robust and significant relationship between average earnings, demand side factors such as relative market power, supply side factors such as technical efficiency and scale, and input costs. The chapter shows that self-management models provide a very good explanation of Yugoslav income dispersion after 1965, and one which is significantly better than these offered elsewhere in the literature (e.g. Vanek and Jovicic, 1975).

We conclude this chapter by considering some of the more important limitations of our study. In the first place, we use a very narrow interpretation of self-management theory, restricting ourselves to the particular branch of the subject in the tradition of Ward (1958), Vanek (1970) and Meade (1972). This assumes cooperatives to be income maximising in a certain environment, and limits the analysis to issues of static allocative efficiency. In fact, numerous more sophisticated models and alternative frameworks are beginning to appear in the literature, referring to questions of welfare maximisation, dynamics and uncertainty (see Bonin, 1980; Sapir 1980b; Ireland and Law, 1982). However, these have not yet yielded significant numbers of testable propositions about the operation of the system as a whole. Therefore we must base our work on the simpler textbook models for which the implications are at least fully specified, in the hope that our findings will encourage further theoretical work. Moreover, given the paucity of empirical results on the effects of self-management, one may wish to commence research with the simplest available propositions.

A second limitation is that we will only consider other interpretations of Yugoslav behaviour in so far as they have a bearing on the predicted effects of self-management. Thus, we never focus directly on such critical issues of Yugoslav economic history as the pattern of development and capital accumulation or the effects of regional disparities, except as factors specifying the environment in which self-managed firms operate. The advantage of this approach is that we can deduce very specific answers to the narrow questions at issue, but there is no doubt that breadth of coverage has been sacrificed for analytic precision. In consequence, our study cannot provide a balanced overall description of the post-war Yugoslav economy.

These methodological points can be clarified by considering how we deal with the most important alternative explanation of Yugoslav allocative inefficiencies: capital market imperfections. Yugoslavia has developed a special property rights system for capital, which excludes many of the more conventional elements of ownership. Moreover, the country's capital markets are thin and severely imperfect, with interest rates regulated at well below the scarcity value of capital which causes rationing (see World Bank, 1975). These facts have motivated the development of two relatively distinct models associating general allocative problems with capital market imperfections. One approaches the issue from the perspective of property rights (e.g. Furubotn and Pejovich, 1970, 1972) and the other regards the problem as an institutional or a structural defect of the Yugoslav system (e.g. Vanek, 1973). Our analysis precludes any direct consideration of propositions from the former approach, and treats the latter as determining one element of the Yugoslav environment.

Furubotn and Pejovich (1970) point out that Yugoslav property rights in capital are severely restricted. Cooperative members can use the capital stock as they wish, but they cannot sell it, nor recover from it any investments they have made during their association with the company. Moreover, the book values of the assets must be maintained by appropriate depreciation. It is argued that these arrangements will lead Yugoslav firms to invest less than their capitalist counterparts or even than cooperatives which rented all their capital stock, and to rely relatively more on external than internally generated funds. The argument hinges on the members' inability to recoup their principal which raises the implicit cost of funding investment internally. However, although this approach does generate empirically testable propositions, our focus on issues of static resource allocation precludes them from consideration in this study. It is not clear how restrictive this omission is, since the property rights analysis has been questioned both theoretically and empirically (see Stephen, 1978, 1979, 1980; Tyson, 1977a). Indeed, the model is not really concerned with the effects of self-management at all, but rather the consequences of a particular legal constraint on private Yugoslav choices. The organisation and performance of cooperative enclaves such as Israeli Kibbutz's or the Mondragon group (see Barkai, 1977; Thomas and Logan, 1982) argues against any straightforward link between property rights and self-management itself. In consequence, it may not be too misleading to treat the property rights system as an exogenous element of the Yugoslav environment.

A second school of thought, best represented by the later works of Vanek (1975, 1977), stresses the widespread consequences of Yugoslav capital market imperfections. Some analysts go so far as to suggest that most Yugoslav allocative problems can be attributed to capital shortages, inefficient rationing procedures and low or negative real interest rates.[2] A considerable empirical literature has emerged to measure the scale of capital misallocation (see World

Bank, 1975; Miovic, 1975) and relate it to other allocative problems such as income differentials (see Vanek and Jovicic, 1975).[3] Our approach is to treat these imperfections as characteristic of Yugoslav institutional structure. The aim is then to isolate significant phenomena in the Yugoslav economy which can be attributed to self-management, even when all other sources of allocative inefficiency have been taken into account. Unfortunately, there are still sometimes identification problems because allocative inefficiencies in different factor markets tend to be closely associated. However, it is hoped that our robust and detailed picture of inter-related labour and product market inefficiences provides a sufficient case for the influence of self-management forces on the Yugoslav allocation of resources.

PART I

ECONOMIC THEORY

2

The theory of a self-managed economy

2.1 ASSUMPTIONS AND DEFINITIONS

In this chapter, we briefly survey the relevant literature on resource allocation under market self-management. Particular stress is placed on the configurations of variables for which Yugoslav data are readily available, and on the functional forms appropriate for model estimation. We develop the analysis from first principles so the treatment of the material is self-contained and no prior knowledge of the literature is required. However, our interest is restricted to income maximising models along the lines of Ward (1958), Vanek (1970) and Meade (1972), and readers who wish to approach the subject from other perspectives are referred to Jones and Svejnar (1982) and Ireland and Law (1982).

There are five sections in the chapter, with the remainder of this one devoted to outlining our definitions, assumptions and notation. The following section is micro-economic, analysing cooperative decision-making under perfect competition. It shows how shifting control from private entrepreneurs to the labour force influences factor demand and the choice of equilibrium production technique and output. Decisions at the micro-economic level are brought together in the third section for a description of system-wide resource allocation under competitive self-management. We also compare the modes of adjustment to efficient general equilibria under self-management and capitalism, highlighting the relative weakness of labour market forces in the former system. The effects of monopoly power under self-management are the subject of the fourth section, which explains the link between product and labour market misallocation. Our empirically testable hypotheses are summarised in the final section.

From a theoretical perspective, a self-managed firm can be defined as a production unit in which the labour force as a whole takes all the economic decisions through some democratic process.[1] This group, which will henceforth be referred to as the collective, assumes the entrepreneurial role, and in return for bearing this organisational function and risk, receives the surplus of revenue over cost which is distributed among the group according to some pre-arranged mechanism. We will generally assume that the labour force is homogeneous and has agreed to distribute the surplus, or pure profit, equally amongst the membership.[2] The collective is also assumed to have borrowed the entire capital stock, for which it is paying a market determined interest rate. Thus, the case of worker-owned firms which typifies Western experiments with cooperatives is not considered.[3] In the self-managed system, labour hires capital rather than capital hiring labour or an entrepreneur hiring both factors. For the economic analyst, the main differences between such firms and their capitalist counterparts arise from the assumed objective of the organisation – to maximise average earnings per head rather than profits, or any of the other possible objectives discussed in the literature (e.g. Scherer, 1980). This maximand was first proposed in Ward's seminal paper (1958), and was strongly justified as a first approximation by Vanek (1971), who pointed out that the membership would always prefer outcomes with higher incomes to those with lower ones. The case for income maximisation is straightforward. In their simple models, industrial economists always assume that entrepreneurial groups maximise the residual per member. But since the surplus is assumed to be invariant with respect to the membership of the group in capitalist firms, the objective can be reduced to simple profits. However, under self-management the labour force undertakes the entrepreneurial role, and the quantity produced varies with the size of the entrepreneurial group, so this simplification is no longer possible. The identification of the entrepreneurial role with that of a productive factor requires that the objective remains the surplus per entrepreneur, or average earnings per head.

However, the assumption of income maximisation severely restricts the questions which can be considered. We can certainly construct enterprise and general equilibrium models comparable with the textbook descriptions of competitive capitalism, but many proponents of self-management would argue that this misses the most essential characteristics of the system. They propose instead a utility maximising framework in which the alleged advantages of cooperatives with respect to worker satisfaction, employment security and collective consumption could be modelled (see Vanek, 1970, 1971; Jan Vanek, 1972). Such models do yield some interesting and important insights into behaviour under self-management (see Law, 1977; Berman, 1977; Smith, 1982), but do not yet generate many testable hypotheses about the behaviour of the system as a whole. The findings are generally enterprise specific and often depend on assumptions about the arguments and form of the utility function. Moreover, for our limited purposes the loss of generality may not be too serious since the models normally have the same results as income maximising ones for the set of variables analysed by both if income enters the utility function.[4] Rather, they generate new propositions about a wider range of variables, for which Yugoslav data are not generally available. Thus, in sticking with income maximising models, we narrow the range of our inquiry and exclude from consideration the numerous alleged benefits of self-management. This necessarily restricts the generality of the conclusions which can be drawn.

We have asserted that the collective must exert its control over economic decisions through a 'democratic process', but this has been left deliberately vague. We may wish to follow opponents of the self-management system (e.g. Coyne, Chiplin and Sirc, 1977) in pointing out that such a mechanism could be seriously inefficient in practice if internal dissension slows or prevents rational economic choices. There is also the potential for a social choice approach, analysing the consequences for enterprise decisions and resource allocation of alternative social choice rules to aggregate from individual members to an entrepreneurial group preference set (see Sen, 1966, for a development of these ideas). It is likely that impossibility theorems for aggregating from private to social choices of the sort developed by Arrow (1963) are just as relevant within each individual self-managed firm. We avoid this problem by drawing on the Yugoslav division of authority between executive and policy-making powers.[5] Our model is consistent with the following institutional arrangements. In the first instance, each member is assumed to be identical in that they desire the cooperative to maximise the same objective function – average earnings per head. The collective appoints a director who is given completely autonomous powers to execute this policy, subject to dismissal for failure. The labour force has exercised its control of the enterprise by determining the maximand, but the firm is actually run in precisely the same way as its capitalist counterpart. This approach could also be appropriate for studying social choices, or internal dissension if preferences were not identical, within a utility maximising framework. Our description of enterprise self-management is more closely akin to models of representative democracy than the more participative notions implicit in much of the cooperative literature.

Turning to the formal assumptions and notation, self-managed firms choose levels of output (denoted q), membership or employment (denoted L) and capital stock (denoted K and evaluated in financial terms) in order to maximise average earnings per head (denoted y). It will be assumed that each firm produces only one output using two inputs, since this considerably simplifies the exposition and permits geometric representation of the results. However, extensions to the case of multiple inputs and outputs are analytically straightforward, and have been considered in Domar (1966) and Vanek (1970).[6] The technically efficient feasible combination of inputs and outputs, will be represented by a production function ($q = f(L, K)$), which is assumed to have continuous first and second order derivatives and to be locally concave around the equilibrium.[7] The following section models cooperative decisions on the assumption that they produce for competitive output markets. By this, we mean that the firm is sufficiently small for its choices not to affect the market outcome, so that it is a price-taker. At the system level, the assumption of competitiveness is also taken to imply that prices (denoted p) are set to clear markets. Enterprises operating in imperfectly competitive product markets are assumed to be sufficiently large for their output decisions to influence price, although they are assumed to know their own product demand curve ($p = p(q, \Delta)$, where Δ is a shift parameter; $\partial p/\partial \Delta > 0$). Individual cooperatives are always assumed to lack monopsony power on the capital market, and therefore face an exogenously determined interest rate (r). However, we do not necessarily assume that interest rates are set in order to clear financial capital markets, nor even that different firms are necessarily required to pay the same interest rate for their capital stock.

There is no labour market in a self-managed economy because each cooperative chooses its own level of earnings and labour

Table 2.1. *Notation*

y = average earnings per head
p = product price
r = rate of interest
q = output
L = employment (membership of cooperative)
K = capital
$q = f(L, K)$ = production function
$p = p(q, \Delta)$ = demand function
f_L = marginal product of labour, etc.
$\lambda = \lambda(q, L)$ = returns to scale function
$\lambda_{\hat{q}}$ = how returns to scale vary with output along a ray in capital–labour space
λ_L = how returns to scale vary with employment at a fixed level of output
λ_q = how returns to scale vary with output at a fixed level of employment
π = profits
w = market wages under capitalism
$C(q)$ = cost function
Superscript m denotes monopoly
Superscript c denotes capitalist
$*$ = equilibrium value
E = ratio of price to marginal revenue

demand, subject only to the constraints set by production technology and the economic environment. However, it will be convenient to assume a single labour type and equal distribution of the surplus among the membership for reasons discussed above. Moreover, many of our results will be compared with the findings under capitalism, so an appropriate basis for comparison must be defined. Enterprises will be referred to as 'comparable' or 'counterparts' when their common set of parameters are identical. Thus, a competitive capitalist firm which maximises profits (denoted π), equal to revenue (pq) minus costs (denoted $C = C(q)$) including the hiring of a labour force at the market wage (w), is comparable to its self-managed counterpart when the product price, interest rate and production function are the same in either system, although average earnings would not necessarily equal wages. Incidentally, it is irrelevant whether average earnings are defined as net value added per member $(pq - rK)/L$ or in terms of deviations from a notional market wage $(w + \pi/L)$.[8] Equilibrium values will be denoted by a star (*), and derivatives by the appropriate subscript to the original function.[9] Table 2.1 summarises the notation employed in the remainder of the book.

2.2 DECISION-MAKING IN THE COMPETITIVE SELF-MANAGED FIRM

2.2.1 *The general problem and short-run analysis*

The general optimisation problem for the competitive self-managed firm takes the following form.

Given p, r,

$$\underset{q,\,L,\,K}{\text{maximise}} \quad y = \frac{pq - rK}{L}, \tag{2.1}$$

$$\text{subject to} \quad q = f(L, K), \tag{2.2}$$

with first order conditions

$$y = pf_L, \tag{2.3}$$

$$r = pf_K. \tag{2.4}$$

The second order conditions are satisfied by local concavity of the production function, and are the same as those for a capitalist firm, but the first order conditions are surprising. Equation (2.4) states that capital (or any other non-labour input if we generalise the problem to the case of multiple inputs) should be hired until its marginal value product equals its parametric price. Equation (2.3) appears at first sight to be the same as the labour hiring rule under capitalism, requiring the collective to add members until the marginal value product of the last recruit equals his income. However, while wages, like every other factor price, are parametric under capitalism, average earnings are a choice variable for the cooperative. In fact, the membership rule under self-management is to increase the collective only when this raises everyones' incomes, but the maximum actually occurs where earnings equal the marginal product of labour. Looking at it another way, cooperatives will increase employment when the new member would add more to revenue than cost per head. Denoting revenue per head by R $(= pq/L)$ and costs per head by F $(= rK/L)$, the collective adds to the membership until $\partial R/\partial L = \partial F/\partial L$. A rearrangement of terms reveals that the slopes of the revenue and cost per head functions happen to be equal at the point where earnings equal the value marginal product of labour.[10] Thus, equation (2.3) may appear to be the same as the equivalent condition under capitalism, but it actually has a very different interpretation. The profit maximising firm hires labour until its value marginal product equals exogenous market wages, and parametric shifts only affect the former variable. Under self-management, recruitment occurs to maximise earnings and ceases where these equal the value marginal product, but changes in parameters affect both sides of the equation. The effective 'cost of labour' is an endogenous variable, dependent on both the level of employment and the values of the full set of parameters to the optimisation problem.

The remainder of this sub-section considers cooperative decision-making in the short-run; an analytic 'period' in which the capital stock is assumed to be fixed ($\bar{K}$) so production changes must result from adjustments to the membership. In terms of the general problem of equations (2.1)–(2.4) above, the assumption of a fixed capital stock means that we can truncate the system by dropping equation (2.4), and the production function becomes:

$$q = f(L, \bar{K}). \tag{2.2a}$$

The cooperative solves this system (equations (2.1), (2.2a), (2.3)) for equilibrium values of output and membership, and the short-run equilibria and comparative statics can be represented with two diagrams. Diagram 2.1 describes the equilibrium choice of employment (and therefore implicitly output through the short-run production function (2.2a)) and earnings in terms of revenue and fixed cost functions. In value-employment space, the cooperative chooses the labour input where the slope from the intersection of fixed cost function ($r\bar{K}$) on the vertical axis to the revenue function ($pq = pf(L, \bar{K})$) is maximised. The slope from the intersection to any point on the revenue function is average earnings for that level of employment, which the cooperative is seeking to maximise (for example, at L^*, AL^* is revenue and AB is revenue net of fixed costs so y^* is the level of earnings). In equilibrium, earnings equal the value marginal product of labour, or the slope of the revenue function.

Diagram 2.2 directly plots the cooperative earnings function in value-employment space, which can be used for comparisons with capitalist behaviour. The self-managed firm chooses the combination (y^*, L^*) to maximise incomes, and the value marginal product function passes through the maximum income from above. A

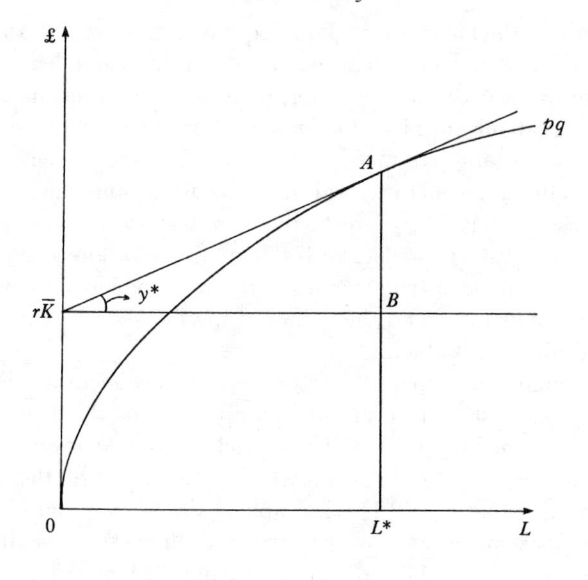

Diagram 2.1

comparable capitalist firm hires labour until its marginal product equals parametric wages, which allows us to examine the relationship between cooperative earnings, capitalist wages and profits, as well as to compare employment and output decisions in each system. The two enterprise forms, if comparable, make precisely the same short-run production choices if wages equal earnings (i.e. $L^* = L_2$ if $w_2 = y^*$). This is the case when the capitalist firm is earning zero pure profits,[11] and underlies the result in the literature that the introduction of self-management into a fully competitive capitalist economy will not affect resource allocation or income distribution (see Pearce, 1977). If wages exceed maximum average earnings, when the capitalist enterprise is operating at a loss, the cooperative produces a relatively greater output with a larger labour force ($L_1 < L^*$ when $w_1 > y^*$ or $\pi < 0$). On the other hand, if self-management is introduced into a profitable capitalist firm ($w_3 < y^*$ or $\pi > 0$), the cooperative produces a relatively smaller output with fewer workers ($L_3 > L^*$). This finding has led some authors to stress the employment-creating role for cooperatives in declining industries (see Clayre, 1980).

As can be seen from Diagram 2.1, the cooperative will alter

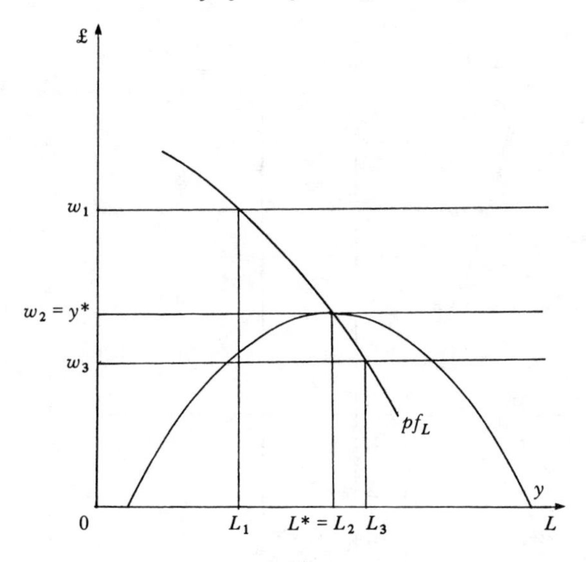

Diagram 2.2

membership and output in the short run in response to any event which changes either the revenue or the fixed cost functions. The revenue function will be shifted upward by either an increase in product price or technical advance which increases output for each labour input, while the fixed cost function will vary according to the rate of interest. Diagram 2.3 describes the short-run comparative statics. It can be seen that under self-management any upward (downward) shift in revenue function or reduction (increase) in the interest rate leads the cooperative to reduce (increase) equilibrium membership and output in order to raise average earnings. Thus, self-managed firms are predicted to reduce production in the short run when product price (and therefore market demand) increases, capital costs decline or there is technical advance. These results are striking, counter-intuitive and have no counterpart: under a capitalism the supply function is upward sloping, the production response to technical progress is generally positive, and short-run decisions are independent of capital costs. For example, an increase in price raises the value marginal product of labour relative to the exogenous market wage of a profit maximising firm, which therefore hires additional workers. Under self-management, an increase in price

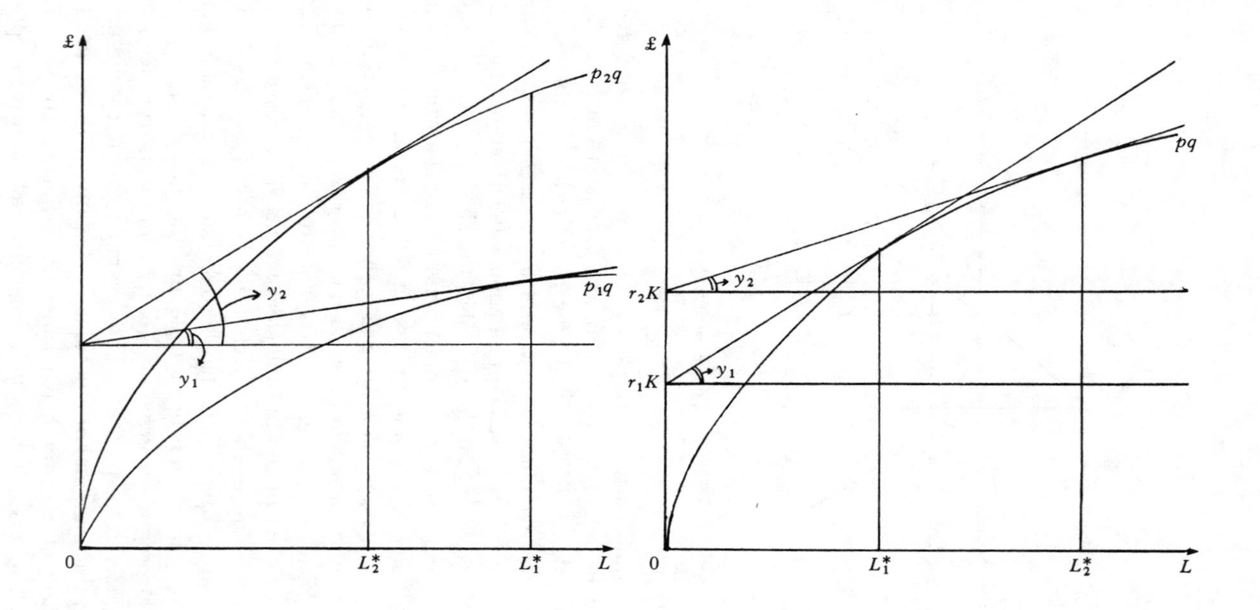

Diagram 2.3. A change in the revenue function and a change in fixed costs

raises earnings more than the marginal product, so cooperatives respond in the opposite way to capitalist firms. This is because, given diminishing returns to a factor, the marginal product of labour is always exceeded by the average product. This can be seen by comparing value of earnings and the slope of the revenue function after the shift in parameters at the initial level of employment (L_1^*) in Diagram 2.3. Further insight can be gained by an intuitive description of the equilibrium and responses. The average revenue per head of the cooperative will increase as the membership declines because of diminishing returns to labour so the enterprise would seek to become as small as possible without the constraint of fixed costs. These force the cooperative to larger membership because per capita they are inversely related to employment. Any equilibrium must reflect a balance between these forces; where the marginal gain to the collective, in terms of revenue per head, of reducing membership exactly balances the marginal loss in terms of fixed costs per head. Technical advance or an increase in product price does not affect the marginal loss from reducing membership, but increases the marginal benefit by raising revenue per capita at each level of employment. Thus, the relaxation of the constraint leads the cooperative to reduce membership, and therefore production, in order to raise average earnings. Similarly, an increase in the interest rate raises the marginal loss to the collective of reducing membership while leaving the marginal benefit unchanged, so the cooperative chooses to increase employment and output.[12]

These results are the best known in the literature, and have motivated significant further research (see Ireland and Law, 1982, for a summary). In addition to the direct predictions, they also imply that a self-managed system will be unable to transmit the correct signals between consumers and producers in the short run. Increases in the relative scarcity of a commodity actually signal suppliers to reduce their production of it, generating allocative inefficiency. They also raise the possibility that markets will be unable to reach or sustain equilibria under self-management, depending on the relative elasticity of demand and supply functions.

Thus the short-run framework offers a plethora of findings, and might appear to provide an obvious basis for empirical work on Yugoslav self-management, oriented towards the estimation of supply elasticities and labour demand functions. However, much of the literature has been dissatisfied with the approach and particularly the deduction that collectives would lay off members to raise the incomes of those who remained. Many authors have tried to reverse the results, generally by imposing additional restrictions on the problem[13] or rejecting the purely material maximand in favour of a broader utility function.[14] For reasons discussed in the next section, our own study is not based on the short-run framework, which is considered to offer few insights of practical relevance for the Yugoslav environment.[15] Instead, we employ deductions from long-run models which, as the next section shows, provide unambiguous propositions about incomes and the choice of technique independent from assumptions about supply elasticities. These hypotheses are associated with more general issues of resource allocation in the later sections of the chapter. Therefore, this discussion has been for the most part at a tangent to our main purpose and was mainly included for completeness. The only short-run results which carry through to the long run and the system levels pertain to the way that enterprise incomes vary according to demand and cost conditions.

2.2.2 *Long-run analysis under competitive self-management*

This sub-section examines cooperative decision-making when all inputs are variable. The main innovation will be to establish that the full optimisation problem (equations (2.1)–(2.4) above) can be reformulated to generate tractable comparative static results which differ from those under capitalism.[16] Moreover, the sensitivity of output results to technical assumptions highlights the critical role that the shape of technology will play in specifying our estimating equations. The findings provide the micro-economic basis for our empirical work. The literature has gone little further than deriving complex expressions for the comparative statics of the long-run optimisation problem, which have ambiguous signs and limited economic interpretation.[17] However, the system can be respecified in terms of a returns to scale function which drives the comparative statics. Substituting equations (2.3) and (2.4) into (2.1) and re-arranging terms;

$$\frac{Lf_L + Kf_K}{q} = 1. \tag{2.5}$$

Starrett (1977) defines returns to scale, denoted λ, as the elasticity of output with respect to all inputs or, in the two-factor case:

$$\lambda = \lambda(q, L) = \frac{Lf_L + Kf_K}{q} \qquad (2.6)^{18}$$

so that equation (2.5) can be rewritten as:

$$\lambda^* = 1. \qquad (2.7)$$

Thus, self-managed firms can only satisfy the first order conditions simultaneously when production technology displays constant returns because the total product must be entirely exhausted by paying factors their marginal products. The fact that an equilibrium will only exist if the production function displays increasing returns in the output range below equilibrium explains the earlier assumption of only local concavity to satisfy the second order conditions. Indeed, cooperatives will only have a unique optimal level of production if returns to scale decline monotonically with output along a ray in capital–labour space from an initial value exceeding unity (i.e. $\lambda(0) > 1$, $\lambda_{\hat{q}} < 0$).

Replacing equation (2.3) by (2.7) allows us to consider the cooperative optimisation problem in terms of the parameters of the returns to scale function, and thereby to derive tractable comparative static results in terms of variables which can be readily estimated. Totally differentiating and rearranging terms, we can show that:

$$\frac{\partial (K/L)^*}{\partial p} > 0, \quad \frac{\partial (K/L)^*}{\partial r} < 0, \qquad (2.8)$$

$$\frac{\partial y^*}{\partial p} > 0, \quad \frac{\partial y^*}{\partial r} < 0, \qquad (2.9)$$

$$\frac{\partial q^*}{\partial p} = \frac{-f_K^2 q}{pLH} \lambda_L \gtrless 0 \text{ as } \lambda_L \lessgtr 0, \qquad (2.10)$$

$$\frac{\partial q^*}{\partial r} = \frac{f_K q}{pLH} \lambda_L \gtrless 0 \text{ as } \lambda_L \gtrless 0,$$

where H, the determinant of the Hessian matrix, is assumed to be positive to satisfy the second order conditions. The results in equation (2.9) are unambiguous, and establish that the short-run association between cost or demand conditions and average earnings continues to hold in the long run.[19] Moreover, there is a similar unambiguous relationship between the choice of technique and the price parameters, which is entirely independent of technological assumptions though the direction of the separate input responses actually depends on the sign of λ_q (see the Appendix for further exposition of this point). Thus, the remainder of this study concentrates on income and choice of technique functions rather than the separate input demand equations, the comparative statics of which depend on the shape of technology. It is particularly interesting to note that the capital–labour ratio is always an increasing function of product price under self-management, which is not always the case under capitalism.[20] Finally, equation (2.10) reveals that the direction of the long-run output responses depends solely on a derivative of the returns to scale function; λ_L, which describes how returns to scale vary around the equilibrium isoquant. This occurs because the output responses are driven by the need to satisfy the returns to scale constraint, and means that an appropriate specification of the production function will allow us to focus on earnings and the capital–labour ratios without considering long-run supply curves.

One can provide an intuitive interpretation of these results with the aid of Diagram 2.4 below, which represents long-run cooperative adjustment in terms of factor substitution and scale effects analogous to the substitution and income effects of demand analysis.

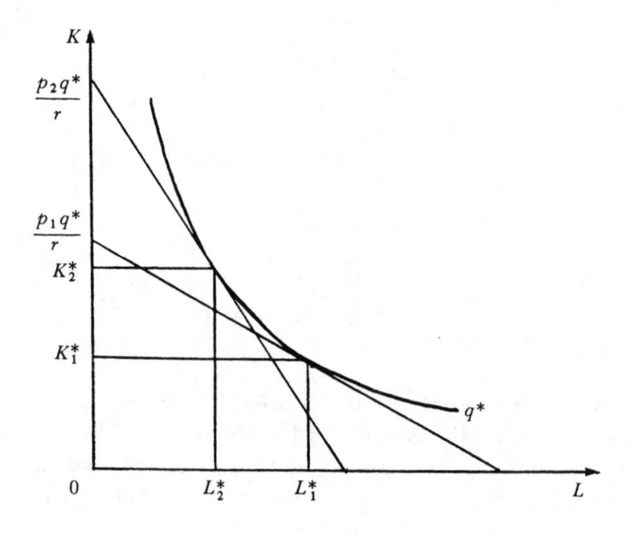

Diagram 2.4

Consider the response to an increase in product price from a unique equilibrium, on the initial assumptions that returns to scale do not vary with factor proportions (i.e. $\lambda(0)>0$, $\lambda_{\hat{q}}<0$, $\lambda_L=0$). The cooperative is assumed to have chosen its unique equilibrium output (q^*) to ensure that returns to scale equal unity, which gives us the isoquant q^* in Diagram 2.4. The capital–labour ratio and earnings are then chosen simultaneously with reference to an 'isocost' line derived from equation (2.1). This relationship between capital and membership, given the parameters and any chosen level of average earnings, is mapped by:

$$K=\frac{pq}{r}-\frac{yL}{r}. \tag{2.11}$$

The collective chooses factor proportions (K_1^*, L_1^*) around the isoquant q^* in order to maximise the slope of the isocost curve from the exogenously determined intercept with the capital axis (pq^*/r), which occurs at the tangency from the intercept to the isoquant. Thus, any technical assumptions which would generate a unique equilibrium permit us to separate the choice of equilibrium output from the simultaneous decision about factor proportions and average earnings.

An increase in product price to p_2 shifts the intercept of the isocost curve with the firm substituting capital for labour around q^* until (K_2^*, L_2^*). The 'factor substitution' effect means that the capital–labour ratio and earnings are always positively related to product price (and inversely related to the rate of interest). The change in desired factor proportions has been assumed not to affect returns to scale, so equilibrium will not be adjusted at all; there is no 'scale effect' when $\lambda_L=0$. However, if we permit returns to scale to vary around the equilibrium isoquant, the direction of the output response depends on how factor substitution influences returns to scale at the initial equilibrium. If $\lambda_L<0$, the reduction in desired membership at the initial level of production increases returns to scale above unity, so production must be increased to restore constant returns. Conversely, the scale effect will be negative if $\lambda_L>0$ because the change in desired factor proportions will reduce returns to scale at q^* so output must be reduced to satisfy the returns to scale constraint (see Estrin, 1982a, for further details).

These results have important implications for any empirical or econometric work on the behaviour of self-managed firms. In the first place, we have to assume that technology has a shape which satisfies the conditions for an existence of an equilibrium, that is, convexity in the range below equilibrium output. This means ruling out any homogeneous production function, such as the Cobb-Douglas form, in the competitive case since returns to scale do not vary with output.[21] To find the technical assumptions which will allow us to test our results about income and choice of technique dispersion without entering the tangled web of supply elasticity, we need to know how parameters of the returns to scale function influence the shape of the production function. The most important point is that returns to scale do not vary with factor proportions if production functions are homogeneous or homothetic. Homogeneity implies that $\lambda_L = 0$ because the distance between isoquants could not be constant or alter at a constant rate along every ray from the origin and simultaneously be different at each level of employment around an isoquant. Homothetic production functions have factor marginal products declining at the same rate along each ray in capital–labour space so λ_L, which measures the difference in their rates of decline, must equal zero.[22] Neither description of production technology has been regarded as excessively restrictive for empirical work about capitalist behaviour. However, the assumption of homogeneity is ruled out if we wish determinate equilibria to exist under self-management. Therefore, the econometric work in Chapter 6 will be based on a homothetic production function which allows us to analyse income and factor proportion responses in the context of perfectly inelastic long-run supply curves.[23]

The fact that supply responses are determined solely by the shape of technology while all the other enterprise choices depend on the set of parameters allows us to highlight the different ways that cooperatives and their capitalist counterparts adjust to demand or cost changes. If we assume that production technology is homothetic and each enterprise type is initially in full market equilibrium (i.e. $\pi^* = 0$ so $w = y^*$ and all choices are identical), an increase in product price leads the capitalist firm to raise production but leaves the desired capital–labour ratio unchanged. In comparison, its self-managed counterpart would substitute capital for labour to raise average earnings, but would not alter the level of production. General equilibrium effects are required under capitalism to ensure a socially efficient level of output, but will not influence factor markets and the choice of technique if relative input costs are exogenous to the firm. The level of production by each individual cooperative will always be socially efficient because each firm always produces at minimum efficient scale. Even so, the market supply curve is perfectly inelastic in the long run so entry or exit may be required to get overall production right. On the other hand, general equilibrium pressures are always required under self-management to bring about social efficiency in the private choice of technique and to ensure that labour value marginal products and incomes are equal in different uses. These allocative differences are explored in more detail in the following section.

However, before proceeding we must justify the use of a long-run framework in our empirical work. The main reason is that these planning models offer unambiguous predictions about observable variables without any problems of identification or interpretation. The essence of the method outlined above is that income and choice of technique functions can be separated out from the rest of the enterprise optimisation problem. Thus, these important variables can be analysed independently of the more ambiguous supply side. Moreover, the long-run models have important allocative corollaries for the system as a whole, especially when general equilibrium effects are relatively weak as is the case in Yugoslavia (see Chapter 4). These arguments are strengthened by considering the options available using the main alternative approach: short-run models. As we have seen, these point attention to perverse employment and supply functions which may be harder to identify empirically. Moreover, the implications of the models may actually be misleading in this case. Industrial economists have normally divided enterprise adjustment into the short and long run to reflect the relatively greater variability of employment than capital under capitalism. However, this assumption may not be valid under self-management, because the required adjustments personally affect the decision-making group. This is not to argue that cooperative membership should be treated as invariant, but that it should not be regarded as relatively more flexible than the capital stock. One may never therefore observe perverse supply responses in practice.

2.3 GENERAL EQUILIBRIUM EFFECTS

Vanek (1970) and Drèze (1974, 1976) have shown that a competitive self-managed economy can sustain the same efficient allocation as its capitalist counterpart. The price vector which will simultaneously clear all markets is therefore independent of the enterprises' objectives in a competitive economy with given production technology and tastes. This indicates that self-management is not necessarily inconsistent with the operation of a free market system, and can support efficient allocations. However, this finding is not directly relevant for our study, which concentrates on the pattern of allocative inefficiencies outside competitive equilibrium. We have already established that, unlike their capitalist counterparts, individual cooperatives respond to changes in demand and cost conditions by adjusting incomes and capital–labour ratios. In this section, we go on to analyse the allocative effects of changes in parameters for the system as a whole, as well as to consider the type of competitive forces acting to restore economic efficiency.

We commence with our earlier example of market adjustment in the two systems when technology is homothetic. It will be remembered that an increase in product price leads each profit maximising firm to increase supply by hiring more capital and labour in the same proportions as before, if factor prices are unaffected. From an allocative point of view, the change in parameters does not affect the capitalist choice of technique, which therefore remains efficient by assumption. The product response is also in the right direction, raising the output of a relatively more desired commodity. Indeed, the production response by existing firms may be sufficient to ensure an optimal supply of the product at the market level. However, under certain conditions profit maximising levels of production by additional firms will be required, motivated by and eliminating any remaining pure profit.

There is a different adjustment process under self-management, which relies more heavily on entry and exit to restore efficiency. When every existing firm has fully adjusted to the new product price, individual enterprise and market level supply will be unchanged, while capital–labour ratios will have risen in response to the increased implicit cost of labour in each enterprise. The responses of each cooperative have actually made the allocative situation rather worse than before. This means, as Vanek (1970) and Meade (1972) point out, that general equilibrium forces have more to achieve under self-management. In the first place, under these assumptions the entire increase in market supply required for efficiency must come from the entry of new producers into the sector.

Moreover, the initial disturbance is amplified by the mechanism distributing pure profits to members as income. This distorts the choice of technique and means that misallocation, from whatever source, must immediately be reflected in the labour market.[24] As under capitalism, the competitive forces acting to restore efficiency are the entry of new producers into the sector, in search of higher incomes. However, the resulting increase in market supply and reduction in product price has more to achieve – eliminating income differentials and choice of technique distortion as well as raising production to eliminate pure profit. For any given change in demand or cost conditions, the number of entrants required to restore efficiency will necessarily be greater under self-management than capitalism because, prior to their entry, market supply will have responded relatively less and each new firm will be smaller than its profit maximising counterpart. Although it is risky to draw any dynamic implications from this essentially atemporal analysis, it does seem likely that the general equilibrium effects will be weaker under self-management.

The allocative effects of a price disturbance under self-management occur largely because conventional labour market forces are absent. Under capitalism, changes in product price affect market supply (relative to the new efficient level) and profits, but do not spill over into factor markets because the wage rate is a parameter to the firm, set to clear the labour market. One can discern two differences in the responses of self-managed firms. It has already been noted that the market supply response will necessarily be smaller. Moreover, the allocative effects are always transmitted into factor markets because there is nothing acting to clear the labour market. Cooperatives which choose output, factor proportions and incomes simultaneously have no demand curve for labour, but merely an enterprise-specific demand point which is a function of all the constraints to private optimisation. These cannot be aggregated to a market labour demand curve. This means that incomes and the capital–labour ratio will always vary with parameters to the enterprise choice, even if capital costs and technology are identical for different firms. If product price increases, earnings and labour value marginal products will rise above the levels attained elsewhere in the economy, and although there are material incentives for workers to transfer to that sector, the existing membership will prevent such movements in order to maintain their own incomes. This use by the cooperative of its labour market monopoly power is precisely analogous to the choice by capitalist monopolies of their own price-output point on the market demand curve. It means that there are no conventional forces to ensure efficiency in the allocation of labour, or even that labour markets clear at all in the absence of enterprise entry and exit. The desire and ability of existing cooperatives to maintain above-average incomes after changes in parameters prevents the labour market from transferring workers from low to high value marginal product uses. From an allocative point of view, enterprise entry must therefore act to alter the parameters of enterprise choice until the maximal level of incomes is equal in different uses, as well as to ensure an efficient level of market supply.

These arguments hold for more general technical assumptions, as can be seen by analysing the responses of a two product economy to preference changes under capitalism and self-management. We shall be largely following the presentation by Meade (1972), and therefore distinguish between the short and long run in this case. The two input (L and K) and two output (A and B) world is assumed in the first instance to have attained a competitive equilibrium which is Pareto efficient, and we then compare the modes of adjustment to a change in tastes in favour of product A, which raises its relative price. If the economy were capitalist, the increase (decrease) of value marginal products in A (B) would lead profit maximising firms to hire (sack) workers, so labour would be attracted from the low to the high value marginal product use until efficiency was restored in the labour market. Precisely the same movements would occur in capital markets until the value marginal product of capital was the same in the two uses. These adjustments by existing firms would have altered the structure of production to some extent, but if further shifts from B to A were required, they would occur because enterprises changed their production line in the desired direction until pure profits were exhausted. Each stage of the adjustment acts to restore efficiency in the appropriate market. If the economy were self-managed, the increase (decrease) in price would raise (lower) earnings and marginal products, and labour would not be transferred in order to equalise them. Indeed, it is quite possible that labour would be shifted from the high to the low value marginal product use, further increasing the allocative inefficiency.[25] As in the capitalist case, capital is transferred from the low to the high value marginal product use, which will reduce the income disparity between sectors to some extent. However, it is entry into sector *A* and exit from *B* which must ultimately restore the efficient structure of production and equalise incomes in the two sectors by altering relative product prices. Thus, the differences in the manner whereby the two systems adjust between efficient equilibria are independent of technical assumptions and the precise nature of cooperative short-run responses.

Therefore, allocative inefficiencies from whatever source should be reflected in a misallocation of labour under self-management if the system has not attained competitive equilibrium. Our empirical work is devoted to exploring various aspects of this hypothesis. It entails the assumption that each enterprise has attained an income maximising optimum with respect to all inputs, though the system as a whole is not in competitive equilibrium. Thus, enterprises are viewed as being able to adjust relatively rapidly, but continual changes in production technology and tastes create disturbances which are never fully eradicated by the more sluggish general equilibrium effects. The appropriateness of this approach is examined empirically in Chapter 4.

2.4 THE SELF-MANAGED MONOPOLIST

This section will examine the long-run behaviour of a monopolist under self-management,[26] with particular reference to the way that product market monopoly power leads us to adapt our propositions about the choice of technique and incomes. It will be shown that output is restricted under monopoly to increase revenue and product price, relative to a competitive counterpart. Thus, monopoly power is precisely analogous to increases in product price in the competitive case, raising average earnings above the level attained elsewhere in the economy and distorting the choice of technique. Since product market imperfections have the same allocative effects as these other changes in parameters, and are transmitted to factor markets through the same mechanism, monopoly power provides a further source of labour misallocation under self-management. However, the additional degree of freedom for the monopolist, because his demand curve slopes down, relaxes the technical assumptions required for the existence of equilibria and positive supply responses.

The monopolist solves a similar optimisation problem to the

competitive firm (equations (2.1)–(2.4)), except that equilibrium price must be chosen from the demand curve:

$$p = p(q, \Delta), \tag{2.12}$$

where p_q is assumed to be negative and Δ is a shift parameter, $p_\Delta > 0$. Moreover, marginal revenue replaces price in the first order conditions (equations (2.3) and (2.4)) which become:

$$(p + qp_q)f_L = y, \tag{2.13}$$

$$(p + qp_q)f_K = r. \tag{2.14}$$

Thus, equations (2.1), (2.2), (2.12)–(2.14) are solved for equilibrium values of output, capital, labour and product price. Substituting equations (2.13) and (2.14) in equation (2.1) and rearranging terms, the long-run condition, superscripting m for monopoly, becomes;

$$\lambda^{m*} = \frac{p^{m*}}{p^{m*} + q^{m*}p_q} = E^*, \tag{2.15}$$

where the function $E(q, \Delta)$ describes the ratio of price to marginal revenue. Alternatively, denoting the elasticity of demand by e:[27]

$$E(q, \Delta) = \frac{e}{1 - e(q, \Delta)}. \tag{2.16}$$

Equation (2.15) is a generalisation of the condition for competitive markets in which E always equals unity because product price is parametric (so $e = \infty$ or $p_q = 0$). It implies that production will always be in the range of increasing returns, or below minimum efficient scale, under monopoly, and both λ and E must exceed unity at some positive level of output for an equilibrium to exist. This is less restrictive than under competition since we no longer require $\lambda_{\hat{q}} < 0$ (or $H > 0$), so the monopolist can produce with homogeneous technology.[28] Thus, for estimation purposes the appropriate specification of technology depends on the structure of product markets.

We require further assumptions about the returns to scale and demand functions to consider the equilibrium in more detail. Diagram 2.5 is constructed on the assumption that equilibrium output is unique and can be compared with the outcome under competition. Therefore returns to scale are assumed to diminish monotonically from an initial value exceeding unity and the ratio of

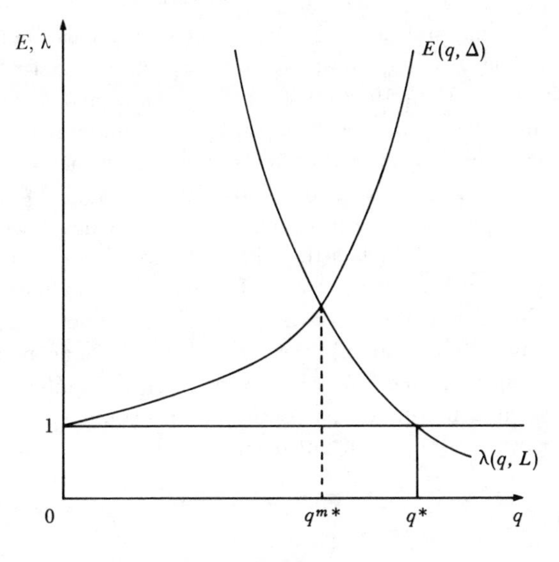

Diagram 2.5

price to marginal revenue is assumed to be an increasing function of output, which is consistent, for example, with linear demand curves.[29] The monopolist maximises income by producing at q^{m*}, at the intersection of the two curves. The diagram shows that in the circumstances when equilibrium outputs can be uniquely compared, it is always greater under competition than monopoly. A brief run through the arguments of section 2.2 quickly ties down all the other comparisons. Product price will necessarily be higher under monopoly because the product demand curve is assumed to be downward sloping. This means that granting monopoly power to a firm acting on a hitherto competitive market would have exactly the same effects on average earnings and the choice of technique as an increase in product price for a competitive self-managed firm.[30] Monopolists under self-management act to restrict production relative to their competitive counterparts, in order to raise product price and average earnings, therefore leading to a more capital-intensive production technique through increases in the implicit marginal cost of labour.

It is interesting to note that cooperatives have precisely the same incentives to attain product market monopoly power as their capitalist counterparts, namely raising the value of the enterprise objective function, and that the consequences for allocation are also analogous. Just like its capitalist counterpart, the self-managed monopolist restricts production, preventing efficient allocations in product and factor markets and generating monopoly welfare deadweight losses. However, the effects are more serious because the product market inefficiencies are transmitted through to earnings and the choice of technique in exactly the manner described in the previous sections, and the fact that they arise from monopoly power means that they will not be eliminated by entry. In the first place, it can be shown that the allocative inefficiency and deadweight monopoly loss will be relatively greater under self-management than capitalism, superscripted c. A rearrangement of the familiar marginal revenue equals marginal cost condition for a counterpart capitalist monopoly reveals that output is chosen where:[31]

$$\lambda^{cm*} = E^{cm*}\left(\frac{1-\pi^{c*}}{p^{cm*}q^{cm*}}\right). \tag{2.17}$$

Since we can assume that capitalist monopolies always make positive profits, this is equivalent to shifting the E function in Diagram 2.5 downwards. Thus, if profits are positive, the capitalist monopoly always produces more than its self-managed counterpart, and sells the output at a lower price. This implies that the deadweight monopoly loss for comparable firms is always relatively greater under self-management than capitalism, as is the deviation from Pareto efficiency caused by the difference between marginal revenue and marginal value products of inputs. Thus, even without taking account of the consequences for labour market allocation, monopoly power will be a relatively more serious problem for efficiency and welfare under self-management. Since these problems arise from a relatively higher product price, the arguments of the previous sections show how these initial inefficiencies will be transmitted to the labour market, generating further dispersion in income per head and the choice of technique. Finally, one can no longer rely on general equilibrium effects ultimately to restore efficiency since these rely on enterprise entry and exit, the restriction of which is the essence of monopoly power. Thus monopoly power is analogous to improvements in demand or cost conditions for the firm, in terms of its effects on incomes and the choice of technique, but will be even less desirable because its effects will be permanent rather than only lasting until general equilibrium effects have worked through the system. Product market monopoly power will be an objective for self-managed firms because it enables them permanently to raise average earnings, but from the allocative point of view it represents a further source of inefficiency which cannot be eliminated by market forces.

The appendix shows that the comparative static results for incomes and the choice of technique can be generalised to the imperfectly competitive case. As before, equilibrium average earnings and the capital intensity of production always increase when either demand or cost conditions improve. However, the output results become more complex for shifts in the demand curve because the ratio of price to marginal revenue as well as the returns to scale function may be affected.[32]

The long-run response is;

$$\frac{\partial q^{m*}}{\partial \Delta} = \frac{q}{LH} [f_K^2 p_\Delta \lambda_L - AE_\Delta + p f_K^2 \lambda_L E_\Delta], \tag{2.18}$$

where A is assumed to be positive. The first term in the bracket is analogous to the expression derived for competitive firms, and the latter two describe shifts in the ratio of price to marginal revenue at the initial equilibrium and cross effects. The ratio of price to marginal revenue at the initial equilibrium would be reduced by an upward shift in the demand curve unless the slope were altered sufficiently to reduce the elasticity of demand at q^{m*}. Thus, the long-run supply response will be positive for a relatively broad class of assumptions about production and demand functions. These do not have to be specified in detail because one can determine the general conditions with reference to Diagram 2.5. The self-managed monopolist will always increase production if an upward shift in the demand curve leads to a downward movement in the ratio of price to marginal revenue and an upward movement in the returns to scale function at the initial equilibrium. The supply response will also be positive whenever a movement in one of these directions by either function outweighs shifts in the opposite direction by the other, for example when technology is homothetic and the family of demand curves is linear and parallel.

Thus, self-managed firms will desire monopoly power for exactly the same reasons as their capitalist counterparts, and its allocative and welfare consequences will be even more serious. The existence of imperfect competition does not, in principle, affect the performance of a self-managed economy as described above, particularly the transmission of allocative inefficiency to the labour market, but it does provide an additional source of welfare loss and impede the operation of general equilibrium effects in the system. However, although monopolists are relatively more restrictive than their competitive counterparts, the degree of freedom added by the more relaxed sufficiency conditions means that the conditions for the existence of equilibria and positive supply responses are less restrictive. The former point will be used in Chapter 6, but the latter would primarily affect studies of Yugoslav output functions.

Apart from generalising the framework to imperfect competition, the main result of this section has been to show that monopoly power will be an independent source of dispersion in incomes and the choice of technique under self-management.

2.5 FROM THEORY TO APPLIED WORK

The models in this chapter have defined the variables which ought to prove of interest in Yugoslavia and specified how they should be inter-related. It has also clarified the role of technical assumptions in developing estimating equations. The empirical validity of these propositions will be evaluated in the second part of this book. We conclude this chapter by summarising how our findings will affect the applied work.

The most obvious feature distinguishing capitalist and self-managed market economies is the allocation of labour. We have argued that this is best studied on the assumption that enterprises have attained their planning optimum, though the system as a whole is not in competitive equilibrium. Under these circumstances the allocation of labour will be not Pareto efficient, and there will be income and capital–labour ratio dispersion across firms. We commence our empirical study with reference to market structure and general equilibrium pressures in Chapter 4. This also gives the opportunity to see whether earnings are the motivating force for entry and exit, as argued in section 2.3. We then discover whether average earnings dispersion did emerge in Yugoslavia after self-management was introduced; a proposition unique to the labour-managed market economy. The analysis is developed in the final chapter by estimating reduced form earnings equations, the specification of which draws heavily on the findings in this chapter. We also examine the predicted association between product and labour market imperfections by testing the independent effects of concentration on incomes, and study empirically assorted other propositions about the choice of technique and labour market clearing.

Finally, we return to the issue of capital market imperfections, and the way that they will influence our analysis. Of course, market pressures would necessarily equalise capital as well as labour marginal products so this institutional problem strengthens the case for assuming that Yugoslavia has not attained competitive equilibrium. Capital market imperfections which lead to inter-firm differences in the cost of capital charged pose no problem for our framework. The effects on income, output and the choice of technique are the same as those of interest rate dispersion. However, if capital is entirely rationed according to arbitrary criteria,[33] it becomes exogenous to enterprise choice and an independent determinant of earnings and the choice of technique. Thus, the stock of capital itself replaces the cost of capital as a parameter of the economic system. This notion has fostered empirical work by Vanek and Jovicic (1975) and other members of the 'capital school' (reviewed in Estrin and Bartlett, 1982). However, we show in the next chapter that the Yugoslav capital stock changed rapidly over time, with firms having sufficient autonomy to determine their own investment pattern. We therefore treat the capital stock as an enterprise choice variable and analyse the constraints from the capital market in terms of implicit marginal capital costs which vary between firms.

Mathematical appendix to Chapter 2

Table 2.1 summarises the notation employed in this appendix. The competitive self-managed firm solves the following general optimisation problem, given p and r,

$$\underset{q,\, L,\, K}{\text{maximise}} \qquad y = \frac{pq - rK}{L}, \tag{A1}$$

$$\text{subject to} \qquad q = f(L, K), \tag{A2}$$

with first order conditions

$$y = pf_L, \tag{A3}$$

$$r = pf_K. \tag{A4}$$

where (A2) satisfies local concavity conditions around the equilibrium for sufficiency; that is:

$$f_L, f_K > 0, f_{LL}, f_{KK} < 0;$$
$$f_{LK} = f_{KL} \text{ and } H = f_{LL}f_{KK} - f_{LK}^2 > 0. \tag{A5}$$

The short run is defined as the period in which production can only vary via changes in membership, so that the capital stock is taken as fixed. Relative to the general optimisation problem, this entails omitting equation (A4) and assuming the capital stock in equation (A2) to be invariant. The comparative statics of this truncated system are:

$$\frac{\partial L^*}{\partial p}, \frac{\partial q^*}{\partial p} < 0; \frac{\partial y^*}{\partial p} > 0;$$
$$\frac{\partial L^*}{\partial r}, \frac{\partial q^*}{\partial r} > 0; \frac{\partial y^*}{\partial r} < 0 \tag{A6}$$

and are described in Diagram 2.3 of the main text.

Returning to the planning problem, equations (A1), (A3) and (A4) together imply,

$$\frac{Lf_L + Kf_K}{q} = 1. \tag{A7}$$

Returns to scale (λ) describe the elasticity of output with respect to all inputs according to function,

$$\lambda(q, L) = \frac{Lf_L + Kf_K}{q} \begin{matrix} > \\ = \\ < \end{matrix} 1 \Rightarrow \left.\begin{matrix} \text{increasing} \\ \text{constant} \\ \text{diminishing} \end{matrix}\right\} \text{returns to scale.} \tag{A8}$$

From equation (A7), competitive equilibrium under self-management implies

$$\lambda^* = 1, \tag{A9}$$

a condition which has no equivalent under capitalism.

Returns to scale are normally considered to vary along a ray in capital–labour space ($\lambda = \lambda(q, K/L)$). The sign of the output derivative of this function, denoted $\lambda_{\hat{q}}$, is inversely related to the sign of the determinant of the Hessian matrix, H. Thus, $\lambda_{\hat{q}} < 0$ around the equilibrium from (A5). However, in the self-managed case it is more convenient to consider the derivatives of the returns to scale function with respect to employment and output, as defined in (A8). The total derivative of this returns to scale function is:

$$\partial\lambda = \frac{(Lf_{LL} + Kf_{KL} + f_L)}{q}\partial L - \frac{(Lf_L + Kf_K)}{q^2}\partial q + \frac{(Lf_{LK} + Kf_{KK} + f_K)}{q}\partial K. \tag{A10}$$

Using the total derivative of the production function,

$$\partial q = f_L \partial L + f_K \partial K, \tag{A11}$$

when $\partial q = 0$ implies $\partial K = -f_L/f_K \partial L$, so

$$\lambda_L = \frac{\partial\lambda(L, q)}{\partial L} = \frac{1}{qf_K}[f_K(Lf_{LL} + Kf_{KL}) - f_L(Kf_{KK} + Lf_{LK})]. \tag{A12}$$

Similarly, when $\partial L = 0$ so $\partial K = \partial q/f_K$,

$$\lambda_q = \frac{\partial\lambda(L, q)}{\partial q} = \frac{q - Lf_L - Kf_K}{q^2} + \frac{Kf_{KK} + Lf_{LK}}{qf_K}. \tag{A13}$$

Hence, with constant or decreasing returns to scale, a negative sign on f_{LK} or f_{KL} is sufficient to determine the sign of λ_q. However, the sign of λ_L is, in general, indeterminate though it equals the expression in Ireland and Law (1982) describing the difference between the rate of change of factor marginal products along the expansion path. Thus, $\lambda_L = 0$ when production technology is homothetic.

Returning to the general optimisation problem of equations (A1)–(A4), the comparative statics are:

$$\frac{\partial L^*}{\partial r} = \frac{-1}{pLH}(Lf_{LK} + Kf_{KK}), \tag{A14}$$

$$\frac{\partial K^*}{\partial r} = \frac{1}{pLH}(Lf_{LL} + Kf_{KL}), \tag{A15}$$

$$\frac{\partial L^*}{\partial p} = \frac{f_K}{pLH}(Lf_{LK} + Kf_{KK}), \tag{A16}$$

$$\frac{\partial K^*}{\partial p} = \frac{-f_K}{pLH}(Lf_{LL} + Kf_{KL}). \tag{A17}$$

The sufficient condition for capital to respond in the same way as under capitalism is that $f_{LK} = f_{KL} \leqslant 0$, which is satisfied when $\lambda_q < 0$. If we impose this and the second order conditions,

$$\frac{\partial K^*}{\partial p}, \frac{\partial L^*}{\partial r} > 0; \quad \frac{\partial L^*}{\partial p}, \frac{\partial K^*}{\partial r} < 0. \tag{A18}$$

However, the optimal choice of technique responds unambiguously to changes in demand or cost conditions. This can be seen from equations (A14)–(A17), in which the inputs respond to any change in parameters in the opposite direction whatever the sign of f_{LK}. The result can be deduced directly from the earnings function (A1) along the lines of Ireland and Law (1982). Optimal incomes are described by,

$$y^* = y^*(p, r), \tag{A19}$$

where $\partial y^*/\partial p > 0$ and $\partial y^*/\partial r < 0$. Evaluated at the optimal levels of employment and capital, the homogeneity of degree zero of y_p and y_r and the convexity of (A19) with respect to p and r implies,

$$\frac{\partial (K/L)^*}{\partial p} > 0; \quad \frac{\partial (K/L)^*}{\partial r} < 0. \tag{A20}$$

The competitive output comparative statics are

$$\frac{\partial q^*}{\partial p} = \frac{-f_K}{pLH}[f_K(Lf_{LL} + Kf_{LK}) - f_L(Lf_{KL} + Kf_{KK})], \tag{A21}$$

$$\frac{\partial q^*}{\partial r} = \frac{1}{pLH}[f_K(Lf_{LL} + Kf_{KL}) - f_L(Lf_{KL} + Kf_{KK})]. \tag{A22}$$

The sign of the complex bracketed expressions in equations (A21) and (A22) is determined by the relationship between returns to scale and factor proportions at a constant level of output. Hence, given equation (A12) and the second order conditions,

$$\frac{\partial q^*}{\partial p} = \frac{-f_K^2 q}{pLH}\lambda_L, \tag{A23}$$

$$\frac{\partial q^*}{\partial r} = \frac{f_K q}{pLH} \lambda_L. \tag{A24}$$

It is interesting to note that a similar rearrangement of the capitalist optimisation problem (equations (A2), (A4), (A25), (A26) below) leads to condition (A27):

$$\pi = pq - rK - wL, \tag{A25}$$

$$q = f(L, K), \tag{A2}$$

$$pf_L = w, \tag{A26}$$

$$pf_K = r, \tag{A4}$$

$$\lambda^{c*} = 1 - \frac{\pi^*}{pq^{c*}}. \tag{A27}$$

Denoting the capitalist cost function as $C(q) = wL + rK$, equation (A27) can be seen to be equivalent to the familiar condition that marginal cost equals price ($\partial C/\partial q = p$). A consideration of equations (A7) and (A27) facilitates a comparison of long-run equilibria under the two systems. The direction of the output response under capitalism depends only on the slope of the marginal cost curve, or the sign of $\lambda_{\hat{q}}$. The long-run supply curve is upward sloping if $\lambda_{\hat{q}} < 0$ or $H > 0$.

The self-managed monopolist solves the following general optimisation problem,

$$y^m = \frac{p(q, \Delta)q - rK}{L}, \tag{A28}$$

$$p^m = p(q, \Delta), \tag{A29}$$

$$q^m = f(L, K), \tag{A2}$$

$$y^m = (p + qp_q)f_L, \tag{A30}$$

$$r = (p + qp_q)f_K, \tag{A31}$$

where $p_q < 0$ and $p_\Delta > 0$ by assumption. Substituting equations (A30) and (A31) into (A28) and rearranging terms yields the returns to scale constraint under monopoly,

$$\lambda^{m*} = \frac{p^{m*}}{p^{m*} + qp_q}. \tag{A32}$$

The ratio of price to marginal revenue is denoted by the function $E(q, \Delta)$. If the elasticity of demand, e, equals $-p/qp_q$,

$$E(q, \Delta) = \frac{p^m}{p^m + qp_q} = \frac{e}{1 - e}. \tag{A33}$$

Therefore, equation (A32) becomes,

$$\lambda^{m*} = E^*. \tag{A34}$$

The capitalist monopolist solves a similar optimisation problem to equations (A2), (A28)–(A31) except that the maximand is profits (equation (A25)), and the marginal revenue product of labour in equation (A30) is set to equal market wages rather than average earnings. The long-run equilibrium condition is,

$$\lambda^{cm*} = E^{c*}\left(1 - \frac{\pi^{m*}}{p^{cm*}q^{cm*}}\right). \tag{A35}$$

Imperfectly competitive equilibria under the two systems can be compared (with reference to equations (A34) and (A35)).

The comparative statics of the self-managed monopolist are derived from equations (A2), (A28)–(A31). Letting an upward shift in the demand curve play the role of a change in price under competition, the comparative statics for the equilibrium choice of technique and earnings are the same as in the competitive case. However, the output response is,

$$\frac{\partial q^{m*}}{\partial r} = \frac{E_q f_K}{pLH}\lambda_L \lesseqgtr 0 \text{ as } \lambda_L \gtreqless 0, \tag{A36}$$

$$\frac{\partial q^{m*}}{\partial \Delta} = \frac{-f_K^2 p_\Delta q}{pLH}\lambda_L + AE_\Delta + \frac{f_K^2 E_q E_\Delta \lambda_L}{LH}\lambda_L, \tag{A37}$$

where $A < 0$. The capitalist monopolist will increase production in response to an upward shift in the demand curve provided that the long-run marginal cost curve is upward sloping ($H > 0$ or $\lambda_{\hat{q}} < 0$) and the shift in the demand curve increases marginal revenue at the initial equilibrium ($E_\Delta < 0$).

3

The Yugoslav environment

3.1 INTRODUCTION

This chapter summarises the historical and institutional material which will be relevant in specifying the economic environment for our models and for interpreting our findings. Yugoslavia was chosen as the testing ground for our propositions from self-management theory because it remains the only country in which the entire allocation of resources is based on some approximation to market self-management.[1] This chapter investigates the robustness of that approximation, and warns that the complexity of the system, as well as such structural characteristics as underdevelopment and regional disparities, mean that our equilibrium propositions must be carefully adapted and interpreted. The following section provides a general introduction to the country itself, and highlights a number of institutional and historical points relevant to our study. The legacies of previous experiences and methods on contemporary economic behaviour and structure are the subject of the third section, while the fourth briefly outlines the relevant aspects of post-war economic history. The period is divided into three distinct phases characterised by different mechanisms for allocating resources, of which only the second is argued to approximate the market self-management analysed in the previous chapter.

The complexity of the Yugoslav environment leads us to think more carefully about the precise implications of our propositions and warns against simplistic interpretations of our results. This institutional and historical material will be used in interpreting our results and specifying alternative explanations for observed phenomena. We try to take account of the most important elements of the Yugoslav environment in the remainder of our analysis. But it is part of our purpose in writing this chapter to offer readers sufficient information to form their own judgements on our findings. Even so, we can only provide a brief summary of the large literature on this subject, and further references are contained in the Yugoslav bibliography at the end of this book. The general texts include Horvat (1971a), Dirlam and Plummer (1973), World Bank (1975), Schrenk, Ardalan and El Tatawy (1979), Tyson (1980) and Estrin and Bartlett (1982). The contents of the chapter are culled from the material referenced in the Yugoslav bibliography, but in order to simplify the exposition, specific references will not in general be given point by point in the text except for data sources.

3.2 NATIONAL CHARACTERISTICS

As in any other country, national characteristics – historical, social and institutional – necessarily influence Yugoslav economic behaviour and therefore our expectations about the implications of theoretical models. The problem is particularly acute in Yugoslavia because the country is unusually complex, heterogeneous and dynamic. This section will consider three general features of contemporary Yugoslavia, each with numerous important implications for observed behaviour: regional diversity, underdevelopment and communist government. The regional heterogeneity of the country, with its consequences of social enmity and economic fragmentation, has been an important determinant of government policy, and goes a long way towards explaining the frequent institutional changes discussed in the fourth section. Moreover, the fact that the country is not fully integrated economically necessitates caution in interpreting any country-wide empirical work, and the need to check that observed phenomena are not caused by regional factors. Because Yugoslavia remains a relatively less developed country, a competitive general equilibrium framework is an inappropriate tool of analysis, and this underlies the choice of methodology outlined in the previous chapter. The structural problems of a less developed country also provide some of the alternative explanations of the observed phenomena. Finally, the fact that communists have ruled throughout the period brings into question the appropriateness of our market self-management model to discuss Yugoslav behaviour. There is no doubt that the government's orientation brought certain strong biases to economic policy, including the suppression of numerous market forces, and meant that the economy was rather more regulated than our model would suggest. It will be argued that the limited extent to which the Yugoslav system actually approximates theoretical market self-management explains many of the deficiencies of our empirical work.

Yugoslavia is an abnormally fragmented national entity. Thus, for example, the country contains five relatively distinct ethnic groups as well as two substantial minorities, organised on approximately ethnic lines into the six republics (one republic, Bosnia, has a mixed Serb and Croatian population) and two autonomous provinces. Between them, these groups speak four languages and follow three major religions.[2] Unlike most of Western Europe, regional considerations have retained a central significance for Yugoslavia, perhaps because the national state itself was only recently created to unite an area with a long history of enmity. Indeed, at the start of the post-war period the very existence of the country as a stable political entity was in question, and the demise of President Tito in 1980 has reawakened some fears of fragmentation into the constituent regional parts. Many aspects of recent Yugoslav policy can be interpreted as a consequence of inter-republican disagreements over substantive issues. Indeed, it might be argued that a major theme of government policies since the war has been to discover a political and institutional framework which will act to hold the country together against the strong centrifugal force of ethnic differences (see Hoffman and Neal, 1962; Milenkovitch, 1971; Rusinow, 1977).

This point is best amplified with reference to a very brief history of the area. The northern parts of contemporary Yugoslavia were contained in various Western European empires (for most of the period, Habsburg or Austrian) from the Middle Ages, while the southern parts of the country were under Turkish sovereignty over the period. Apart from the inevitable consequences for language, culture and religion, this separation caused differences in the level and pattern of development in the two regions, as well as the product and trade orientation and the property rights structure, which continued after the creation of a united South Slav state[3] in 1918. Moreover, there was a heritage of political and social instability and, in all probability, some local enmity left in this boundary area between two large and intermittently feuding empires, both centred far away.

Yugoslavia was created at the end of the First World War, but was not able to integrate into a single, properly functioning political entity during the inter-war period. The country was founded around the Serbian monarchy and state. Serbia was a small South Slav country which had successfully fought for its independence from Turkey during the nineteenth century. It had nurtured the concept of a united Slavic entity in the Balkans, and had fought on the victorious side in the First World War. The main disagreements in the inter-war period were between the Croats, who had achieved some degree of self-determination in the later years of the Austrian empire, and the Serbs, who had succeeded in imposing their hegemony over the area. However, there were numerous other sources of disagreement in the fledgling state arising from ethnic, religious and political differences, which explained the existence of forty political parties during the brief period of parliamentary democracy before 1929. The were also serious problems of economic adjustment in creating a common market between regions at differing stages of economic development which hitherto had not traded extensively and which were oriented to produce and exchange on very different markets. Thus, the relatively more developed and industrialised northern regions were united with the less developed, primary producing south. For each area, much of the trade which had been internal prior to unification became external, while the relatively smaller north–south exchanges become internal. In the light of the ethnic and social differences, and their numerous political ramifications, it is hardly surprising that the new country did not fully develop a unified market system in the inter-war period, particularly for labour and capital (see Hoffman and Neal, 1962).

Democracy gradually gave way to monarchical dictatorship under the pressure of inter-regional strife in this uneasy first period of unification. This culminated in a virtual civil war between the ethnic groups after 1939. In fact, the Second World War was a very confused period, in that it comprised simultaneous ethnic and religious wars, with some elements of genocide between regions, as well as conflicts between communists, royalists and the occupying Germans and Italians. This chaos ended in 1944 with the emergence of the communists as the ruling group. They led a large, ethnically heterogeneous liberating army committed to the maintenance of a united Yugoslavia, and thereby, not merely by force of arms, they were in a stronger position to fill the power vacuum left by the collapse of the Axis occupation than any of the numerous feuding regional parties. This unhappy period had some important consequences for post-war developments. The new administration was profoundly concerned to avoid the bitter internal dissensions of the inter-war period, and was therefore pragmatic with regard to policies which might act to hold together the unlikely Yugoslav entity. Moreover, the regime started with considerable internal support, and rapidly developed unifying myths of self-liberation which acted to underline the relative independence that these communists sought from Moscow. However, the logic of their actions clearly pointed to frictions with Yugoslavia's closest immediate post-war ally – the Soviet Union under Stalin.

In 1948, the disagreements came to a head. Yugoslavia was expelled from the Eastern bloc and an economic blockade was imposed. After an initial period of dismay and confusion (see Ross-Johnson, 1972), the internationally isolated party leadership established the joint goals which have been important to this day: the development of a socialist system different to that in the Soviet Union and the maintenance of internal unity. The frequent social and institutional experimentation which followed had to ensure that the communists[4] would continue to rule over a one-party socialist state and avoid Soviet-type central control (which was often associated with Serbian hegemony over the country) without fostering fragmentation of the national entity into its regional components. These complex problems led to a gradual, erratic process of decentralising political and economic authority – the former to republican and local governments and the latter to self-managed firms – while seeking to strengthen certain national institutions such as the communist party itself and the army. The requirement to delegate authority while maintaining the terminology of marxism as well as unifying institutional principles was an important reason for the introduction and later developments of the self-management system. As a result of these changes, economic and political authority had largely shifted to the republican governments by the time of Tito's death, with the bulk of federal policies requiring consensus from the different regions (see Rusinow, 1977; Comisso, 1979; Tyson, 1980). Indeed, the rotating Presidency, which has ruled the country in recent years, cements the effectively confederal nature of modern Yugoslavia. The decentralisation of considerable decision-making authority around agreed national institutions, including self-management, means that economic environments are not necessarily the same in different republics. These differences include legal requirements and structures, economic policies and government regulations, as well as the level of economic development[5] and industrialisation, and means that results from country-wide data may hide more than they reveal.

One would hope to offset this problem to some extent by bringing precise information about the nature of inter-regional differences to bear on our findings, and this approach will be employed in our empirical work. However, there are limits to how far this can be taken because of the frequency of reforms, which also presents its own problems, and the possibility of regionally disparate divergences between legal forms and practice. The frequent changes to the Yugoslav system after 1952, including the intermittent overhaul of the entire institutional structure (see section 4), were in part driven by the deep regional differences in the country and the resulting search for acceptable compromises. The consequence was that most economic arrangements and policies were very short-lived, so decision-makers operated in a constant state of flux. For example, the rules governing the internal distribution of wages were changed twelve times in twenty-five years, and even the definition of enterprises was altered, especially during the 1970s. This brings into question whether one can sensibly distinguish between 'economic systems' in Yugoslavia as the basis for empirical work, which is considered in the fourth section. It also indicates that any observed behaviour is likely to contain at least an element of adjustment. While our models will continue to be based on the assumption that enterprises have attained their own optima, this points to the examination of dynamic lag structures in our economic work.

It is also difficult at times to tie down the precise implications of the legal changes and the relationship between constitutional forms and actual practice. The large number of reforms do not help in this respect, and the problem is aggravated by the official descriptions of events. Most official documents (and academic studies) are based on marxist categories which can be confusing or empty for Western readers. More seriously, the official view of historical events, including some arguments accepted in the Western literature, may not be entirely accurate or may fail to stress important events.[6] This seems to arise from the general tendency of official histories to rationalise the changes into a broad historical pattern, though many were in fact pragmatic, ad hoc or the consequence of a short-lived victory by a party faction (see, for example, Rusinow, 1977, on this point). Moreover, it is possible that some of the legal changes, being imposed by a victorious regional coalition in the party, were never properly enforced in the areas ruled by opposing factions. This appears to have occurred in Serbia in the few years following the major Reforms of 1965, and is also argued to have been slowing the impact of the 1974 Reforms (see Milenkovitch, 1971; Tyson, 1980). Since these were fundamental changes of direction, one might suspect even more endemic failures with regard to minor new regulations. Thus, even if one could be sure of actual implications of legal reforms, there always remains the possibility that they were never properly enforced, or were enforced differentially in different regions. Finally, there remains the role of the League of Communists itself. Although the regime has generally made more conscientious attempts to live within its legal code than its Eastern European neighbours, the fact remains that the party represents an extra-legal chain of authority in the system. Unfortunately the decentralisation, especially since 1965, means that it is impossible to determine the extent of the interference by the League of Communists, and even its direction. Although the party has generally remained united, republican leaders have considerable autonomy in their regions, and the previous discussion suggests that they do not always act as a monolithic entity. Thus, to the problem of regional differences in the economic environment, we must add the consequences of differences in the extent and direction of party interference in private decision-making. In conclusion, regional diversity in Yugoslavia is a central element in the determination of political and economic policy. The resulting decentralisation of authority, combined with the problems of discovering what actually occurred, make it difficult to specify the economic environment at a national level. Indeed, because regionalism has remained a potent force in Yugoslavia, most of the serious political or economic problems, including those outlined in the empirical work below, have tended to develop a distinctly ethnic hue. This is a point to be borne in mind for the remainder of the study.

The second important characteristic of post-war Yugoslavia for our discussion is its level of development. The country was relatively less developed in 1945, to approximately the same extent as Greece and Turkey. Despite very rapid growth, particularly during the

1950s and early 1960s (see Sapir, 1980a), it has only reached an intermediate level of development (see OECD *Country Yearbooks on Yugoslavia*). One inevitable consequence is that Yugoslav economic policies have been directed towards growth and industrialisation rather than static resource allocation. The structural problems normally faced by a less developed country are an important reason why our marginalist propositions could be inappropriate for Yugoslavia, and the development literature will furnish several of our hypotheses.

The very low initial level of development reached by the disparate Balkan states before unification was not greatly improved during the inter-war period. Growth averaged around 2% per year, and was founded on small, foreign-owned enclaves in the North (who produced for German and Italian markets), the extraction of raw materials in the South, and state-owned monopolies in transport, salt and tobacco. The trade pattern was typical of less developed economies, with agricultural and forestry products accounting for around 62% of total exports, and non-ferrous and metal ores a further 20%, while 65% of imports were consumer goods and machinery, and a further 20% intermediates (Hoffman and Neal, 1962). As has been noted, regional differences hindered the establishment of a unified national market in labour and capital, as well as many traded products.

This fragile economic base was seriously damaged during the Second World War, in which there were 1.7 million casualties (more than 10% of the population) with around 40% of manufacturing capacity being destroyed or damaged and some 3.5 million people being rendered homeless. Thus the communists inherited a divided, poor, backward and war-damaged economy, in which about a quarter of the population over ten years of age was illiterate, infant mortality was 118.6 per thousand live births, and only around 300,000 of the approximately eight million labour force worked in industry and mining (World Bank, 1975; Dirlam and Plummer, 1973; Hoffman and Neal, 1962). Central planning until around 1950 restored pre-war production levels, and was oriented towards development through heavy industry based on nationalisation and centralised control. Even so, at that time agriculture generated around 33% of GDP at factor cost, while industry produced only 17% (the figures for employment were 66% and 7% respectively). Thus, self-management was introduced in 1952 to a system with a small industrial base. It relied on decision-making by a poorly educated and new industrial labour force and was oriented to mobilise resources for development.

As has been noted, the low average level of development disguised serious regional disparities, both within and between republics. Generally the northern republics and areas (Slovenia, Croatia, Vojvodina and Belgrade) were relatively better off than the southern ones, with the most extreme poverty in Kosovo, Macedonia, Montenegro and parts of Bosnia and Serbia. Thus, in the early fifties the average per capita income in the less developed republics was two-thirds of the developed ones, with an overall range between Slovenia and Kosovo of 3.6:1.[7] The rapid post-war growth has raised the average, but widened the internal dispersion, so per capita income in the less developed republics had fallen to less than half of the northern ones in the seventies, and the range widened to 6.7:1 (World Bank, 1975). These disparities fuelled the regional enmities discussed above and helped to determine the economic environment, reforms and their degree of implementation in each republic. Generally, the more developed North favoured increased liberalisation, trade with the West and a reduction of state control and planning. The southern republics and Serbia sought a transfer of resources to their republics, planned investment and accelerated development for the poorer regions. In political terms, the 1965 Reforms came about because the northern republics formed a coalition with the South to defeat centralised control, which had overtones in Yugoslavia of Serbian hegemony from Belgrade (see Milenkovitch, 1971; Rusinow, 1977). The market system did not last because of the increasing possibility of national disintegration, and because the victorious coalition disagreed about the future path of development. The implications of underdevelopment for our study will be examined in detail in the relevant sections of the text.

The last general theme of Yugoslav economic development relates the consequences of Communist Party rule (League of Communist rule since 1952). The ruling group was committed to certain aspects of a Soviet-type ideology and perspective despite the split, and this introduces important biases to the economic system. There is a certain pattern to the behaviour of Soviet-type regimes, which were clearly relevant in the Yugoslav case from 1946 to 1950 and continued to affect decision-making until at least the 1965 Reforms. In the mode of Wiles (1962), one can regard a communist party ruling in a relatively less developed economy as primarily concerned with mobilising resources for the industrial sector, if necessary by appropriating surpluses from the agricultural and service sectors. The ideology, as well as the exigencies of the planning system, would favour producer goods, intermediates and heavy industry over the production of commodities for final demand, and would rely on small numbers of very large plants. Investment planning would militate against the development of agriculture, services and small-scale industry, and there would be pressures towards either autarchy or the strict regulation of international trade. There would be profound mistrust of the market mechanism, particularly the free operation of capital markets, entrepreneurial activity and the price mechanism, and prices would generally be set to reflect planners' preferences and revenue needs rather than relative scarcities. Despite the split with Moscow, the Yugoslav leadership showed all of these biases to some extent during, at the very least, the 1950s and early 1960s (see sections 3 and 4), with important consequences for the industrial structure and degree of government regulation during the self-management period. Moreover, the independent effects of ideology on decision-making should not be underestimated in any communist regime, and especially in Yugoslavia where the leadership was trying to discover a new path to socialism.[8] Many important decisions were made in order to conform with ideological principles without serious consideration of their efficiency and practicality, and while the world may have gained information from the experiment, there is little doubt the Yugoslav economy has suffered for its inventiveness (see Sirc, 1979; Moore, 1980). For example, agriculture was briefly collectivised in 1948, at considerable cost, to prove socialist conformity, and technical groups in each firm were made the basic decision-making units after 1974 (the BOALs – see Comisso, 1979; Sacks, 1982), despite the potential losses of efficiency and control to ensure effective self-management in large firms.

We have seen that regional disparities, underdevelopment and communist rule imparted important legacies and biases to the Yugoslav economic environment. Not all of these can explicitly be taken into account in our study although all should be borne in mind. Some of the literature goes further in suggesting that one or more of these factors is the fundamental determinant of economic behaviour, and these studies often relegate self-management to an unimportant role. For example, many political scientists focus on aspects of regional heterogeneity and communist rule (i.e. Pavlowitch, 1971; Gregory, 1973; Rusinow, 1977), while much of the empirical economic research looks at questions which are relevant to a decentralised planning system (i.e. Granick, 1975; Mieczkowski, 1976) or the process of adjustment from plan to market (i.e. Marschak, 1968; Wachtel, 1973; Sirc, 1979). Finally, numerous economists have preferred to view Yugoslavia as basically a developing economy (i.e. World Bank, 1975; Schrenk, Ardalan and El Tatawy, 1979), with attention paid to such issues as growth and industrialisation (i.e. Moore, 1980; Sapir, 1980a), employment (i.e. Bartlett, 1979, 1980) and foreign trade (i.e. Amacher, 1972). Especially, given the wealth of material on these topics, we feel justified in dealing with a hitherto underplayed aspect of the Yugoslav economy: the effects of self-management on resource allocation.[9]

However, this section has shown that the Yugoslav environment is far more complex than our models would suggest. Thus, even if we alter our propositions, whenever possible, to take account, for example, of enterprise adjustment through lag structures, and we are fully aware of the identification problem in establishing self-management rather than, say, structural causality for our findings, we cannot be entirely sure of the conclusions from our empirical work. This means our case for the relevance of self-management will have to rest on as many separate pieces of evidence as possible, so that we can draw general conclusions from the findings as a whole rather than any particular result. The exclusion of numerous important factors from our modelling, such as the ones enumerated above, means that our evidence will have to be interpreted relatively loosely in each particular case, in the hope that we can still gradually build up a general picture of economic behaviour which is broadly consistent without theoretical expectations. Thus, a proper interpretation of our findings must rely as much on the broad outlines of the story we are telling, treated as a totality, as the robustness of each constituent part.

3.3 THE 'LEGACIES'

Economic and political history prior to 1952 bequeathed the Yugoslav 'experiment'[10] with a number of legacies for industrial structure, economic behaviour and attitudes. The contemporary economic system was also affected by aspects of the Soviet-type regime which functioned immediately after the war. This section will consider briefly some of these legacies, the ramifications of which extend across the range of current economic decision-making.

An important consequence of the initial Serbian hegemony over the area was that a Turkish form of legal system was introduced across the country. By this, we mean a vast complex of laws in existence at any one time, some of which were seriously inconsistent, and many of which were randomly enforced. This provides an inadequate basis for the property rights structure fundamental to the free operation of a market system, particularly with respect to the notion of legally enforced voluntary contracts (see Furubotn and Pejovich, 1972; Manne, 1975). Indeed some of the problems discussed in the previous section can be better understood from this perspective. This legal heritage, and the resulting weak assimilation of the essential rules of market behaviour, continues to have consequences to this day. For example, the widely noted illiquidity of the Yugoslav financial system during the 1970s (see Tyson, 1977b; Estrin and Bartlett, 1982) was largely caused by enterprises which maintained their incomes or investment in times of recession by defaulting on or delaying external contractual obligations without facing any legal retribution. Similarly, the effective guarantee against enterprise closure (see Chapter 4) permits weaker enterprises to default on outstanding credits without facing serious consequences. Although these phenomena may also be caused by the relative unfamiliarity of Yugoslavs with the market mechanism itself, which should disappear over time, it brings into question the precision with which marginalist propositions from market models should be interpreted.

There was certainly little understanding of competitive forces or the market framework before 1945, and even less respect. Mining, industry and trade were run by state monopolies or foreign corporations before and during the inter-war period, and frequently there were government-sponsored cartels operating in the highly centralised, inefficient and corrupt environment. Industrial production was highly concentrated and directed to the preferences of the ruling group rather than to demand. There was also a serious shortage of indigenous entrepreneurship and limited domestic capital accumulation outside the state apparatus. We have noted that ethnic differences and previously established trading patterns had hindered the development of an integrated market system after 1918, and financial and insurance markets were either thin or non-existent. One must add to this picture an inadequate transport network between north and south, and within the resource-rich mountainous regions. Therefore, industrial production and distribution in the inter-war period was largely in the hands of regional monopolies and cartels, with a few foreign-owned national corporations, and with very little capital or labour mobility between the richer and poorer areas.

Certain of these problems, common to many less developed countries, were exacerbated when the communists assumed power after the Second World War. Their emulation of the Soviet experience reinforced the anti-free market attitudes of the earlier period, although some effort was made to equalise the distribution of resources between regions (see Gregory, 1973). Since the industrial sector was developed as one giant firm under strict central control, some of the regional barriers, particularly for labour and capital, were undermined, but central planning built on the previous legal structure with an intertwining of state and industry and negative attitudes towards competition, entrepreneurship and the private accumulation of capital. The use of very large-scale technology also had important consequences for industrial structure when a regulated market system was introduced after 1952. The planners chose large-scale equipment because the machinery was largely Soviet, and therefore huge in relation to domestic production, because it was easier to create and control a small number of plants, and because there was a shortage of managerial staff. The consequences are the subject of the next chapter. The new industrial system was based on a small number of very large companies, so there were problems of monopoly power after the introduction of the market mechanism.

We have noted that the communist regime adopted a political and planning system closely modelled on the Soviet Union. Although the plan was effectively abandoned after the economic boycott in 1948, the particular way that the first stages of industrialisation were undertaken left important legacies for the operation of self-management. The First Plan, scheduled to run from 1947 to 1951, provided for a 500% increase in industrial output and a 20% rise in agricultural output over the pre-war level, to be attained from a high rate of accumulation within the state sector (see Waterson, 1962). Many of the production units which could provide a basis for later development, including the creation of an electricity generation and transport system and a heavy industrial base, were either constructed or designed in this period, and much of the growth during the 1950s arose from the completion of these projects. The failure of the plan to achieve its numerical goals should not obscure the fact that a high investment rate was established (in excess of 20% of gross material product) and a large new cohort of managerial and industrial workers recruited, the former largely for their political rather than organisational talents. It will be argued in the following section that the introduction of a new system after 1952 left the strategy, if not the tactics, of development – industrial growth, distributed equitably around the regions and based on high rates of investment – largely unchanged. Hence, the legacies of planning endured well into the 1960s. Finally, it should be noted that the industrial, mining, banking, transport, wholesale, retail, catering and parts of the agricultural sectors had been nationalised by 1948, so private ownership was restricted to small-scale services, crafts and the bulk of agriculture. Both the market and self-management were therefore introduced into a highly regulated environment with limited experience of the price mechanism and with social rather than private ownership of the means of production. The industrial labour force was relatively new and the managerial group was better schooled in marxist ideology than in entrepreneurial activities.

The dynamic of the new economic system which has been gradually, if erratically, developing since 1950 also has important legacies. The devolution of political and economic authority from the centre has been associated with the de-politicisation of many divisive issues. To define the bulk of areas (except, for example, defence, foreign policy and the political nature of the system itself) as non-political solves the conflict between communist ideology, which implies central control of all political decisions, and regional demands for autonomy. It has allowed important issues, such as education, health and social services, to be determined by local or republican groups on democratic lines because they represented problems outside the governing competence of the League of Communists. This political 'self-management' had a corollary in the economic sphere – enterprise self-management – which necessarily entailed the gradual extension of enterprise autonomy and decision-making powers. This could only be achieved with the replacement of central planning (itself politically suspect after 1948 because of its identification with the Soviet system) by a market mechanism, however regulated or imperfect it might prove to be. But this approach to reform meant that markets and self-management were imposed from above, without any real basis of popular support in the early period. Indeed, the authorities were possibly responding to political necessities, with no real intention of entirely replacing central direction of the economy. They were concerned to decentralise the minimum feasible degree of authority, and differing interpretations of what would be required goes some way to explaining the erratic path of reforms. As a result, they countenanced the creation of a market self-management system without being able to accept all its implications, such as liberalising trade or the free operation of a price system and capital market. The malfunctionings of the market self-managed system, in part because of the legacies discussed above, combined with the ideological predispositions of the regime and their mistrust of the mechanism itself, often led to ad hoc and inefficient intervention. The resulting somewhat incoherent regulatory policies seriously affect the outcomes observed in our empirical work.

3.4 ECONOMIC ENVIRONMENTS SINCE 1952

There were fundamental changes to the Yugoslav political and economic system between 1950 and 1952, in 1961 and 1965, and from 1972 to 1974, involving new constitutions in 1953, 1963 and 1974 and far more frequent alterations to specific laws. For the purpose of our study, the sporadic and erratic evolution which occurred in practice will be schematised into three economic environments:[11] the 'Visible Hand' period from 1952 to 1965, the 'Market Self-Management' era from 1965 until between 1972 and 1974, and 'Social Planning' which has operated to the present day. This characterisation necessarily over-simplifies and would have little justification in a detailed economic history of the entire period (see Sirc, 1979, for an alternative approach or Horvat, 1971a, for a different schematisation). However, for our purposes it is crucial to know when the theoretical propositions are most likely to hold, and the general economic environments during the remainder of the post-war period for the purposes of comparison. We are examining the impact of differing institutional arrangements on economic behaviour, so the robustness of the schematisation is itself an empirical question. We shall be arguing that self-management effects should be most pronounced when government regulation of the economic environment was at its minimum, between the 1965 and 1973/4 Reforms. If the assumption is incorrect, either because the system was never effectively self-managed or because self-management was operational throughout the post-1952 period, this will be observed in our empirical findings. With the general points and legacies in mind, this section outlines the most important characteristics of the three Yugoslav economic systems between 1952 and 1982.

3.4.1 *The Visible Hand period 1952–65*[12]

This period was marked by a compromise between a Soviet-type development strategy, stressing rapid accumulation and industrial growth, and self-managed market tactics. The level and allocation of investment and trade were centrally planned, but the newly created self-managed firms operated within a highly regulated market system for some current commodities. In fact, the system increasingly resembled the contemporary reformed structure in Hungary over the period (see Hare, 1977; Cave and Hare, 1981) with strong central determination of the aggregate sectoral balances and future growth path, but some degree of decentralisation for detailed allocation. Although the balance of authority probably remained at the centre throughout the period, the continuous legal changes in general acted to increase the autonomy of self-managed firms and the effectiveness of the market mechanism over time.

The legal principles of self-management were codified between 1950 and 1953, and remained the basis of the system until 1974, although there were also some changes in the 1950s and 1960s. Prior to 1974, enterprise self-management operated approximately as follows. A Yugoslav enterprise comprised two legal entities – the Collective, being all permanent workers over eighteen years of age[13] (around 97.5% of the total), which produced, managed and distributed the income, and the Assets, which were socially owned. The Collective retained 'usus fructus' rights[14] over the Assets, but were not permitted to distribute them in income, and had to pay taxes on them until 1969.

Economic decision-making was vested in the Collective, though formal control was passed up to an elected Workers' Council if the enterprise membership exceeded thirty. Even so, the Collective retained influence through electing the Council, making personal proposals or choices in general meetings, or voting in the referenda that were called on most central issues. If the enterprises were very large, Economic Units might be formed, which were autonomous decision-making units with their own collective general meetings and Workers' Councils. For multi-plant firms the central Workers' Council became meetings of the unit delegates, and referenda replaced general meetings for enterprise-wide topics. This made self-management feasible in the formal sense for large corporations.

The Workers' Council (the whole collective in small companies, or enterprise-wide councils in the very large ones) determined overall policy and general direction. Its primary functions were legislative, with the executive role played by a sub-committee it appointed – the Board of Management – and the Director. The Council therefore set general aims, and ensured that they were carried out by the executive, using a machinery of reports, rules (called statutes), plans and accounts. It could have between 15 and 120 members (the average was stable at 22), elected for a two-year term (half elected annually), of whom 75% had to be production workers.[15] Initially, the elections were organised by the trade union, but the role was later assumed by the outgoing Council. A rotation principle was introduced to ensure that there was a fast turnover, with members not sitting for longer than two terms consecutively on any self-management committee.

The Board of Management was the executive branch of the Workers' Council, with responsibility for the development and supervision of detailed plans to achieve the general policy goals from collective meetings, referenda and the Council. It included the Director as ex-officio member, had three to eleven members, of whom 75% had to be manual workers, and could appoint specialist committees. Membership of any self-management organs entailed no work exemption, nor higher earnings except for expenses, but did guarantee freedom from dismissal, transfer or ordinary discipline procedures during the term of office.

The Workers' Council appointed the Enterprise Director.[16] On the one hand, he was the principal executive agent; an employee carrying out the general policies of the Collective as interpreted by the Workers' Council and specified by the Board of Management, and appointed in open competition for a fixed period (in the earlier years he was appointed by a committee entirely or partly chosen by the local authority). He could only be dismissed during his (normally four) years of office if he broke the law, or if the enterprise was liquidated. However, his position was ambiguous because he assumed legal responsibility for enterprise behaviour, and had 'the power to suspend any decision by an elected body at variance with law or statutes', which made him, in part, a government (or League of Communist) watchdog over the behaviour of self-managed enterprises. However, the Director's legal responsibility for business practices left the Collective and the members of the various self-management committees free from legal liability. The Director appointed a conventional enterprise hierarchy who were responsible to him in the execution of policy, at the head of which was a 'Collegium' of departmental heads. This enterprise structure is summarised in Diagram 3.1. The fact that the responsibility for ensuring the rule of law fell to the executive branch led to some

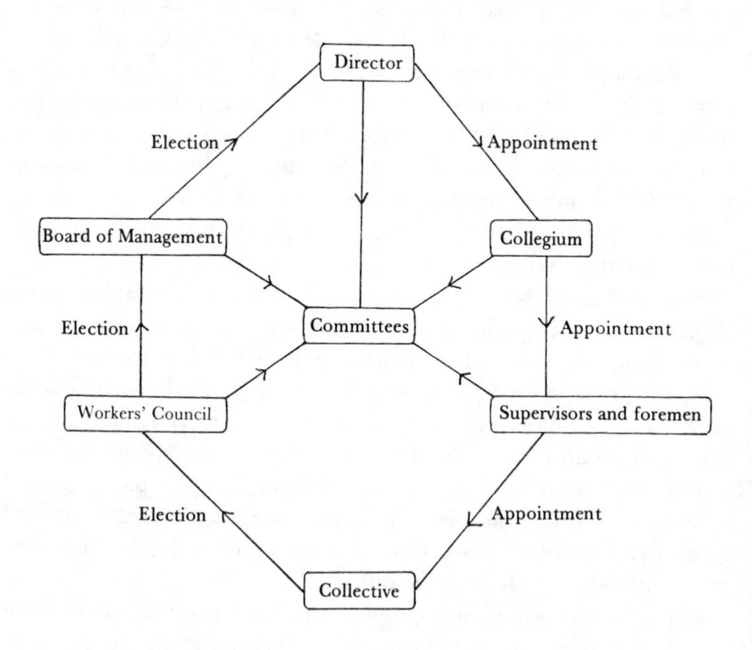

Diagram 3.1. The structure of the enterprise

confusion of authority in practice, especially in the early years. However, in principle, the Yugoslav system of self-management was, and remains to this day, established on a fundamental distinction between decision-making, to be undertaken by the self-management committees, and execution, which is empowered to a managerial hierarchy.[17] The imperfections of this distinction in practice, and in particular the fact that managerial staff appear to dominate much of actual decision-making, has been a major theme of the Yugoslav literature (see Adizes, 1971; Kavcic, Rus and Tannenbaum, 1971; Rus, 1978; Obradovic, 1978; for a survey, see Estrin and Bartlett, 1982). It was a principal factor behind the 1974 Reforms which further devolved decision-making authority to the 'Economic Units', later known as 'Basic Organisation of Associated Labour' or BOALs (see Comisso, 1979; Sacks, 1982).

We shall briefly focus on three of the most important tasks for the self-management organs: the choice of wage distribution schedule, the distribution of net revenue (total revenue minus non-labour costs) between the four available final uses (wages, investment, collective consumption and reserves), and the adoption of internal statutes. Our models assume that labour is homogeneous, but the existence of different labour skill types in Yugoslav firms meant that the self-management committees had to find an agreed way of distributing the surplus amongst the Collective. The approach was to compile a list of rates for each job, proportionate to the least skilled, using complex job evaluation procedures. Collective members were then paid an agreed sum as an advance, with the remaining surplus distributed at the end of accounting periods according to this wage distribution schedule. As will be noted below, this led to considerable variation in the income received over time (for further evidence, see Jan Vanek, 1972). The standard accounting procedure for self-managed firms involved summing total revenues and deducting non-labour costs and depreciation for Enterprise Income. This was divided into contractual and statutory obligations (such as taxes) and net personal incomes which were available for allocation between the final uses. Generally, referenda were used to pass a major change in the distribution schedule or the employment of funds. The Workers' Council also determined the Enterprise Statutes, which fixed the safety and health procedures, labour relations and discipline, holidays and recruitment, and the formal structure of committees and procedures. These were registered with Economic Courts, and the social welfare rules they provided proved a major concern of the self-managed bodies (see Koloja, 1964; Adizes, 1971).

Given the suggested immobility of labour under self-management, employment rules are worth further consideration. Recruitment was organised by a committee of the Workers' Council, normally according to the qualifications for the job-type specified in the statutes, and by open competition. Promotion was similarly based on qualification, so anyone who passed a particular vocational examination had earned the automatic right to a higher skill rating in the distribution schedule. It was relatively difficult to remove individual Collective members since a worker had to be brought before a Disciplinary Tribunal (with two members from the Workers' Council and one from the trade union) and found guilty of a disciplinary breach five times, each with a defence council, prior to dismissal, and the individual retained the right of appeal. However, the low mean and high variance of earnings in sectors of poor demand could still generate quits, and the Director was empowered to determine overall employment policy. Even so, apart from the rare cases when the Collective might close one economic unit, downward labour force flexibility relied on natural wastage, part-time, temporary and sub-contracted employment, and youth under eighteen years.

An enterprise could be founded by federal or republican bodies, the commune (local government), another enterprise, banks or groups of individuals. Once production had commenced, the founders handed over all rights over income or decisions to the self-management organs. The Collective could choose to merge or sub-divide, but not to liquidate (this authority was vested in the commune, and occurred when the firm could not meet statutory and contractual obligations, or broke its own statutes or the law). If the firm ran an operating deficit, liquidation could be temporarily averted by the appointment of a receiver, who assumed managerial control for one year. This left the commune, or republican authorities, with the prospect of subsidising legally 'profitable' collectives (where revenue exceeded contractual payments) which could not generate adequate net income to pay their members' average earnings at even a subsistence rate.

In practice, formal self-management had few consequences for economic decision-making during the Visible Hand period (though rather more for social welfare issues[18]) because the state left few choices to be taken at the enterprise level, and even these were closely guided by an informal chain of command: the League of Communists. In the early fifties, around 40% or less of enterprise revenue was available for disposal by Workers' Councils (the remainder being paid in statutory obligations or non-labour costs), though this gradually rose to 55% by 1964. The scheme for collective choice of the wage schedule was introduced in 1954, but only referred to net profit[19] until 1961 when the net income system described above was properly operational. The state determined the level and allocation of investment providing the funds from the budget through Bank and Investment Fund credits according to the plan. The firms paid the bulk of their revenues to the state and labour, leaving insufficient funds for investment without government assistance. While the projects themselves might be devised at the enterprise level, they were generally only implemented if they meshed with the planned allocation. Thus, in 1955 some 64% of total funds for investment were provided by the state, and only 35% by enterprises (often collectives had to provide a certain proportion of the financial capital themselves, as a condition for bank credits), and even in 1962, these proportions were 59% and 38%. Thus, enterprise investment was, for the most part, centrally directed under the Visible Hand system, though firms could influence the detailed allocation of funds to an increasing extent over time. More generally, as we shall see below, the highly regulated nature of the economic mechanism between 1952 and 1965, especially the control of prices, costs and international trade, combined with the high taxation and direction of investment to leave the inexperienced self-management committees with little autonomy over the period, and particularly during the 1950s.

Not only were the self-management organs given relatively little to control but actual authority was severely constrained by legal and informal pressures.[20] In the early years, the Director retained many discretionary powers, and had dual loyalties to the collective, and state and party apparatus. He, the Collegium, the trade union leadership and senior enterprise committee members generally belonged to the League of Communists, which continued the practice of democratic centralism. While the League, in theory, had relinquished direct control of the state to play a 'leading role' through discussion, education and propaganda (the 1958

Programme), in practice party members held every important job and followed the orders from a well-defined centralised hierarchy. The full effect of this informal chain of command cannot be evaluated, but it seems unlikely that, in a case where the self-managed organs had the desire and means to execute a policy which contradicted central objectives, the Director would carry out their plans. In this early period, the informal network of control and the limited financial autonomy of the enterprise generally ensured that both the self-management organs and the executive branch followed party workers on most major policy decisions, even if questions of social welfare were largely left to collective choice. If, on major issues, the opinions of the Collective diverged from planned objectives, the Director, aided by the Unions, Collegium and senior committee members were sufficiently powerful to prevent the 'anti-social' behaviour. The authorities also ensured that the enterprises fulfilled their social responsibilities through scrutiny, regulations and control by diverse government bodies, such as the Social Accounting Service, tax authorities, the communes and Economic Chambers (Kormora). The latter institutions were formed on an industrial basis in 1954 (and enterprise membership made compulsory by 1958) to formulate and implement economic policy, coordinate enterprise decisions and offer technical advice. The trade unions also played a supervisory role in the earlier years, organising the elections to Workers' Councils and setting wages, but their functions were gradually assumed by the Council itself. Although time gradually reduced the problems of inexperience and indifference, the effective central control of the bulk of enterprise decision variables and the operation of this hidden chain of command meant that self-management could have had little effect on the allocation of resources during the Visible Hand period.

The idea of the Visible Hand system was that the authorities intended to control the development path, planning future production through central determination of the volume and structure of investment, while markets were used to allocate current resources. Moreover, the planners should have permitted information about consumer preferences from the market to influence their proposed allocations of capital. In practice, a freely operating market system was never properly created so the planners dominated every aspect of economic allocation. For example, the investment funds, accumulated from enterprise taxation through the state budget, should have been allocated according to a number of market and development-based criteria including profitability, the proportion of internal financing and the foreign exchange impact. However, these principles were not fully applied, and the most important factors in practice proved to be political and regional (see Neuberger, 1959; Milenkovitch, 1971). More generally, markets were not the primary source of information, motivation and incentives in the system, as one might expect given the persistence of an informal network of central command over the period, and market criteria were not the actual determinants of enterprise success or failure.

Yugoslav markets during the Visible Hand period existed behind a complex wall of protection with multiple exchange rates and numerous tariff systems (see Horvat, 1971a). The authorities determined the vast majority of prices centrally, with the purpose of aiding accumulation and growth. Thus domestic prices were effectively insulated from both the world market and the pressures of internal relative scarcities, and distorted to reflect accumulation possibilities and planner's preferences. The development strategy remained essentially that of the centrally planned era, particularly during the 1950s; growth through industrialisation based on a high share of investment in national product and biased in favour of heavy industry. The system differed from its classic Soviet-type counterpart in that much of the decision-making was decentralised and enterprises could even suggest options to the centre. Yet final strategic decisions rested with the central authorities and were enforced by an extremely tight regulation of the allocative mechanisms, particularly investment, and through the informal network of command. Markets provided a forum for the decentralisation of decision-making, but their limited sphere of operation and the way that they were regulated meant that market forces, as we would understand the term for Western countries, were not the basis for economic choices. This point can be illustrated at the enterprise level. In principle, firms bought inputs and sold outputs on markets, subject of course to price and, in the early years, wage controls. They could also propose investment projects to the centre, which actually determined the allocation of most funds. However, in practice enterprise success or failure (measured, for example, by income per head or profitability) was largely in the hands of the political authorities, who could be induced to raise output prices and lower input costs, lend working capital, allocate investment funds or alter the quantity and terms of foreign trading. Regional factors, ideological biases towards the product and sector, political favouritism and even the formal and informal contacts of the Director and the leading communists in the firm were therefore as important to enterprise profitability as reducing costs or improving the efficiency of production in this period. Although liberalising reforms began in 1961, they failed to endure in full beyond 1962 (see Milenkovitch, 1971) and the system was not thoroughly altered until 1965. Our discussion suggests that the Visible Hand era would not be a suitable period to test our propositions about enterprise behaviour under market self-management.

3.4.2 *Market Self-Management 1965–72/4*

After four years of debate and false starts (see Rusinow, 1977; Milenkovitch, 1971), Reforms in 1965 formalised a fundamental change in economic strategy and tactics. Though the Reforms were inadequately prepared and never fully implemented (see Horvat, 1971a), the resulting system is suitable for testing our hypotheses because the market mechanism was, to some extent, liberalised, and enterprise autonomy was considerably increased.

The new strategy was intended to achieve international competitiveness for Yugoslav goods in an open economy, growth based on domestic demand and consumption, and a major extension of effective self-management. This implied the adoption of high technology and capital intensity, promoted through mergers, joint investment and partnership with foreign corporations (after 1967) to exploit imported techniques and raise factor productivity. The basic tactic was to create a free market system of autonomous self-managed firms, borrowing funds through a form of capital market and operating in an open economy. Thus, the range of decisions taken by the enterprise was to be increased, relative prices restructured and freed, and markets and trade fully liberalised. This was all accompanied, though probably not intentionally, by a significant decline in the control exercised by the League of Communists over the economic sphere.

The machinery for the central collection and allocation of investment funds was dismantled, with the latter function assumed by banks which received the balance of state assets. The banks were directed by their founders – any economic or political organisa-

Table 3.1. *Domestic sources of finance for fixed investment (% total)*

	1960–3	1965	1966	1969	1972
Economic organisations	30	29	39	28	30
Social organisations	7	8	7	6	8
State finance:	60	27	15	16	20
Federal	(33)	(3)	(6)	(9)	(2)
Republican	(8)	(4)	(3)	(3)	(14)
Commune	(19)	(20)	(6)	(4)	(4)
Banks	3	36	39	49	42

Source: World Bank (1975).

tion – who were represented on the Managing Assembly in proportion to their subscription towards the 'Credit Fund', up to a maximum of 10% (see Dmitrijevich and Macesich, 1973). Thus the new system implied the operation of a capital market, with enterprises determining their own investment demand. This would be met by internal financing or borrowed from the banking system that had mobilised private savings and had been given the remainder of the state's investment funds. Table 3.1 illustrates the changing sources of Yugoslav investment, and is derived from the World Bank (1975). It can be seen that, even at the end of the Visible Hand period, most investment was state financed, primarily at the federal or communal level, although projects were backed with a proportion of enterprise funds. The banks and enterprises had largely replaced federal funding as early as 1966, and the importance of the former grew as both self-financing and central allocation declined. Enterprises increasingly relied on external funds after the initial jump following the Reforms, which probably reflects the low or negative real rates of interest over the period; interest rates were pegged at 8% between 1966 and 1972 (except for 1968 when they rose to 10%) while inflation rates varied between 7% and 18%. The shifting balance of political power over the period probably explains why the republics gradually replaced the federal authorities as the major source of government funds.

The abolition of centralised accumulation increased the resources at the disposal of the enterprise. Thus, the proportion of gross value added at the disposal of the self-management committees rose from around 45% in the early 1960s to over 60% in this period. For the first time, enterprises had sufficient resources effectively to determine their own incomes, collective consumption and even investment, though as we have seen the latter continued to be primarily financed by the banks. After some thirteen years of nominal authority, it is likely that the relevant committees had gained the stature and experience to use their decision-making powers. There continued to be central plans, but in the absence of the state direction of investment and the informal chain of command, and since enterprises were now geared to open market criteria and incentives, the authorities lacked the leverage necessarily to implement them. The essential change introduced in 1965 was that, although before the Reforms the authorities had both the information and the power to determine enterprise decisions on the lines of the overall development strategy where necessary, they did not after that date. As a consequence, the planning system came to resemble French indicative planning (see Estrin and Holmes, 1983), except for the projects in which the state acted as founder.

The detailed structure of self-management was also altered in this period. Although the spirit of the earlier form was retained, enterprises become free to choose internally the appropriate arrangements for effective self-management. In general, the Workers' Council and Director were retained, but there was an increased use of collective meetings and referenda. The enterprise gained full control over the choice of Director for the first time, and they were frequently elected directly while the Board of Management often lost its position amongst the plethora of other Workers' Councils' committees. Finally, there was increasing use of hierarchical Workers' Councils and Economic Units; a move culminating in the BOALs rather than the enterprise itself being established as the legal basis of the self-management system in the 1974 Reforms.

All these legal changes were a necessary but not sufficient condition for the operation of a market self-managed system between 1965 and 1974. Even the dismantling of central investment control and the increase in the disposable resources of the enterprise would have had limited significance for resource allocation if the informal chain of command operating through the League of Communists had remained intact. However, the Reforms were pushed through by a coalition of northern republics, who believed that an economic system based on political patronage was inefficient and hindered development, and southern ones, who opposed the Serbian hegemony implied by party control from Belgrade. In the process, regional political authority was devolved to the eight national parties, leaving a power vacuum at the centre until around 1971 (Rusinow, 1977). Moreover, the reformers were apparently sincere in their aims of freeing enterprise decision-making, as is reflected in the 'basic intention' of the 1966–70 plan 'to ensure a gradual redistribution of national income in favour of personal incomes, so that they may not only bring about an improvement in the standard of living, but also become a factor conducive to rational production and spending' (World Bank, 1975). Thus the central party network split and lost direction, while the victorious decentralising factions were agreed at least to relax control in the economic sphere. Therefore, though the local party retained considerable central power in some republics, after the fall of Rankovitch in 1966 (see Rusinow, 1977) the informal network of command was neither willing nor able to prevent enterprises from exploiting the autonomy provided by the Reforms.

It has been argued that, while the Reforms provided enterprise independence, decisions were actually taken by management rather than labour (Rusinow, 1977; Broeckmeyer, 1970; Adizes, 1971). Hence, Yugoslavia should not be used to test the theories of self-management. In fact, the effectiveness of workers' control varies according to Director, enterprise, sector, region, commune and even issue, so no general refutation is feasible, but the literature suggests the following picture (Gorupic and Paj, 1970; Obradovic, 1978). The collective was normally led by skilled and white collar workers (comprising some 80% of the membership of self-management organs by 1970), who were primarily concerned with issues of income and welfare, and left the bulk of production decisions to management. However, they retained rights of consultation over all choices, and an effective veto in cases of disagreement with the Director. Moreover, the operation of the BOALs gave shop-floor workers considerable influence over low-level and organisational decisions. While there was clearly considerable leeway in the interpretation of collective preferences, the Director could not consistently implement decisions in opposition to the membership, and had to accept the general orientation favouring labour incomes and employment security. The effectiveness of Yugoslav self-management is a complex area (see Estrin and Barlett, 1982, for a survey of the considerable literature on the subject), and the interpretation of the findings depends as much on the reader's expectations of self-management as the operation of the system itself. The fact that workers were in a position to influence decision-making, whatever the extent to which they actually did so, justifies examining empirically propositions from self-management theory on Yugoslav data.

However, the Yugoslav system only approximated the market self-management of our models because, although enterprises may have been given considerable decision-making autonomy, the free market element was never properly operational. The 1965 Reforms were introduced during a depression, which was severely exacerbated by the resulting adjustments and labour shake-out. Industrial employment, which had been rising at 7% per annum, fell for two years. This led to almost immediate backsliding on certain of the market principles announced in 1965, and reinforced the tendency not to implement some of the Reforms. Thus, although relative prices had been entirely restructured in 1965, price controls began gradually to creep back to distort the system again, until they covered some 70% of products by the late sixties. The liberalisation of the foreign exchange system was only partially implemented, and then in 1967, some two years after the dinar devaluation. The goal of dinar convertibility on international money markets was never attained. Finally, a new central investment fund, for the less developed regions (the Fund for Accelerated Development), was set up in 1966 (it had been proposed in 1961), operating with 1.85% 'contributions' from enterprise social product (this was raised to 1.94% in 1971).

However, severely regulated and subject to arbitrary intervention from authorities at the various levels though it doubtless was, the post-Reform Yugoslav market mechanism in general still provided some basis for the decentralised coordination of private decisions. The most important area in which this may not have been the case was the newly created capital market, where ideology combined with inexperience to generate severe allocational problems. Yugoslav law permitted virtually no alternative capital flows so financial investment was composed almost entirely of the liabilities of the banking system, which was becoming highly centralised. The number of banks declined from 220 in 1963 to 64 in 1970, primarily through mergers, with the ten largest ones providing virtually all investment credits and 60% of short-term loans in 1968 (Dmitrijevich and Macesich, 1973). The authorities' mistrust of the market mechanism for capital allocation is shown by their pegging of the interest rate to a low or negative rate over the period. It has been argued that this restricted the mobilisation of private savings (World Bank, 1975), and encouraged the adoption of capital-intensive techniques (Sapir, 1980a). Moreover the banks, the only legal channel between savings and investment, faced excess demand for funds, and had to employ rationing procedures which have been blamed for resource misallocation (Sirc, 1979; World Bank, 1975). It would appear that the banks did not apply consistent appraisal criteria between 1965 and 1972, so that even after the 1965 Reforms economic criteria may have taken a second place to political and regional interests. Certainly, as late as 1970–1, some 44% of bank investment funds were 'earmarked' contributions formed from government deposits and therefore heavily influenced by republican or local authorities. Most remaining funds were formed from the founding contributors' pool, so that the group of firms directly involved with the bank doubtless had superior access to credits and a considerable say in their allocation. It is very hard to judge the effects of these imperfections on the system as a whole, particularly since there were widespread semi-legal or illegal transactions between enterprises which doubtless provided a somewhat richer and more effective market mechanism (see Dmitrijevich and Macesich, 1973). There is no doubt that government regulation of markets, particularly of interest rates, product prices and some traded goods meant that the post-Reform system, at best, only approximated the market self-management of our models.

The Reforms were based on the belief that decentralisation would engender rational economic decision-making. However, responsibility was devolved to individuals who had risen through the hierarchy because of their ability to administrate the orders of a superior, and to a relatively new industrial proletariat. Moreover, the industrial structure was highly concentrated to suit the convenience of planners, and there was no prior knowledge of market forces, or the need to fulfil voluntary contracts. There was certainly a shake-out at the management level (some 20% of Directors were not re-elected in 1966, compared with less than 10% during the Visible Hand period), but there is little doubt that many firms responded to the new, more uncertain economic environment (noted by Adizes, 1971) with anti-social or irresponsible behaviour. The former will be considered in the chapter on industrial structure, but the latter was exemplified by the increases in both earnings and investment which were financed by the non-payment of debts and trade credits. Similarly, some collectives raised earnings by increasing prices, or appropriating investment and reserve funds. The authorities had expected a decline in aggregate investment (as a share of GDP) as enterprises chose to distribute more resources for current consumption, but had hoped the more sophisticated technology could maintain previous employment and output growth. The irresponsible financial behaviour, and associated reduction in growth, inflation and illiquidity gradually hardened attitudes against market self-management, and, combined with a reassertion of central communist will in 1971, led to the Reforms between 1972 and 1974.

3.4.3 *Social Planning 1972/4 to the present*

There was increasing disillusion with the performance of the market system in the early 1970s, as well as a revival of central authority and morale in the communist party following the 'defeat' of Croatian nationalism in 1971 (see Rusinow, 1977). Moreover, fears about the effectiveness and relevance of self-management also contributed to a number of atmosphere changes and legal reforms between 1972 and 1974. Chapter 5 indicates the reduction in economic growth, inflation and trade deficits and widening income inequalities, which were blamed on free markets and persuaded the authorities to reassert central guidance over the economy. The idea was that, although the economic strategy would remain largely unchanged, institutions were to be created in which self-managed firms agreed, or were induced, to avoid irresponsible and anti-social behaviour and follow planned guidelines for development. At the same time, the format of self-management itself was radically altered, with decision-making authority devolved from the enterprise to BOALs. It is not yet entirely clear how the new institutional mechanism is operating in practice, nor its implications for economic performance. For the purposes of this study, we shall merely note that the reassertion of central guidance, however imperfect its operation or regional its authority, makes the period after around 1972 unsuitable for testing our propositions about the effects of market self-management in Yugoslavia. Readers interested in more details on the recent institutional developments are referred to the growing literature on the subject (see especially Comisso, 1979, 1980; Moore, 1980; Sacks, 1982; Schrenk, Ardalan and El Tatawy, 1979; Tyson, 1980).

On the coordination front, voluntary contractual arrangements were developed between economic actors and the government (generally at the republican rather than federal level) to ensure the implementation of the policy objectives specified in a revitalised planning system. In principle, this new mechanism once again gave the authorities the power to steer the economy, at a relatively detailed level, in a desired direction. The new planning system was designed to be closely akin to indicative planning, as formalised by Massé (1965) and Meade (1970) (see also Estrin and Holmes, 1983). Economic agents are required by law to exchange pre-specified information about their current position and projected future decisions. The planners search for inconsistencies among these medium-term private plans, transmitting further information back and forth between the enterprises and policy-makers until the set of choices over time is internally consistent and socially desirable. The completed plan which emerges is agreed to by all participants, who are argued to be likely to implement it because of their involvement in its construction. In Meade's type of plan, the target would anyway represent the best outcome that any individual could hope to attain, because the authorities would not have attempted to shift the allocation away from privately desired outcomes. However, in the Yugoslav case the system was built specifically to facilitate the direction of economic development to some degree, so one must presume that there would be a divergence between private and social interests. This explains the role of Social Compacts and Self-Management Agreements, which are contractual arrangements between enterprises, economic institutions and the government which bind their signatories to implement agreed or planned targets. Both arrangements are notionally voluntary. Social Compacts are not legally binding and are primarily concerned with general policy objections, such as income distribution, prices or trade. Self-Management Agreements are legally binding contracts of a specific character between agents, for example concerning investment or collective consumption provision. They are enforced through 'Courts of Associated Labour', which can award financial compensation or dissolve defaulting participants. Loosely, Social

Compacts appear to outline general policy intentions at a republican or inter-republican level, while Self-Management Agreements specify actual policy methods and tactics to attain desired targets. Thus, the post-1974 aim has been an economic system which derives economic objectives as a consensus through a complex structure of negotiations, and enforces them via contractual arrangements between planners and all the other economic actors.

This 'social planning' mechanism is the main way in which the government coordinates the economy, but its effects on resource allocation are not yet clear. In the first place, the authorities would probably have rather more say in the building of 'consensus' than the previous description would suggest, although to a degree which differed between regions and republics. This guidance of the mechanism in practice would be even more marked given the increased authority of the Communist League in recent years, and its desire to reassert some central direction after the perceived incoherence of the 'free market' period. Although enterprises have continued nominally to retain autonomy over the bulk of economic issues, apart from current incomes, prices and the cost of capital, the planning system would offer the centre enough information to make micro-economic decisions if required, and Self-Management Agreements the potential leverage to enforce them. There has also been some increase in the authorities' direction and financing of investment, located at the republican level, and laws in 1971 reduced direct enterprise control over banks (which were no longer permitted to lend more than 30% of their total credit fund to one client). Hence, some producers lost their earlier excellent access to funds which derived from the joint ownership of banks. In addition to their increased role in the allocation of capital, the authorities also gained potentially more control over enterprise decisions via their say in the arrangement of joint ventures and mergers, and the greater activity of such old centralising institutions as unions and Economic Chambers in the new planning mechanism. Many of these changes were associated with the revival of the Communist League, which began to play a greater part in ensuring that development conformed to the planned pattern. Even so, it is very hard to judge the extent to which enterprises actually lost real decision-making authority after around 1974; the answer is probably that they were in a stronger position than in the fifties, and weaker than in the late 1960s. But the environment was highly regulated during even the self-management era, and any reform designed to increase government direction substantially and further reduce enterprise authority, however ineffective, makes one unwilling to continue testing firm-level equilibrium propositions on those data.

The actual operation of the new system has been very mixed. The degree of central guidance has appeared to vary significantly in different years and among regions while the mechanism appears to be rather slow and clumsy in practice, perhaps because the real diversity of interests makes it very difficult to reach harmonious decisions within a region, let alone between republics. In consequence, despite the broad extent of interference at the microeconomic level, no properly planned detailed guidance of the economy has really emerged. The most notable feature of the interventions has been their incoherence, between sectors, republics and regions, which makes it even harder to hypothesise Yugoslavia in terms of an integrated market. It appears that the 1974 Reforms may have brought Yugoslavs the worst of both worlds: eliminating the decentralised coordination of markets without properly replacing it by planned coherence, leaving unsystematic ad hoc interventions. The system does not conform to market self-management, but may not represent planned development either. An important example, which has particular significance for our study, concerns the role of contractual arrangements in the formulation of an incomes policy. Self-Management Agreements were constructed after 1974 to assure that, whatever the net revenue of the firm, the amounts distributed to labour were not too dissimilar across enterprises, industries and regions. If effective, this 'social planning' would of course have repressed precisely one of those suggested effects of self-management upon which this study will concentrate: income differentials. However, in practice such contracts had a differential impact according to sector and region, so the empirical implications are less clear-cut. It should also be noted that such policies could only represent a temporary solution to the problems caused by self-management. The 'excess' net revenue over agreed labour payments was shifted to business funds, leading to enforced differences in investment rates and collective capital accumulation which could amplify real earnings differentials in the future.

The second aspect of the 1974 Reforms was that decision-making authority was formally devolved from the enterprise to the BOAL, which became the basis of the entire self-management system. This radical move appears to have been motivated primarily for ideological reasons, to ensure the effectiveness and relevance of self-management for shop-floor workers. Any group of workers whose product could be evaluated independently from any others could set up a BOAL, and enterprises legally became just another 'voluntary pooling of resources', linked contractually by Self-Management Agreements and distinguished from joint ventures, long-term supply contracts or cartels only by the degree of formal structure. The purpose of the reform was to increase decision-making power at the periphery vis-à-vis the centre of the firm for all choices which could feasibly be made at that level. This was intended to counter the growing remoteness of central self-management committees from the actual labour force and the increasing ineffectiveness of direct workers' participation, particularly over the numerous technical choices to be made in a market environment (see Estrin and Bartlett, 1982, for a survey of the Yugoslav literature expressing doubts about the effectiveness of labour management in Yugoslav firms). It was hoped that the inefficiency threatened by such decentralisation would be offset by the more active role of unifying institutions, unions, Economic Chambers and especially the Communist League, in stimulating ideas and arbitrating disputes. Thus, the apparent decentralisation of economic authority was undertaken in the context of a recentralisation of political power.

It is very hard to evaluate the economic consequences of this reform in practice, not least because the impact on actual decision-making probably varied enormously among firms. In fact, the overall effect may have been slight. It has been suggested that the reform was more nominal than real and authority never really shifted from the central Workers' Council and Director in most cases. A similar institutional structure had existed since 1961, so one can see how the transfer of 'ultimate authority' to the old Economic Units could often leave the actual important marketing, output and investment decisions in the centre. On the other hand, every BOAL, which could be a workshop, technical department or even a plant, was given a potential veto over enterprise-wide decisions after 1974, with the right to secede from the rest of the company over insoluble disputes. One could therefore imagine, for example, the break-up of conglomerate enterprises which practised cross-subsidisation as a consequence of the reforms, since some product branches had been given the incentive and right to leave the corporation. This is a tangled area with few clear-cut results to date (see Comisso, 1979, 1980; Sacks, 1982, for a discussion of the issues), but for our purposes, the main effect of the reform was to render the data on enterprise numbers and industrial structure quite unreliable after the early 1970s. Yugoslav sources provide no series with a consistent definition of the firm over time, so the legal replacement of BOAL for enterprise doubled the number of 'firms' in the industrial sector in two years, even though the actual number of producers and industrial concentration was probably not affected. This is a further reason for not extending our study into the social planning era.

In conclusion, the Yugoslav economic system between 1952 and 1965 represented a decentralised planning process, while the 1965 Reforms introduced a particular variant of market self-management in which enterprises had decision-making autonomy, but the market environment was controlled. Even then serious problems in the design, timing and implementation of the new system, combined with market inexperience, caused both economic problems and irresponsible behaviour. The changes between 1972 and 1974 represented a major constraint, institutional and political, on self-managed behaviour, the consequences of which they were partly intended to suppress, and also brought into doubt the reliability of some of the data. Therefore, the predictions of the model on earnings dispersion and factor proportions will be tested on data referring to the years 1965–72, while the effects of introducing self-management to a planned system will be studied by comparison of the Visible Hand and Market Self-Management periods. The null hypothesis for tests of the model must be derived from the structure that the variables would assume in a planned economy, and the fit might be expected to be worse during the initial years of adjustment after 1965, and slightly before the actual legal changes in 1974, since the political atmosphere had changed one or two years earlier. The background, heritage and institutional instability displayed since the war lead one to interpret the static, equilibrium predictions of the theory with caution in the Yugoslav environment.

PART 2

YUGOSLAV PRACTICE

4

Yugoslav industrial structure

4.1 INTRODUCTION

We examine in this chapter another important element of the Yugoslav environment – the industrial structure. We offer evidence on the degree of product market monopoly power, which has implications for system-wide adjustment as well as for static welfare losses. The chapter is something of a link between the two parts of the book. It provides descriptive statistics about Yugoslavia to help in framing hypotheses and presents the first opportunity to test the relevance of self-management theory. The Yugoslav industrial structure of 1958 is outlined in the following section, and plays the role of starting point for the analysis. The severely non-competitive nature of the findings leads us to stress monopolistic factors for the rest of the study. Entry, exit and mergers between 1958 and 1972 are considered in the third section, with special reference to their consequences for enterprise numbers and market concentration. The data are used to investigate the predicted relationship between entry, exit, average earnings and concentration. Falling market concentration with declining enterprise numbers points to an investigation of overall concentration which is reported in the fourth section, and our findings are summarised in the fifth.

It would be interesting to use these data to analyse competitiveness under self-management in comparison with other market systems. Vanek (1970) claims that the industrial structure will be relatively more competitive under labour-management because each cooperative will be smaller than its profit maximising counterpart. Hence, more firms will be needed to meet a given market demand. However, the assumption of an identical output may be inadmissable, and Estrin (1982b) suggests that markets will actually be less competitive under self-management. Either way, there exist hypotheses about the determinants of industrial structure under self-management which one might hope to be able to test in this chapter. Unfortunately, Yugoslav data are unsuitable for examining these questions, because the industrial structure in this period had not emerged as the result of decentralised private decisions. In effect, the market structure at the start of the self-management era had been determined during the period of planning, to satisfy the needs of development and planners' preferences. It was therefore exogenous to the firms themselves. This interpretation is reflected in the organisation of the chapter, in which we commence by describing the pre-determined environment of 1958 and go on to see how enterprises chose to act in this framework after they had attained decision-making autonomy.

We only consider evidence for the Yugoslav industrial sector, with statistical sources and numerous additional tables on market structure being contained in Statistical Appendix A.[1] Where possible, Yugoslav findings are also compared with the experience in the UK and the USA in order to provide some perspective. Analysis is conducted for the entire industrial sector, classified according to three different levels of aggregation. Published Yugoslav sources subdivide material on the Yugoslav industrial sector into 'sectors', which approximate Standard Industrial Classification (SIC) two or three digit industries, and 'industries', which approximate SIC four or five digit industries. For example, chemicals are a 'sector' and artificial fibres an 'industry'. In addition, Stephen Sacks (1972, 1973) provides evidence on firm numbers at the product level, which is reproduced here for completeness. It is worth stressing that there are considerable problems with data from published Yugoslav sources, not least because the Yugoslav definition of the enterprise is so loose that different tabulations are inconsistent. It will be remembered that the economy comprises a pyramid of self-managed entities with differing degrees of formal structure at each level. The vital question is to determine which, from the host of legal arrangements including economic units, enterprises, joint resources, pooling agreements and long-term contracts, is the autonomous economic decision-making unit. In practice, either economic units or a pooling agreement rather than the 'enterprise' could be the location of economic choices. Data inconsistencies between tables, sources and years suggest that the authorities themselves use a plethora of definitions in their published material. These problems could not be solved without significant additional information, which was not available. Therefore we draw heavily on the earlier literature, and particularly Sacks (1972, 1973), for both data and interpretation. Even so, some of the material, such as the concentration ratios for the later period, must be treated as primarily illustrative. In general, however, we aim for consistency of definition and use over time, and refer in the text to the occasions when this has not been possible.

4.2 YUGOSLAV INDUSTRIAL STRUCTURE IN 1958: THE HERITAGE

The foundations of contemporary Yugoslav industrial organisation and structures were laid by the nationalisation of most companies after the war and the brief period of central planning prior to 1952. Data availability restricts the choice of starting year to 1958, though the relatively small movement observed in later years suggests that this six-year delay will not seriously distort the picture of the nascent markets' industrial structure. We commence with enterprise numbers at the four potential levels of aggregation – the industrial sector as a whole, sectors, industries and products – before proceeding to describe industrial concentration.

Table 4.1 shows the number of firms in Yugoslavia in 1958, as well as their average size and the size distribution, and is derived from Table A1 in the appendix. Comparative material on the United Kingdom and the United States is also offered, derived from the UK *Census of Production* and the US *Statistical Yearbook*.

One might expect that a relatively less developed economy which had recently been centrally planned would contain fewer industrial enterprises than developed economies. However, the extent of the difference is surprising and underlies many of the findings which follow. Basically, Yugoslavia had very few firms in 1958, and these were of a relatively large average size. Manufacturing industry had only 2,500 firms with around 400 workers on average in each. No adjustment for income or population could make this comparable with the hundreds of thousands of firms in the two developed capitalist economies. The difference is explained by the virtual absence of small firms.[2] The vast majority of all producers in the USA and Britain employed fewer than 100 workers and the size distribution of firms was heavily skewed with a low mean. In the

Table 4.1. *Manufacturing firms in Yugoslavia, UK and USA, around 1958*

	Yugoslavia (1958)	USA (1958)	UK (1963)
No. of establishments (UK) or firms	2,500	299,000	174,760
Average labour force	372	62.1	51.8

Size distribution (1958)

No. of workers employed	Yugoslavia (% firms)	No. of workers employed	USA (% firms)	UK (% establishments)
<15	5.5	<20	68.1	
15–29	7.0	<25		52.2
30–60	13.2	25–99	22.8	20.4
61–125	19.6	100–249	5.4	14.0
126–250	19.6	250–999	3.0	3.4
251–500	16.2	1,000–5,000	0.7	5.2
501–1,000	11.3			
1,001–2,000	7.6	>5,000		4.7

Sources: Table A1; UK *Census of Production*, 1963; USA *Statistical Yearbook*, 1958.

UK, only about 10% of firms employed over 1,000 people, and in the US, where the distribution was more skewed and there were more small firms, the percentage was 0.7. The Yugoslav distribution was less skewed, with a high mean, and only 25% of firms could be considered small while about 19% employed over 1,000 workers. The bulk of firms were of medium to large size, with between a few hundred and one thousand workers. Thus, Yugoslavia did not have the large hinterlands of small firms characteristic of Western economies; there were a very small number of firms, each of relatively large scale and similar size.

One can consider firm numbers by sector and by industry in 1959 on the basis of the information in Tables A2 and A3. At the sectoral level, Table A2 shows that three sectors out of eighteen contained fewer than twenty firms and only five contained more than one hundred cooperatives. On average, each sector contained around

Table 4.2. *Concentration ratios in Yugoslavia, UK and USA, around 1958*

	Yugoslavia (1959)		UK (1958)	USA (1963)
Concentration ratio (CR4:sales)	Sectors (%) (18)	Industries (%) (103)	Industries (%) (117)	Industries (%) (416)
0–19				21.4
<30	12	8	57.5	
20–39				38.7
40–59				22.1
60–70	35	31	39.1	
60–79				11.3
>70	53	61	3.4	
80–100				6.5

Sources: IP; Drutter (1964); Sawyer and Aaronovitch (1975); Sacks (1973).

ninety-two enterprises, with a coefficient of variation[3] between the sectors of 103%. In fact, the smallest number of firms was found in the 'heavy' industries – rubber, oil, ferrous metals and ships – while 'light' industries – building, food processing, textiles and wood – were generally characterised by more producers. Table A3 is reproduced from Drutter (1964) and describes the number of firms in each industry in 1959. At this level, there are very few enterprises indeed, with some 18% of Yugoslav industries containing five firms or fewer. Indeed, more than a third of Yugoslav industries had ten firms or less and around two-thirds twenty-five firms or less. Only 5% of industries contained more than a hundred producers, and only 16% more than fifty.

Turning to industrial concentration, we follow the rest of the literature in this area (e.g. Drutter, 1964; Sacks, 1972, 1973) in producing concentration ratios[4] for Yugoslavia. Table 4.2 gives the four firm sales concentration ratio (CR4: sales) for Yugoslavia in 1959, measured at both the sectoral (18) and the industrial (103) levels, as well as comparative data for the UK and the USA. The table is derived from Tables A4 and A5. In effect, Yugoslavia had no competitive sector at all, with fewer than 10% of its industries displaying CR4 below 30%, and the vast majority with CR4 over 70%. Normally, one is unwilling to compare these rough measures between economies, because of definitional problems, but in this case the differences are sufficiently marked to bear consideration. Though the UK and USA are rarely considered to be competitive market economies, in comparison with Yugoslavia they appear so. Table A4 also reveals some association between concentration levels and firm numbers in Yugoslavia. It can be seen that industrial concentration was most marked in the heavy industrial sectors, the planners' preserves of oil, non-ferrous metals, ships and rubber, and lowest in light industry where there were more firms.

The sparsity of firms in each industry had a particularly marked effect on concentration ratios measured at this level of aggregation. Table A5 reveals that 21% of industries were effectively monopolies with concentration ratios of 100%, and over a third of industries displayed a CR4 in excess of 90%. This compares with only 65% of industries in the United States, calculated at a lower level of aggregation. On the other end of the spectrum, the lowest industrial-level concentration ratio recorded for Yugoslavia in 1959 was 14%, in the brickbuilding industry. There were a few other relatively low observations, such as in saw-mills, grain processing and knitting, but they were a tiny proportion of industries. There is therefore no clear pattern to the high concentration measured at the industrial level, though virtually all the heavy sectors fell into the category with the lighter ones, such as wood, textiles or leather, being more likely to contain relatively more competitive industries.

This picture of severely imperfect market structure can be strikingly confirmed with reference to Sacks' (1973) data on specific product markets. Table A14 reproduces Sacks' evidence on the number of firms in 509 Yugoslav product markets in 1959, and shows that 15% of the markets were served by only one firm, with duopoly in a further 12%. Indeed, there were fewer than five producers of more than half of the products considered, and only 18% of the markets contained more than twenty enterprises. Thus, in the late 1950s, Yugoslavia had very few firms, generally of a relatively large scale, and very high measures of concentration which were inversely related to the level of aggregation considered. At the product level, a considerable proportion of markets were monopolies or oligopolies. This markedly non-competitive industrial structure was probably related to the level of economic development and the influence of planners on the industrial sector, and means that our analysis must be based on models with imperfect competition.

4.3 CHANGES IN INDUSTRIAL STRUCTURE, 1958–72

4.3.1 *Institutional arrangements*

This section describes the changes in industrial structure at the various levels of aggregation which occurred because of entry, exit and merger over the period 1958–72. We also attempt to associate the observed movements with the factors stressed by self-management theory. The material spans both the Visible Hand and Self-Management eras, and one would not expect to see the predicted effects of autonomous cooperative decisions until around the mid-1960s. We commence with a brief summary of the relevant institutional material.

During the Visible Hand period, the government was effectively the only body which played the role of entrepreneur, being responsible for enterprise entry, expansion of production and liquidation. This was, of course, the government's intention, and was reflected in the social ownership of capital, and its rationing according to the plan. Even so, groups of citizens and existing collectives were actually entitled to create new firms, though the latter group had virtually no funds for private disposal and were anyway heavily influenced by the informal chain of command. After 1953, groups of citizens could also compete for allocations of state capital. It was claimed that the rationing procedure for the fixed amounts allotted to each sector would be based on a strict rate of return criterion so every potential cooperative had an equal chance of finance. But in fact the authorities were probably biased against such 'capitalist' tendencies. Anyway, history gives little reason to expect an untapped pool of private entrepreneurs to emerge in response to signals inadequately processed by the state and to create a dynamic small-scale sector. Yet, according to Sacks (1973) between 327 and 462 such small firms had been founded in the entire economy by 1969, after which date the laws were tightened sufficiently to eliminate the practice. Generally, these small firms were outside the industrial sector, of a dubious legal and commercial character, and did not survive for long.

Exit from the market by liquidation was, and for the most part remains, impossible in Yugoslavia. The main reasons were political and ideological; the ruling communist party preferred to guarantee job security from plant closure, despite the opportunity cost in terms of failure to relocate unproductive resources. This position makes some sense in a less developed economy, where one may seek a reallocation of labour from unemployment or low productivity uses to relatively more productive sectors such as industry, rather than efficiency within the industrial sector. Whatever the justification, the Yugoslav authorities have been willing to subsidise 'loss-making' enterprises over long periods to maintain employment. Apart from cases of enterprise malpractice or fraud, such exit as there is therefore tends to occur via mergers, with the local or central authorities persuading relatively successful companies to absorb inefficient producers to avoid closure. A further reason for merger activity, which was always permitted but really only became important in recent years, is that existing firms use surplus funds effectively to purchase productive capacity in new markets.[5]

One must therefore look to the state as the primary motivating force for changes in the industrial structure prior to 1965, and expect rather more activity concerning entry than either merger or exit. We cannot know the state's motivation as entrepreneur in this period, but even if entry and exit were being manipulated in the interests of improved resource allocation, this behaviour could not be observed by looking at the price system because markets were so severely regulated. Thus, one would not expect to see any relationship between entry, exit, concentration and average earnings during the Visible Hand era.

The state largely withdrew from the entrepreneurial role after around 1965, but apart from this the institutional arrangements were about the same during the Self-Management period. In the absence of effective entry by groups of private citizens, the burden fell largely to existing producers aided by the banks, which had inherited the state Investment Funds (see Chapter 3). In fact, enterprises were left with more resources from as early as 1960, which gave them some autonomy to frustrate planned priorities on entry and exit before 1965. If firms were motivated materially, one would expect to see entry into relatively high earning sectors after 1965, and mergers if not actual liquidation from low earning ones. The arrangements for exit and merger were for the most part unchanged from the earlier period, though the abrupt restructuring of relative prices and change in the system of rewards and penalties created a new class of unsuccessful firms. Henceforth, these tended to rely on subsidies or contractual arrangements with other firms for the maintenance of their incomes during times of general economic recession, and they were one of the major sources of financial irresponsibility and illiquidity in the system.

There were no effective policies to counter restrictive practices throughout the period, despite the very high levels of industrial concentration. Indeed, as we have seen, government policies favoured collusion, the creation of implicit cartels through the business associations and the encouragement of joint production arrangements. However, there was increasing press attention after 1965 to monopoly power, and the difficulties it could cause in the distribution of income, particularly in the banking and trade sectors. There is evidence (*Absees*; Popov, 1970; and Chapter 6) that the controls on trade, capital costs and prices were all manipulated to some extent during the Self-Management era to increase competition or restrict labour incomes and capital accumulation in the more monopolistic sectors. We have also seen that the Reforms of 1972–4 invalidated the data series employed below by changing the definition of the enterprise (see Chapter 3). In consequence, our study does not proceed beyond 1972. Firm numbers can be observed to increase after 1971 (see Graph A1), which suggests that actual changes followed the Communist League's political victories and preceded the legal adjustments.

4.3.2 *Enterprise entry, 1958–72*

Although Yugoslav sources recognise the entry of entirely new enterprises created by the authorities into various markets, entry resulting from the expansion of existing firms into new production lines must be proxied by the net change of firm numbers per industry. In this section, we examine both forms of entry at the various levels of aggregation, and try to relate them to average earnings as an indication of the relevance of self-management theory.

Commencing with entirely new firms, the state only formed around eleven new companies per annum between 1952 and 1957, mainly in electrical supply (which accounted for between 20% and 50% of the annual total) and in heavy industry (Sacks, 1973). Thus, there was probably little change in the industrial structure between 1952 and 1958, the first year for which we have more systematic evidence. Table A8 covers the period 1960–72, showing the number of firms (E) and new plants (P) created. The data prior to 1968 are derived from Sacks (1973) and for the later years are drawn directly from *Industrija Preduzeca.* The difference in source and definition means that there is a marked discrepancy between the series, which can be particularly observed in 1968. Sack's material is preferable since he is able to distinguish between entry, new capacity for existing firms, enterprise name changes, formal pooling and nominal secessions by BOALs. This could not be done for the raw data from *Industrija Preduzeca.*

The table shows that the number of entirely new firms varied between thirty and forty per year (around 1.5% of the total) from 1960–4. Entry was concentrated in light industries where there were already a large number of producers, and virtually never occurred in sectors with fewer than twenty enterprises. However, Sacks' data suggest that new entry effectively ceased with the end of centralised activity after 1964. Only between three and twelve new firms per year appeared in the period 1964–8, probably founded by republican authorities. Thus, in the absence of government sponsorship, Yugoslav collective entrepreneurship in the industrial sector proved to be very sparse. There are no direct data on the size of these new firms, but Table A1 shows that even while it was reasonably brisk, entry did not prevent an appreciable rise in average enterprise size. Since it did not reduce concentration (see below) and primarily occurred in sectors where there were many producers, this suggests that the average scale of entrants was large by the standards of existing producers, though small relative to market demand.

Using a different source after 1968, there appears to have been a major upsurge in entry, which almost doubled enterprise numbers by 1972 (see Table A1). While one cannot know whether these changes are purely nominal or actually reflect the creation of new autonomous units, one must suspect the former. Activity continued to be concentrated in the lighter industrial sectors and Table A9 details the changes in numbers, output and inputs by sector in 1971 and 1972. The recorded movements were large, creating 12% more firms, 4% more output, 2% more employment and 4% more capital in each year. Firm number changes were greatest in oil, rubber, ferrous and food; added most to output in electrical supply and building; to employment in leather; to capital in non-ferrous metals, building and wood; and to all three in non-metals and electronics. However, the source is inadequate to confirm that there actually was an upsurge in entry in the later years of the period.

Existing enterprises which start to produce in entirely new markets represent the second source of entry in Yugoslavia. There are no direct data on this matter, but the movements can be imperfectly proxied by changes in firm numbers, net of entry. This measure is inadequate because it ignores liquidation and mergers, but the later sections suggest neither were an important reason for changes in firm numbers during this period. The appendix presents material on firm numbers from 1958 to 1972 at three levels of aggregation, total (Table A1), sectoral (Table A2) and industrial (Table A3), from which the relevant information can be deduced. The three data series on enterprise numbers are internally consistent but not comparable.

There was considerable stability in the total number of producers operating in the industrial sector from 1958 to 1970, as can be seen in Table A1 which is depicted in Graph A1. On average there were 2,512 firms operating in any one year with a standard deviation across years of 109.7. One can discern some degree of cyclical variation, however, in that enterprise numbers rose by 287 between 1958 and 1961, after which they gradually declined by around 400 until 1970. Thus, there was some fall in the total number of industrial producers during the Self-Management era. Table A2 indicates that there were rather more changes in the number of firms operating in each sector, though the change in data source mean the two series should strictly not be compared. In general, the number of enterprises in each sector moved with approximately the cyclical trend of the aggregate series. Thus, between 1959 and 1963 enterprise numbers only actually declined in four sectors (building, tobacco, chemicals and electricity supply) and remained approximately constant in a further two (shipbuilding and printing). Every other sector ended the period with more producers than it started, but for the most part the increase was not large. Indeed, it was only significant in areas which already contained many producers – wood, textiles, leather and food processing – so that even in 1963 25% of sectors continued to contain fewer than twenty firms. This gently rising trend for most sectors actually reversed itself for the most part during the Self-Management era. Thus, almost two-thirds of Yugoslav sectors contained fewer producers in 1970 than 1964, which undid much of the progress of the early 1960s.

Turning to firm numbers at the industrial level, the changes are summarised in Table 4.3. This shows that there was a consistent

Table 4.3. *The number of firms by industry, 1959–72 (%)*

No. of firms	1959	1961	1968
<5	18	22	16
5–10	18	11	8
11–24	28	34	40
25–49	20	19	19
50–100	11	7	8
>100	5	7	9

Number of firms by industry: changes over time (%)

Industries in which firm numbers:	1961/59	1963/61	1968/63	1970/68	1970/59
Increased	54	63	47	16	58
Decreased	22	23	45	56	32
Unchanged	24	14	9	28	10
					(excluding new products)

Source: Table A3.

significant rise in the number of producers operating in each industry over the entire period. The data are derived from Table A3, and suggest that the total number of 'firms' acting on each industrial market (as distinct from the total number of enterprises in the industrial sector as a whole, or its various sectoral subdivisions[6]) increased from 1,593 in 1957 to 1,937 in 1961, 2,057 in 1963 and 2,497 in 1968, before falling back to 2,437 in 1970. The total number of firms increased, on average, by 5.7% per annum over the period, with producers entering six entirely new markets between 1959 and 1961, and eleven from 1963 to 1968 (these are included as an 'increase' in the table). Table 4.3 reveals that the proportion of industries containing fewer than ten firms fell quite markedly between 1959 and 1968, with the bulk shifting to the group containing between eleven and twenty-fiive enterprises. There was also a movement in the group containing over fifty firms to even larger numbers, in excess of 100. The second part of the table shows that firm numbers per industry were generally rising before 1968, but actually declined between 1968 and 1970. Firm numbers increased most in the years 1961 to 1963, and the pace appears to have slowed somewhat after the introduction of self-management. Therefore one observes an appreciable rise in the number of producers in each market at the industrial level, which appears to be independent of state-sponsored entry and is not reflected in changes of the total number of firms.

It would be interesting to see whether entry in Yugoslavia, either state-sponsored or by existing firms, followed average earnings in the manner predicted by self-management theory, and whether the relationship changed with the 1965 Reforms. The series on state-sponsored entry restricts the investigation to the sectoral level of aggregation, and the change in firm numbers in each sector net of officially sponsored entry is taken as the proxy for entry by existing firms though it is gross of merger and bankruptcy. The period 1959–70 is divided into three: 1959–63, 1963–6 and 1966–70, and the tests are very simple. Table 4.4 reproduces findings on the association between entry by new firms (ENT), the change in firms numbers net of this state-sponsored entry (DFN) and the level of sectoral average earnings (Y) (the former two series are a percentage of initial firm numbers, and the latter a proportion of the mean). As in all tables, bracketed figures are *t*-statistics.

For the two periods for which there are reliable data before 1966, one cannot isolate a positive significant assocation between average earnings by sector and state-sponsored entry. This may not reflect political distortion of market criterion in the Visible Hand era, but it does suggest that the state did not sponsor entry according to economic criteria in a way that might have reduced income differentials. From 1959 to 1963, entry by existing firms must have largely followed the pattern set by the authorities. The two series were closely associated and neither were related positively to sectoral earnings. However after 1963, when firms had more autonomy in decision-making, the picture alters. Until 1966, firm numbers apparently responded somewhat to the sectoral earnings' dispersion, though they were also related to state-sponsored entry. After 1966, the net change in firm numbers was closely associated with earnings, in a linear relationship which was significant at the 99% level. Thus, there is evidence that, at the sectoral level, state-sponsored entry followed political dictates, as did entry by existing firms before 1963. After the reforms, the latter source of enterprise mobility followed

Table 4.4. *Association between entry and earnings*

Linear regression

1959–63: Y	=	111.31	+	0.025 ENT	−	0.130 DFN : $\bar{R}^2$	=	−.0241
		(18.8)		(0.07)		(1.08)		
1963–6: Y	=	111.08	+	0.76 ENT	+	0.215 DFN : $\bar{R}^2$	=	−.0257
		(12.4)		(0.73)		(1.55)		
1966–70: Y	=	134.7			+	2.10 DFN : $\bar{R}^2$	=	−.4138
		(17.21)				(3.98)		

Partial Correlation Coefficients

		Y	DFN	ENT
1959–63				
	Y	1		
	DFN	−.2996	1	
	ENT	−.1551	.5505	1
1963–6				
	Y	1		
	DFN	.3243	1	
	ENT	−.0685	.2895	1
1966–70				
	Y	1		
	DFN	.6646	1	

market incentives, and therefore acted to improve resource allocation. This is the first evidence in favour of our choice of time period, and of the relevance of self-management theory.

4.3.3 *Mergers*

Material on Yugoslav mergers, also referred to as 'integrations' in the Yugoslav literature, is only available at the aggregate level and it describes the type, location and scale of integrated firms in any year. Moreover, though the absolute number of enterprises involved is given, their combination is not, so the effects on enterprise numbers are unclear. One can assume that the majority of mergers are pair-wise (though the average will clearly exceed two) so the figures presented below must represent approximately double the consequential decrease in enterprise numbers.

Table A10 gives the numbers of firms involved in mergers between 1960 and 1974. The series moved in strong cycles, with peaks in 1962–4 and 1970–1, and troughs in 1967–8 and 1973–4. As one would expect, there appears to have been no significant change of pattern between the two periods. On average, some 4% of firms merged in any year, which implies a reduction of around 1.5% in total producer numbers per annum. Table A11 gives merger by regions and the size of partners (according to employees), and it can be used to illustrate Yugoslav exit procedures. Most integrated firms were of medium size (50–100 workers), with few very large or small companies, and the activity generally occurred in a commune or neighbourhood between producers of different commodities. Thus, in 1974 only 2% of mergers were between republics, and only around 24% within a particular product market. This is consistent with the argument that Yugoslav mergers involved the linking of loss-making firms to more successful ones by local authorities to prevent plant closure. The changes in the pattern over time (from commune to neighbourhood, and less related products) imply an increasing paucity of viable local firms producing a similar output, forcing the authorities to cast their net over wider areas.

Since around 90% of mergers between firms occurred in a very small region and around 24% were between firms producing similar outputs, one can surmise that only some 15% of the total (perhaps involving six or seven firms in a given year) were voluntary mergers to exploit scale economies or market power. Some 85% of integrations (fifteen to seventy firms) per year could therefore be regarded as liquidations. Of course, if the integrated firms did not cease production, such mergers would not act to improve resource misallocation, but merely shift the burden of subsidy from the government to local producers. There are no data on actual liquidations, but the legal arrangements, attitudes and literature (Vanek, 1972; *Absees*) suggest that it was insignificant in the industrial sector.

4.3.4 *Changes in concentration*

The entry and exit of firms in various markets can be expected to influence industrial concentration, and in this subsection we describe changes in market structure over the period. There is also an

Table 4.5. *Changes in sectoral concentration over time*

Concentration	1961/59	63/61	67/63	68/66	70/68	74/70
Increase	39	15	55	50	32	59
Decrease	39	80	35	41	54	36
Unchanged	22	5	10	9	14	5

Source: Table A4.

attempt to relate these adjustments to changes in firm numbers, whether due to state-sponsored entry, movements by existing firms or merger, at the three levels of aggregation, and further examine some simple self-management hypotheses.

Before proceeding, it will be useful to examine in more detail the changes in total firm numbers, to take account of entry and merger. Three relatively distinct sub-periods can be observed, commencing with 1960–6, when state-sponsored entry was relatively brisk. However, between 1962 and 1964 this entry was swamped by the first large merger boom, so that over the sub-period total firm numbers increased at first but then declined. New entry slumped between 1965 and 1968, but there were relatively few integrations so the total number of firms declined slowly. From 1968 to 1970, a second merger boom reduced the total rather more quickly since the pace of entry did not greatly change. Thus, aggregate firm numbers were primarily determined by integration over this period with state-sponsored entry playing a minor rôle after 1964. There was a close association between the rate of merger and the trade cycle over the period (see Chapter 5) since integrations peaked during upswings in output and employment and troughed during periods of low growth. The partial correlation coefficient between the rate of growth of industrial output and mergers is 0.578, which could represent evidence of economic motivation to combine during booms. Alternatively, Table A11 might indicate that the authorities could only find sufficient viable enterprises to assume the subsidy burden of failing enterprises during upswings.

With this background of relatively stable total enterprise numbers, Tables A4, A5 and A14 contain data on concentration at the sectoral, industrial and (indirectly) product level. Concentration measured at the sectoral level is described in Table A4, and is

Table 4.6. *Concentration (CON) regressed on firm numbers (FN) and state-sponsored entry (ENT), 1959, 1963, 1966*

CON59	=	74.11	–	0.116 FN59	+	0.09 ENT59	:	$\bar{R}^2 = .12$
		(8.29)		(1.98)		(0.24)		
CON63	=	77.33	–	0.133 FN63	+	0.33 ENT59	:	$\bar{R}^2 = .4195$
		(11.13)		(3.81)		(0.11)		
CON66	=	62.20	–	0.182 FN66			:	$\bar{R}^2 = .5620$
		(11.38)		(5.29)				

derived from two sources. Sacks (1973) provides four firm sales concentration ratios, aggregated from industry to sector using sales proportions as weights 1959–68, and from Yugoslav sources there are unweighted value added concentration ratios for the largest four firms over the period 1966–72. Both series present problems of interpretation; the former measures may be misleading because of the aggregation, and the latter ones refer to large sectors producing non-homogeneous outputs. However, they give the same rank order of concentration ratios except for metals, non-metals and tobacco where the simple measure of the later years indicates a higher rank. Table 4.5 indicates the proportion of sectors in which concentration altered in a particular direction over time. As can be seen from the table, changes in concentration showed no unambiguous pattern at the sectoral level over the period. The four firm concentration ratio fell in most sectors, 1961–3 and 1968–70 but increases predominated from 1965–7 and after 1970. The changes were evenly matched between 1959 and 1961. Thus, at least at the sectoral level, changes in concentration showed no relationship with the pace of state-sponsored entry or movements in total firm numbers. There appears to have been a negative association with mergers, but this may merely reflect the impact of the trade cycle. Taking these points together, the following possible explanation emerges, medium sized firms grew fastest in cyclical upswings and existing firms entered new markets in search of higher earnings which reduced sectoral concentration. Simultaneously, pressure from the authorities led to relatively more mergers, which reduced total firm numbers. The converse could have taken place during cyclical downswings.

The data at the sectoral level can be brought together for a series of relatively simple-minded exercises to test predictions from self-management theory. The discussion is based on the earlier division

Table 4.7. *Regressions explaining changes in concentration (DCON), 1959, 1963 and 1966*

DCON59 =	12.077	− 0.247DFN59	− 0.15CON59	+ 0.229ENT59:	$\bar{R}^2$ = .2812
	(1.31)	(2.95)	(1.15)	(0.92)	
DCON63 =	14.20	− 0.164DFN63	− 0.183CON63	+ 0.139ENT63:	$\bar{R}^2$ = .5265
	(2.81)	(4.41)	(2.25)	(0.48)	
DCON66 =	−4.79	− 0.807DFN66	− 0.0734CON66		: $\bar{R}^2$ = .2061
	(0.06)	(2.71)	(1.46)		

of sectoral data into three sub-periods (1959–63, 1963–6 and 1966–70) and covers the nineteen or twenty-two (1966–70) industrial sectors of Table A4. In the first place, one can confirm that the hypothesised association between average earnings (as a percentage of the mean) and industrial concentration did emerge after the introduction of market self-management in 1965. The partial correlation coefficient between the two variables, measured at the sectoral level, was only 0.2817 in 1959 and 0.3676 in 1963. However, it had risen to 0.517 by 1966, and continued to climb slightly during the 1960s. Simple linear regressions revealed a statistically significant relationship between earnings and concentration at the 99% level.

Moving to the determinants of concentration ratios at the sectoral level, Table 4.6 reveals a negative significant association between concentration and the number of firms in a sector (FN). However, monopoly power appears to have been unrelated to either current or previous state-sponsored entry in any of the sub-periods, which further indicates that the state did not found new companies to reduce market concentration.

Table 4.6 also suggests that the level of market concentration (and therefore earnings) only become closely related to the number of firms in the sector after market forces were liberalised in the mid-1960s. This implies that changes in concentration measured at the sectoral level (DCON) might be explained to a significant degree by changes in firm numbers net of state-sponsored entry (DFN), the variable we have constructed to indicate the scale of entry by existing producers into new sectors. Table 4.7 reports the results of regressions to explain changes of concentration in terms of DFN, state-sponsored entry (ENT) and the level of concentration (CON). Current levels of concentration in each sub-period are included in the equations because barriers to entry could hinder the reduction of market power and above-average incomes in severely non-competitive sectors. Conversely low income relatively competitive sectors might experience exit and therefore increasing concentration. A positive coefficient on CON indicates that entry barriers were effective; a negative one that rationalisation was taking place in competitive sectors. A balancing of the two forces could result in no relationship. In practice, the equations offer a reasonable explanation of changes in Yugoslav concentration, particularly for 1963. There was always a significant inverse relationship between changes in firm numbers and concentration, which confirms that this was the most important factor among those we have identified. On the other hand, state-sponsored entry was never significantly associated with changes in concentration ratios, and the relationship actually had a positive sign. The coefficient on the level of concentration was negative before 1963, and became positive for the Self-Management period, which may indicate that the effectiveness of barriers to entry had begun to balance the consequences of rationalisation. However, such conclusions must be purely speculative since the variable was only significant in 1963.

This material can be combined with the full list of partial correlation coefficients reported in Table 4.8 for an intuitive exposition of the determinants of changes in concentration at the sectoral level. Most changes occurred because of entry by existing firms which was motivated to some extent by the level of earnings after the introduction of market self-management. Thus, there is some evidence that private agents in Yugoslavia, when permitted, were motivated by economic incentives to improve resource allocation and reduce monopoly power. On the other hand, state-sponsored entrepreneurial activity was never very great, particularly with respect to entry, and appears not to have been directed towards improving allocative efficiency. Moreover, industrial structure was sufficiently imperfect for existing producers to erect effective barriers to entry around high income sectors after 1963, and the tables indicate that firm numbers and concentration altered least in those sectors where potential gains were the highest. Thus, there was some entry though very little exit from Yugoslav sectors over the period. It tended to take place in areas where concentration initially was not very high and there already existed a reasonable number of firms.

Data limitations mean that these exercises cannot be repeated at the industrial level, but such evidence as there is supports a similar

Table 4.8. *Partial correlation coefficients, 1959, 1963, 1966*

	Y	FN	CON	DFN	DCON	ENT
*Y*59	1					
FN59	−.4634	1				
CON59	−.2817	−.1285	1			
DFN59	−.2990	−.1285	−.0971	1		
DCON59	.4786	−.4241	−.1317	−.5757	1	
ENT59	−.1511	−.2342	.1616	.5505	−.2090	1
*Y*63	1					
CON63	.3076	1				
FN63	−.4322	−.6954	1			
DFN63	.3224	−.1838	−.1831	1		
DCON63	−.5758	−.2309	−.5443	−.6839	1	
ENT63	−.0685	−.2992	−.4282	.2895	−.2586	1
*Y*66	1					
FN66	−.3022	1				
CON66	.5166	−.7635	1			
DFN66	.6646	−.0377	.2855	1		
DCON66	−.2164	.0202	−.0641	.5232	1	

interpretation of events. Table A5 shows the four firm concentration ratios (CR4: sales) for 103 Yugoslav industries over the period 1959 to 1968, from which we have constructed Table 4.9 to describe the changes in industrial concentration. The first part of the table describes the distribution of industries according to the level of concentration in 1968, and offers evidence about Britain for the purpose of comparison. The second part provides a summary of changes in the two countries over time. It can be seen that even in 1968, some sixteen years after a market system had been formally introduced and three years after effective self-management became operational, no industries in Yugoslavia had a concentration ratio of less than 10%, while 31% had a measure between 90% and 100%. Indeed, 19% of Yugoslav industries still contained four firms or fewer in 1968. It can be seen that Yugoslavia had proportionately more highly concentrated industries than Britain, with 57% of industries displaying CR4s in excess of 70% compared with 48% in the UK, and slightly fewer less concentrated industries; 22% having CR4s below 50% as against 27%. However, although the British

Table 4.9. *Industrial concentration in Yugoslavia and the UK*

Distribution of Sellers by CR4(%) 1968

CR	% Yugoslav sectors	% UK sectors
0–10	0	0
11–20	4	2
21–30	3	6
31–40	8	8
41–50	7	11
51–60	10.5	14
61–70	10.5	11
71–80	16	12
81–90	10	14
91–100	31	22

Changes in Concentration, 1959–68

Percentage of industries in which concentration	Yugoslavia (103 industries) (CR4)			
	59–68	61/59	63/61	68/63
Increased	24	36	29	30
Decreased	58	40	49	44
Unchanged	18	24	22	26

Sources: Table A5; Sawyer and Aaronovitch (1975).

data set is considerably more disaggregated (concerning 209 industries rather than 103), the differences between the two countries are not all that marked. It is the second part of the table which contains the striking results. It indicates a persistent and considerable decline in concentration measured at the industrial level in Yugoslavia over the period 1959–68, and most particularly in the period 1961–3. Between 1959 and 1968, market concentration actually declined in well over half of Yugoslav sectors, and only increased in less than a quarter of them. The four firm concentration ratio fell most in industries with moderate market imperfections, and most of the increases occurred in relatively competitive sectors with a large number of firms. However, those industries with very high concentration ratios tended to remain unscathed by entry; for example, most of the industries which experience no change in concentration ratios commenced the period with CR4s of 100%. This is further evidence for the view that there was considerable mobility by existing firms into relatively high earning products and some rationalisation in markets with declining demand, but there were also effective barriers to entry in the high income, concentrated, heavy industries such as oil, glass, non-ferrous metals, engineering and artificial fibres.

Finally, Sacks (1973) provides data for a more detailed insight at the level of product markets, with statistics on specific products which are reproduced in Table A14. There were 509 producers in 1959, and 542, 580, 667 and 684 respectively in the remaining years of the table for 759 products. In 1959, around 15% of products were produced by a monopolist and 27% by two firms or less, while only 33% of products were offered by more than ten firms. There was a decline in the number of products produced by less than five firms, between 1959 and 1961, filled largely by the six to ten category, but there was some retrenchment from 1961 to 1963 as the less than five and greater than ten producer categories gained from the middle. From 1963 to 1968, the group with less than five producers increased while that with more than ten declined. Thus, Sacks' data do not confirm the findings at the sectoral and industrial level of declining concentration in moderately imperfect markets. This may be because the data are excessively disaggregated for our purposes. Given that there are always fewer producers than products, most firms must produce more than one product, so some of Sacks' 'products' must be very close substitutes for each other.

Thus, from the initially highly imperfect market position, there was a movement over time towards declining measures of concentration at the sectoral and industrial levels, except in competitive and highly monopolistic sectors. This occurred in the context of almost no changes in the numbers of firms, though there was considerable variation in producer numbers at the sectoral and industrial levels. In general, these movements were motivated by average earnings and therefore acted to improve resource allocation, though there is some evidence of barriers in the most concentrated sectors.

4.4 OVERALL CONCENTRATION

In this section, we examine overall concentration in the industrial sector, 1966–72. Our material is from Yugoslav sources only and concerns size category groups rather than enterprises. There is no evidence from other sources, because the issue has not previously been investigated. Hence, consistent measures such as the proportion of output provided by the top 100 firms can only be approximated imperfectly and the evidence must be regarded as, at best, indicative of true movements. The previous discussion would lead to predictions of increasing overall concentration provided that the firms diversifying their production were relatively large and therefore would be included in the list of the largest Yugoslav companies.

Table A12 shows the proportion of net product supplied by each firm size group as a cumulative percentage of their respective totals from 1966 to 1972. The picture initially appears rather confused since, apart from 1966 and 1968, no two years are easily comparable. This is because there is a simultaneous shift of both firms and net product to the higher groups over the years, at differential rates. The relevant question is whether the latter increases faster than the former, implying an increase in overall concentration, and the answer is clearly affirmative. In 1966, the smallest 20% (approximately) of firms produced around 1% of output, while the largest 5% (124 firms) produced 41.2%. By 1972, the smallest 30% produced only 2%, while the top 1.7% (75 firms) supplied over 30% of net product. Moreover, in 1966, the top 15 firms used 9.9% of staff employed, 12.4% of the capital; the top 124 firms 32.7% and 38% respectively. By 1969, the top 150 firms used 49% of the capital, and 38.4% of labour, and in 1971 the top 296 firms used 63.7% and 54% respectively. Finally, in 1972, the largest 75 firms used 34.3% of the capital, and 24.8% of the labour employed. This confirms that the largest firms are also more capital-intensive than the average.

The sales of the ten largest industrial, and five largest trading, corporations are given for 1970 in Table A13, along with other information. The first thing to note is that some have become very large indeed, especially in relation to the domestic economy. The top ten industrial firms are responsible for 18.44% of Yugoslav sales, and the largest five trading companies for a further 11.2%. There are four enterprises, each responsible for producing nearly 3% of national sales, and the largest ten companies overall are supplying 22.8% of output. The industrial firms operate for the most part in a single sector, though they probably produce in several 'industries' and a wide range of 'products'. However, the trading corporations

Table 4.10. *Share of largest firms in net output, 1958–72 (%)*

	Yugoslavia			USA			UK		
Share of	1966	1970	1972	1958	1963	1970	1958	1963	1970
Top 50 firms	25	25	27	23	25	24	25	28	32
Top 100 firms	36	37	38	30	33	33	32	37	42
Top 200 firms	51	52	54	38	41	43	41	48	53

Sources: Table A12; Sawyer and Aaronovitch (1975); Hannah and Kay (1977).

are normally conglomerate. For example, Inex (Interexport) is concerned with hotels, an airline, travel agencies, department stores, a brewery and film production, as well as international trade and financial services. Yugoslavia is not really a fully unified market, but perhaps can best be viewed as a free trade area between relatively distinct republican markets. In this case, the power of the largest companies is significantly greater. The largest fifteen companies, assuming that their sales are entirely within their own republic, are responsible for 10% of Croatia's trade, 15.66% of Slovenia's and 72.6% of Serbia's.

Table 4.10 provides comparative data on overall concentration for Yugoslavia (from the approximations of Table A12), the USA and the UK for the years 1958–72. On these data, Yugoslavia had achieved a very high level of overall concentration by international standards in 1965, which was after the period when most of the entry by existing firms at the industrial level had already taken place. The differences in total firm numbers (the top 200 firms in Yugoslavia represent nearly 10% of the total) and the fact that the Yugoslav figures concern only the industrial sector make comparisons highly questionable, but even so it is rather surprising that Yugoslav measures compared unfavourably to Britain or the United States in 1963. Yugoslav and American overall concentration increased gently over time, while the British level grew more rapidly, to reach that of Yugoslavia on this measure by 1970.

4.5 SUMMARY AND CONCLUSIONS

This chapter has sought to describe Yugoslav industrial structure in the manufacturing sector over the Visible Hand and Self-Management eras, and to investigate whether the changes could be associated with self-management factors. There are serious problems of definition, interpretation, inconsistency and even reliability with the data drawn directly from Yugoslav sources. This has led us to build our picture at several different levels of aggregation and stress findings which confirm or extend the results of the existing literature. Hopefully the fact that diverse sources tell a similar story about industrial structure over the period means that our findings are at least indicative of Yugoslav reality, despite the data imperfections.

We have seen that both markets and effective self-management were introduced into an industrial sector with very few producers in total and almost no small firms. The market structure was severely imperfect at all the measured levels of aggregation. This implies that any empirical work on Yugoslavia should assume the environment to be non-competitive and a major theme of this study will be to examine whether monopoly power influences Yugoslav enterprise choices in the predicted way. The simple exercises reported in this chapter indicate that there was an association between average earnings and industrial concentration, though only after the introduction of market self-management in 1965. The analysis in Chapter 6 will attempt to establish the relationship more formally.

The changes in industrial structure over the period approximately followed expectations. The most important finding was that the system did display a gradual decline over time from the initial very high measures of concentration, except in the most competitive and most monopolistic sectors. However, there was very little entry by entirely new firms and virtually no exit or liquidations, so enterprise numbers in total did not change greatly over the period. The bulk of entirely new firms in the industrial sector were founded by the state rather than private citizens, and the choice of sector does not appear to have been based on any market criteria. In so far as one can judge, the majority of mergers were also government sponsored and played the role of bankruptcy in a system where, for political reasons, actual closures almost never occurred.

There were also very strong indications that the major reason for declining concentration measured at the various levels of aggregation was entry by existing firms into new markets. It is hard to be certain that this phenomenon was taking place given the quality of the data and the imperfect approximations used, and the finding could also be consistent with differential rates of enterprise growth within each market. However, one observes considerable changes in the number of firms operating in each market despite the limited formal entry, and these changes in firm numbers were closely associated with the declining concentration ratios. If this interpretation is accepted, one can go rather further in explaining the dynamics of the system. In the first place, product diversification by existing firms was apparently not motivated to any great extent by earnings during the Visible Hand era, but enterprises did enter new markets in search of higher average earnings after the introduction of market self-management. However, potential entrants failed to break into sectors of very high concentration and earnings, which suggests that there were some very effective barriers to entry in Yugoslavia over the period. Secondly, enterprise diversification between markets in the context of approximately the same small number of firms in total suggests overall concentration would be high and perhaps rising; an hypothesis which has worrying political and social implications and which was confirmed by the data.

In conclusion, this chapter has provided a description of industrial organisation in Yugoslavia's industrial product markets, data for later analysis and initial evidence for the relevance of self-management theory. The material also confirms that the initial environment was sufficiently imperfect, and the changes were sufficiently slow, to justify our assumption of inadequate adjustment between efficient equilibria for the system as a whole. There was some entry of a particular sort, and even perhaps some exit, with the former at least moving the economy towards efficiency, but the period was too short and the changes too few to eliminate, or even considerably reduce, monopoly power and other allocative inefficiencies. Thus, we shall assume for the remainder of the study that Yugoslav firms operating in an imperfectly competitive environment have reached a long-run equilibrium while the system as a whole has not. The changing firm numbers at the enterprise level during the self-management era suggest that observed inefficiencies could have been eroded to some extent by general equilibrium effects by the end of the period.

Appendix A: Yugoslav industrial structure

The data concerning the industrial structure in Yugoslavia are derived from both primary and secondary sources. The three primary sources are *Statisticki Godisnak Jugoslavie* (SGJ), the Yugoslav *National Statistical Yearbook* and two statistical supplements, *Industrija Preduzeca* (IP) and *Statisticki Bilten* (SB). We do not, in general, quote table numbers because our series normally run over time and the precise number of the table, and even the section, is altered in each source across years. However, the material is generally derived from the sections describing the industrial sector. Indeed, except for Table A11 which refers to the whole social sector, we only consider data on the industrial sector including mining. The main secondary sources were Drutter (1964) and Sacks (1973), whose evidence was based on otherwise unavailable social accounting data. Figures for the UK were drawn from the *Census of Production* and Sawyer and Aaronovitch (1975), while those for the USA came from the American *Statistical Yearbook*. Yugoslav industrial concentration is generally measured by four firm concentration ratios (CR4), on a net product (Drustveni Proizvod) basis.

As was stressed in the text, there are enormous problems with the data from primary sources, to such an extent that the findings must be regarded as primarily illustrative. These relate to differences in the definition of the enterprise itself, which may refer to a BOAL, plant, enterprise, conglomerate or cartel. Founders of new firms, generally existing producers, can create nominally 'independent' units which are actually subsidiaries. On the other hand, effective mergers may be disguised as contractual arrangements. The result of all this is that the data series from various sources are inconsistent before 1972, after which date the material becomes utterly unreliable. For example, Drutter (1964) reported that the industrial sector contained 2,239 firms in 1963, Sacks (1973) 2,334 and SGJ 2,507. However, the series are more reliable over time provided that one sticks to a single source, and they tell approximately the same story. Our general method has therefore been to stress the evidence from secondary sources and concentrate on the pattern over time with reference to consistent primary sources, with our analysis ending around 1972. The text refers to the occasions when we have not even achieved this degree of consistency.

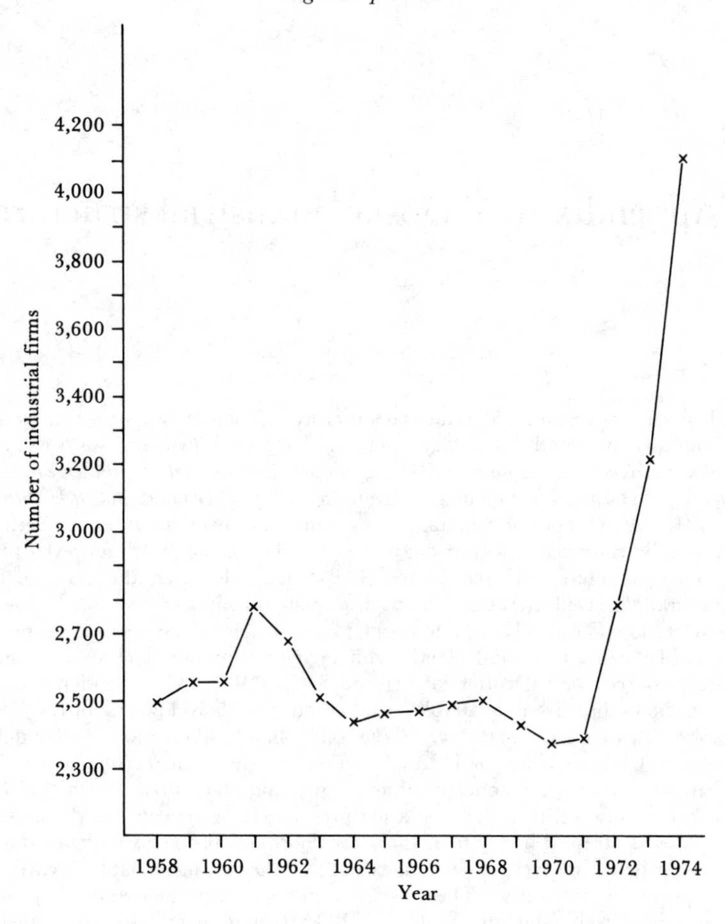
4,200
4,000
3,800
3,600
3,400
3,200
3,000
2,700
2,500
2,300
Number of industrial firms
1958
1960
1962
1964
1966
1968
1970
1972
1974
Year

Graph A1

Table A1. *Number of firms, average labour and fixed assets per firm, 1958–74*

Year	No. of firms	Average labour per firm (1)	Average capital per firm (2) (000.D)	Average sales per firm (3) (000.D)	Index (1)	Index (2)	Index (3)
1958	2,500	372	20.178	5.894	100	100	100
1959	2,537	387	20.956	6.619	104	104	112
1960	2,556	420	22.724	7.515	113	113	128
1961	2,787	405	23.136	7.323	109	115	124
1962	2,684	434	28.883	8.281	117	143	140
1963	2,507	489	31.341	10.349	131	155	176
1964	2,445	540	34.514	12.382	145	171	210
1965	2,466	559	37.342	13.184	150	185	224
1966	2,467	553	40.228	13.805	149	199	234
1967	2,492	543	42.424	13.772	146	209	234
1968	2,505	542	45.281	14.637	146	221	248
1969	2,434	570	50.781	16.852	153	252	286
1970	2,374	612	56.057	19.000	165	278	322
1971	2,398	643	61.640	20.837	173	305	354
1972	2,773	583	57.430	19.323	157	285	328
1973	3,217	518	54.904	17.542	139	272	298
1974	4,100	530		15.320	116		260

Source: SGJ.

Table A2. *Number of firms by industrial sectors, 1959–72*

Sector	1959	1961	1963	1964	1965	1966	1968	1969	1970	1971	1972
1. Elec. supply	45	36	39	94	84	80	81	70	84	98	112
2. Coal	70	73	91	71	72	68	56	50	47	48	53
3. Oil	9	9	12	6	6	4	3	3	5	5	19
4. Ferrous	12	16	14	13	12	14	13	11	13	15	18
5. Non-ferrous	26	29	35	32	31	33	31	28	26	22	36
6. Non-metals	51	59	64	77	90	89	89	84	85	83	87
7. Metals	163	191	222	334	345	347	357	335	331	328	357
8. Ships	20	19	20	21	20	19	19	19	20	20	22
9. Elec.	54	44	53	53	57	73	78	77	77	79	84
10. Chem.	87	105	108	143	151	145	150	148	142	142	168
11. Building	302	294	228	262	254	244	243	246	233	224	235
12. Wood	166	240	333	250	251	268	273	261	254	248	278
13. Paper	21	34	37	37	40	38	38	39	40	39	45
14. Text.	219	300	370	313	320	328	338	338	328	342	377
15. Leather	42	100	102	94	92	91	94	88	91	94	107
16. Rubber	6	8	12	12	12	16	16	16	15	15	15
17. Food	292	338	391	249	234	201	203	198	189	192	258
18. Printing		121	120	274	281	305	328	313	308	314	389
19. Tobacco	76	76	75	60	60	53	38	41	37	38	51
20. Films				11	13	12	18	16	16	17	30
21. Mining Expl.				15	16	16	15	14	14	14	15
22. Miscell.		6	8	24	25	23	19	19	19	21	17

Source: IP.

Table A3. *The number of firms in Yugoslav industry, 1959–72*

Industry	1959[a]	1961[a]	1963[a]	1968[b]	1970[b]	1972[b]
1. Hydro-elec.				23	21	22
Thermo	45	36	39	13	8	13
Other elec.				45	55	77
2. Collieries	45	45	54	51	42	48
Coke/gas	0	4	6	5	5	5
3. Oil Production	3	3	5	1	1	10
Oil refineries	4	4	5	2	4	9
4. Iron mines	2	5	5	3	3	3
Iron works and steel	10	11	9	10	10	15
5. Non-ferrous mines	13	14	15	13	9	7
Non-ferrous factories	5	7	11	11	10	25
Non-ferrous rolling mills	8	8	9	7	7	4
6. Non-metal mines	17	20	17	46	43	41
Salt	6	7	5	5	5	4
Glass	12	11	19	13	13	16
Refractories	5	5	9	3	4	4
Ceramics	7	12	10	10	10	9
Other non-metals	—	—	—	11	10	13
7. Metal reproduction	51	64	79	96	88	92
Metal structures	4	3	13	11	14	20
Metal machinery	39	40	47	98	85	86
Precision goods	12	16	18	16	14	16
Rail/road	5	5	3	18	17	20
Road vehicles	26	25	25	46	45	49
Household	26	38	36	47	45	43
Other metals	—	—	—	24	23	31
8. Ships	20[a]	19	20[a]	19	20	22
9. Electronics machinery	20	17	18	22	19	22
Electronics household	9	7	8	10	9	6
Cables	3	3	4	3	4	5
Radio	9	5	6	14	14	16
Other elec.	—	—	—	29	31	35
10. Basic chemicals	38	37	41	34	22	23
Artificial fibres	1	1	1		10	22
Drugs	11	13	11	12	12	15
Other chemicals	—	—	—	104	98	108
11. Stone quarries	30	32	42	68	64	61
Bricks	244	233	158	145	140	131
Cement	10	11	11	12	11	11
Other building	18	18	17	18	18	19
12. Saw-mills	101	113	116	111	97	99
Finished wood	54	116	152	150	146	168
Chemical wood	9	9	12	12	11	11

(cont.)

Table A3. (*cont.*)

Industry	1959[a]	1961[a]	1963[a]	1968[b]	1970[b]	1972[b]
13. Paper factories	21	20	25	27	29	31
Paper processing		14	11	11	11	14
14. Hemp/flax spinning/weaving	—	40	32	15	6	8
Cotton spinning/weaving	50	53	63	60	63	63
Wool spinning/weaving	35	30	31	31	30	31
Silk spinning/weaving	—	—	—	11	12	12
Other spinning/weaving	15	15	16	13	12	11
Knitting	71	91	92	103	99	110
Underwear	14	23	24			
Overwear	28	39	59	81	81	112
Other	—	—	—	24	25	30
15. Leather factories	47	49	49	44	37	46
Leather footwear	31	41	42	38	43	46
Moroccan leather	11	10	10	12	11	15
16. Rubber	6	8	12	16	15	16
17. Food – grain mills	121	132	132	46	44	58
Paste/bakeries	—	—	—	10	9	11
Canning	66	79	121	74	67	92
Sugar	9	9	13	3	3	9
Sweets	20	18	18	14	12	12
Oil	18	17	17	10	10	15
Spirits	22	27	28	33	31	41
Starch	2	2	3	13	13	20
18. Printing works	—	121	121	136	137	142
Newspapers	—			192	171	247
19. Tobacco – fermenting	65	65	60	27	29	41
Cigarettes	11	11	14	10	8	10
20. Motion picture	—	—	—	18	16	30
21. Mining exploration	—	—	—	15	14	15
22. Teaching equipment	—	2	3	2	2	1
Sports equipment	—	3	4	3	3	2
Musical equipment	—	1	1	1	1	1
Records	—	0	0	2	2	5
Other	—	—	—	11	11	6

Sources: a. Drutter (1964); b. IP.

Table A4. *Sectoral concentration ratios: four firm (CR4) sales and net product (NP) concentration ratio*

Sector	1959[a] (sales)	1961[a] (sales)	1963[a] (sales)	1967[a] (sales)	1966[b] (NP)	1968[b] (NP)	1972[b] (NP)	1970[b] (NP)
1.	28	36	35	33	18	12	20	17
2.	60	71	62	67	40	43	48	43
3.	100	100	99	95	100	100	65	100
4.	81	78	80	80	66	58	59	59
5.	95	94	92	94	61.5	53	62	58
6.	89	88	84	86	30	25	26	27
7.	77	76	54	58	11.4	17	16	14
8.	88	88	85	89	79.4	81	78	75
9.	80	88	84	79	43	37	45	45
10.	79	77	77	71	25	27	26	21
11.	58	58	55	58	21	23	25	22
12.	27	24	21	24	9.5	9	13	9
13.		54	57	50	32	29	29	27
14.	40	38	30	33	14	11	9	10
15.	50	53	40	45	24	25	23	24
16.	88	88	80	79	83	83	85	84
17.	49	57	39	47	16	26	10	11
18.		29	36	26	15	17	20	19
19.	47	54	51	55	49	58	62	66
20.					85	73	51	57
21.					61	72	72	65
22.		100	100	100	35	50	55	48
All	64	65	56	58				

Sources: a. Sacks (1973); b. IP.

Table A5. *CR4 (sales) for 103 Yugoslav industries*

Industry	1959	1961	1963	1968
Elec.	28	36	35	34
Stone coal	99	99	91	98
Brown coal	39	49	46	56
Lignite	68	80	66	78
Gas	–	100	91	100
Petrol	100	100	100	100
Refining	100	100	99.1	95
Carbon black	100	100	99	100
Iron mine	100	99.5	100	100
Iron & steel	79	76	79	77
Lead & zinc	91	92	75	72
Bauxite	93	93	81	81
Copper	100	100	100	100
Lead	100	100	100	97
Aluminium	100	100	100	100
Ferroalloys	100	100	100	100
Non-fe. rolling mills	89	85	84	91
Asbestos mines	93	97	100	100
Magnesite mines	94	96	100	79
Sand	100	87	75	72
Salt	99	93	99	99
Glass	100	100	100	100
Brown glass	74	74	65	68
Refractors	98	99.7	89	99
Ceramics	81	80	84	80
Asbestos	100	100	100	100
Foundries	65	58	53	38
Cutting tools	71	70	62	57
Wire tools	51	48	41	31
Containers	72	77	71	62
Structures	100	100	85	79
Boilers	100	100	100	98
Building materials	78	69	55	64
Metal machines	94	92	81	69
Agr. machines	79	74	79	76
Precision machines	57	45	53	53
Railways	94	93	100	100
Vehicles	78	82	87	52
Bikes	97	96	100	100
Household metal goods	51	46	49	49
Ocean ships	88	89	86	90
River ships	94	89	83	83
Elec. machines	68	77	68	48

Table A5 (*cont.*)

Industry	1959	1961	1963	1968
Household machines	75	81	78	72
Cables	100	100	100	100
Radio	72	99	99	83
Elec. materials	87	94	80	55
Light bulbs	100	100	100	100
Batteries	97	100	98	90
Chemicals	70	72	54	42
Artificial fertilisers	100	100	100	79
Plastic materials	100	100	92	83
Paints	79	81	85	81
Fibres (artificial)	100	100	100	100
Drugs	80	76	84	86
Soap	72	66	70	70
Plastics	58	44	43	50
Crushed stone	63	49	44	56
Lime	50	48	49	50
Bricks	14	17	18	17
Cement	75	76	71	71
Cement products	55	47	52	61
Tar	100	100	100	97
Saw-mills	17	16	18	18
Plywood	61	56	55	64
Furniture	25	19	14	18
Wood	61	66	56	57
Matches	100	100	100	100
Paper	53	49	52	41
Paper products	53	71	85	79
Hemp	53	26	34	52
Cotton	29	28	28	21
Wool	44	50	41	44
Rayon	61	55	52	63
Knitting	23	21	22	15
Underwear	58	47	48	50
Overwear	51	49	36	40
Carpets	94	87	81	77
Leather hides	33	36	39	38
Leather pigskin	33	95	100	100
Leather lining	80	80	80	83
Leather fur	80	100	100	92
Footwear	47	51	39	33
Handbags	72	73	71	60
Rubber	88	88	85	79

(*cont.*)

Table A5 (*cont.*)

Industry	1959	1961	1963	1968
Grain	21	43	25	21
Can. fruit	52	51	35	48
Can. meat	45	51	28	35
Can. fish	52	71	61	79
Dairy	73	66	55	61
Sugar	70	79	61	58
Sweets	62	66	62	61
Oils	72	73	71	72
Brewing	41	44	42	39
Liquor	59	47	48	62
Starch	100	100	100	100
Cattle feed		100	100	82
Printing		29	36	24
Tobacco	29	39	40	34
Cigarettes	60	65	68	74
School goods		100	100	100
Sporting goods		100	100	100
Musical		100	100	100

Sources: IP; Drutter (1964); Sacks (1973).

Distribution of sectors by concentration category

(% sector)

Concentration category	1959	1961	1963	1968
Low (≤33%)	9	6	7	9
Medium (34–67%)	28	28	34	34
High (68–100%)	63	66	59	57

Table A6. *Size distribution of Yugoslav firms*

a. *By staff employed*

Groups (No. of workers)	1958 No. of firms	1958 %	1965 No. of firms	1965 %
<15	137	5.5	55	2.2
15–29	176	7.0	56	2.3
30–60	329	13.2	171	6.9
61–125	489	19.6	407	16.5
126–250	490	19.6	547	22.2
251–500	406	16.2	542	22.0
501–1,000	283	11.3	349	14.0
1,001–2,000	190	7.6	216	8.8
>2,000	0	—	123	5.0

b. *By net product*

Groups		1966 No. of firms	1966 %	1972 No. of firms	1972 %
<15,000	(A)	14	0.6	21	0.75
15,000–50,000	(B)	8	0.3	1	0.04
50,001–150,000	(C)	15	0.6	21	0.75
150,001–500,000	(D)	95	3.9	53	1.9
500,001–1.5 m	(E)	345	14.0	193	7.0
5 m	(F)	795	32.2	524	18.9
15 m	(G)	666	27.0	856	30.9
50 m	(H)	405	16.4	719	25.9
150 m	(I)	109	4.4	310	11.2
>150 m	(J)	15	0.6	75	2.7

Sources: IP; SGJ; Drutter (1964).

Table A7. *Distribution of firms in each sector: by net product: 1966, 1972*

Sector and year	Size group (% of firms)									
	A	B	C	D	E	F	G	H	I	J
1. 1966	1.3	1.3			2.5	11.3	26.3	47.5	10.0	
1972	0.9		0.9	0.9	2.7	8.9	23.2	36.6	21.4	4.5
2. 1966					13.2	25.0	32.4	16.2	11.8	1.5
1972			1.9	1.9	5.7	26.4	20.8	24.5	5.7	13.2
3. 1966						25.0			50.0	25.0
1972					5.3	5.3	15.8	21.0	31.6	21.0
4. 1966	7.1				7.1	7.1		14.3	42.9	21.4
1972						11.1	11.1	5.6	44.4	27.8
5. 1966			3.0		6.1	6.1	33.3	24.2	21.2	6.1
1972						8.3	27.8	33.3	25.0	5.6
6. 1966				2.3	22.5	36.0	23.6	11.2	4.5	
1972	3.4		1.1	2.3	3.4	19.5	35.6	23.1	11.5	
7. 1966		0.3	0.3	7.0	8.9	29.4	31.4	19.6	8.1	0.3
1972	0.6		0.6	0.3	3.4	15.4	28.0	32.8	14.8	4.2
8. 1966						5.3	31.6	31.6	10.5	5.3
1972	4.5			4.5		13.6	36.4	18.2	9.1	13.6
9. 1966					2.7	6.9	24.7	30.1	23.3	4.1
1972	1.2			2.4	3.6	15.5	20.2	30.9	17.9	8.3
10. 1966				4.8	8.3	31.7	31.0	17.9	5.5	0.7
1972	1.2		0.6		4.8	17.8	34.5	25.0	10.1	6.0

11. 1966	0.4			5.3	29.9	45.9	14.8	2.9	0.8	
1972			0.4	0.8	8.9	31.1	0.4	15.9	2.1	0.8
12. 1966	0.8			1.1	12.7	42.5	29.5	12.7	0.8	
1972				0.7	2.9	18.7	37.4	30.6	9.0	0.7
13. 1966	5.3				7.9	29.0	18.4	34.2	5.3	
1972	2.2				8.9	15.6	20.0	37.8	13.3	2.2
14. 1966	0.3			1.2	5.8	31.4	35.4	22.9	2.7	0.3
1972	0.3		0.3		2.9	9.5	35.3	36.9	14.0	0.8
15. 1966			1.1	1.1	7.7	36.3	37.4	15.6	1.1	
1972			0.9	1.9	3.7	13.1	37.4	31.8	10.3	0.9
16. 1966					12.5	25.0	25.0	18.8	12.5	6.2
1972						13.3	40.0	13.3	20.0	13.3
17. 1966	0.5		1.0	4.5	11.4	32.8	26.9	20.4	2.5	
1972	0.4		0.8	1.5	5.0	15.9	33.7	27.9	14.3	0.4
18. 1966	1.6	2.0	3.0	13.4	28.2	26.6	18.0	6.9	0.3	
1972	1.3	0.3	2.6	7.4	22.4	32.9	20.6	9.0	3.1	0.5
19. 1966				5.7	13.2	35.9	18.9	18.9	7.6	
1972	2.0				5.9	21.6	33.3	19.6	11.8	5.9
20. 1966			8.3		8.3	58.3	8.3	8.3	8.3	
1972	6.7			16.7	23.3	20.0	26.7	6.7		
21. 1966				18.8	18.8	18.8	31.3	6.3	6.3	
1972				6.7		26.7	33.3	13.3	20.0	
22. 1966				4.4	17.4	34.8	34.8	8.7		
1972					11.8	11.8	41.7	23.6	11.8	

Sources: IP; SB.

Table A8. *New industrial firms (E) and plants (P): 1960–72: by sector*

Sector	1960 E	1960 P	1961 E	1961 P	1962 E	1962 P	1963 E	1963 P	1964 E	1964 P	1965 E	1965 P	1966 E	1966 P	1967 E	1967 P	1968 E	1968 P	1968	1969	1970	1971	1972
1.	2		1		1			2			3		1			1		7				11	4
2.								1								1		2				7	2
3.														1		2		6				3	6
4.				2			1	2		2				2	1	3		6				5	4
5.	1		1	4	1					4				3		2		8				5	6
6.		5		4		5	2	5		13	3	2	4	1	1			3				19	16
7.	3	4	9	5	2	12	2	14	3	13	1	3	3	1	1	4		11				23	33
8.									1													1	1
9.		2		2	1	3			2	1				3				5				10	10
10.	8	8	3	16	2	14	2	12	5	6		1	1	6		5	1	10				27	39
11.	5	4	2	7	2	14		5	3	10		1		3		1		16				33	58
12.	3	25	3	13	4	27	2	21	2	11		2		3			1	12				36	33
13.	—	4		6	1	2	1	22	3	1			1	2		3		4				6	6
14.	6	4	11	18	10	19	3	25	7	9		2	1	3		4		11				34	37
15.	1	1	5	2	1	4	2		2		1							2				11	18
16.	—	3		—	3	1	1		2													6	4
17.	3	9	2	4	3	8		7		15		5		13		2	1	16				48	64
18.	1	2	2	3		1		3	1	2			1			1		4				4	2
19.	1	1	2	1	1	1		1														1	1
20.	—	—		—																			
21.	—	—		—																			
22.	—	—																1				2	3
Total	34	72	41	87	32	111	16	100	31	87	8	16	12	41	3	29	3	124					
Overall total	106		128		143		116		118		24		53		32		127		234	328	327	292	347

Sources: Sacks (1973); IP.

Table A9. *New firms: size and effect per sector: 1971, 1972*

	1971				1972			
Sector	% Firms	% NP	% Labour	% Fixed K	% Firms	% NP	% Labour	% Fixed K
1.	11.2	21.4	3.5	4.9	3.5	5.0	0.87	2.8
2.	14.5	3.9	4.2	7.0	33.7	1.3	0.5	1.8
3.	60.0	0.3	0.1	0.8	34.5	4.4	0.6	1.5
4.	33.0	2.1	1.7	6.8	22.0	3.9	1.7	5.3
5.	22.7	4.1	0.6	3.4	16.6	2.4	2.8	21.5
6.	22.8	11.2	4.5	7.0	18.3	4.9	4.4	18.9
7.	7.0	1.2	1.3	1.8	9.2	2.7	2.6	7.0
8.	5.0	0.1	0.1	0	4.5	0	0.1	0
9.	12.6	3.1	1.1	1.5	11.9	3.1	1.0	2.7
10.	19.0	17.3	4.0	5.6	23.2	7.2	3.6	10.8
11.	23.2	6.0	3.2	5.2	24.6	10.4	4.3	10.9
12.	14.5	4.2	2.5	5.3	12.2	3.2	2.5	11.9
13.	15.3	2.7	2.5	3.2	13.3	2.1	2.8	2.1
14.	9.9	4.4	2.9	1.9	9.8	3.9	3.1	6.0
15.	11.7	6.2	3.0	6.7	16.8	3.6	4.2	4.4
16.	40.0	2.7	2.0	3.2	26.8	2.1	1.7	1.3
17.	25.0	1.8	1.7	3.3	24.8	2.8	3.9	0.9
18.	1.2	4.5	0.2	1.3	0.5	0	0.3	0.4
19.	2.6	2.3	0.5	0.2	1.9	3.0	0.5	0.2
20.								
21.								
22.	9.5	1.4	3.1	5.1	17.6	1.5	1.6	3.8
All	12.2	5.2	2.2	3.9	12.5	3.9	2.5	5.0

Source: IP.

Table A10. *Number of enterprises integrated in the industrial sector, 1960–74*

	Year														
	1960	1961	1962	1963	1964	1965	1966	1967	1968	1969	1970	1971	1972	1973	1974
Number of firms	87	96	110	160	133	88	68	46	28	73	144	105	81	75	46

Source: SGJ.

Table [illegible]. *Forms of integration*

	1965 (all soc. sector) % integration	1966 (all soc. sector) % integration	1974 (industry) % integration	1974 (soc. sector) % integration
Integration by activity				
Same group	25.5	25.6	23.9	32.1
Same branch	42.0	40.0	21.8	23.4
Same kind	10.1	8.4	15.2	12.7
Different kind	22.4	26.0	39.1	31.8
Integration by region				
Within a commune	81.5	72.8	67.4	69.2
Neighbouring commune	8.1	11.3	8.7	13.1
Within a republic	9.7	14.7	21.7	16.4
Between republic	1.2	1.2	2.2	1.3

Number employed in integrated organisations, 1974

No. of workers	% integrated organisations
<10	—
10–25	2.3
26–50	4.7
51–125	18.6
126–250	30.2
251–500	30.2
501–1,000	9.3
1,001>1,000	4.7
All	100

Source: SGJ.

Table A12. % *Net product provided by % firms, by net product size groups*

Firm size group	1966 % F	1966 % NP	1968 % F	1968 % NP	1969 % F	1969 % NP	1970 % F	1970 % NP	1971 % F	1971 % NP	1972 % F	1972 % NP
A	0.6	0	0.7	0.01	1.0	0	0.4	0	0.33	0	0.76	0
B	0.9	0	0.96	0.01	1.3	0	0.53	0	0.96	0	0.8	0
C	1.5	0	2.2	0.02	2.5	0	1.3	0	0	0	1.56	0
D	5.4	0.1	6.5	0.12	5.3	0.01	3.2	0	2.8	0.02	3.47	0.04
E	19.4	1.2	18.6	0.95	15.7	0.62	11.8	0.42	8.54	0.22	10.4	0.24
F	51.6	8.3	51.1	7.25	46.46	6.1	38.3	4.3	30.6	2.7	29.55	2.0
G	78.6	26.0	78.0	23.0	74.7	21.0	68.9	17.1	62.0	12.8	60.2	11.8
H	95.0	58.8	95.0	58.6	93.8	53.2	91.4	47.2	87.7	39.4	86.1	36.9
I	99.4	85.8									98.3	69.5
J	100	100	100	100	100	100	100	100	100	100	100	100

Source: IP.

Table A13. *Information about the largest Yugoslav firms in 1970 in rank order*

Firm		Rank 1969	Sector and republic	Value of sales (m. dinar)	% Yugoslav sales	% Own republic sales
Industrial firms						
INA	(1)	1	Petrol: Croatia	4,367	2.87	10.0
INKOTEX	(2)	9	Textiles: Serbia	3,367	2.21	9.0
JADRANBROD	(3)	4	Ships: Serbia	3,302	2.17	8.9
RMK ZENICA	(4)	2	Iron and steel	2,982	1.96	
ISKRA	(5)	3	Electronics	2,876	1.89	
CRVENA ZASTAVA	(6)	6	Cars	2,505	1.64	
S. PENEZIC-KRCUN	(7)	5	Copper	2,487	1.63	
NAFTAGAS	(8)	26	Petrol: Vojvodina	2,114	1.39	14.7
RTB BOR	(9)	11	Copper	2,057	1.35	
ZEPS	(10)	7	Electricity supply: Serbia	2,024	1.33	5.43
Trading firms						
CENTROPROM	(1)	1	Serbia	4,284	2.81	11.5
JUGOMETAL	(2)	2	Serbia	4,137	2.71	11.1
INTEREXPORT	(3)	3	Serbia	4,102	2.69	11.0
METALKA	(4)	4	Slovenia	2,832	1.85	9.68
EMONA	(5)	9	Slovenia	1,750	1.15	5.98

Source: Yugoslav Survey, 1971.

Table A14. *Number of products, categorised by number of producers*

Number of producers	% Total number of producers					
	1959	1961	1963	1964	1967	1968
1	15	13	14	15	14	16
2	12	12	11	12	12	11
3	11	11	9	10	11	10
4	8	7	9	7	6	6
5	6	5	5	6	7	7
6–10	15	18	16	15	17	17
11–20	15	14	14	15	13	13
>20	18	21	22	21	20	20

Source: Sacks (1973).

5

Some consequences of self-management

5.1 INTRODUCTION

In this chapter we examine propositions empirically from the first part of the book. We commence by considering the pattern of Yugoslav earnings dispersion by industry and firm, as well as its association with the capital-intensity of production. We then go on to discuss the changes in the structure of economic growth, associated with the introduction of market self-management in 1965. The remainder of this section reviews briefly the main hypotheses to be studied.

We would expect that the introduction of self-management into the imperfectly competitive Yugoslav economy would lead to increases in inter-firm and inter-sectoral dispersion of average earnings and capital–labour ratios. The absence of labour market forces was stressed in Chapter 2 to be the distinguishing characteristic of a self-managed economy. In consequence, workers' incomes become enterprise specific, and may be unequal in different firms or industries. Thus, even if market forces have secured wage equalisation on the margin via entry and exit, earnings could vary among firms in an industry because of differences in technology or costs. On the other hand, we have seen that incomes earned within a sector as a whole are sensitive to market indicators such as demand, industrial structure or cost conditions. Changes in parameters of this type would lead to wage differentials between sectors. Earnings dispersion would be reduced by entry and exit, but we have seen in the previous chapters that the initial market conditions were severely imperfect and the self-management period very short. As a result, it seems likely that the factors acting to increase differentials were stronger than the equalising forces of enterprise entry and exit. In the following section, we examine these ideas with reference to various measures of Yugoslav income differentials and using international data for the purpose of comparison.[1]

The distribution of average earnings per head should also map into dispersion of equilibrium capital–labour ratios by firm and sector. Moreover, we have established in Chapter 2 that if technology is homothetic there is no analogous association between factor proportions and profitability under capitalism. But, contrary to the suggestions elsewhere in the literature (e.g. Vanek and Jovicic, 1975), our predicted relationship between incomes and capital–labour ratios under self-management is not causal. It merely reflects the simultaneous choice of factor proportions and earnings in income maximising cooperatives, so that changes in constraints which permit an increase in equilibrium earnings also involve an increase in the equilibrium capital–labour ratio. The relationship between the two variables is examined briefly in the third section, which thereby provides a link between our study of earnings and the consideration of production technology and growth patterns in the fourth section.

Self-management theory also generates a series of linked hypotheses about the choice of technique and labour market clearing. Cooperatives are viewed as restricting employment to raise incomes above their scarcity value, and being in a position to maintain these differentials in the absence of effective entry despite any excess supply of labour. These relatively higher implicit labour costs will distort the choice of technique towards more capital-intensive and labour-productive methods. In the fourth section, we investigate how the pattern of Yugoslav industrial growth was affected by the 1965 Reforms, focusing in particular on changes in the capital–labour ratio. We also consider labour market clearing directly, for the industrial sector as a whole and between the rural and urban sectors.[2]

Thus, the theme of this chapter will be an examination of how certain variables, the key endogenous ones of our model, actually reacted to the introduction of Yugoslav self-management in 1965. Our approach is purely empirical and descriptive; we offer no evidence on the pattern of exogenous variables or their association with the data series under consideration. The study can only establish consistency with predictions from self-management theory. In the next chapter, we use econometric methods in an attempt to relate the endogenous and exogenous variables more formally, but lack of data restricts the work to the sectoral level of aggregation. The detailed evidence which follows indicates that this restriction may entail a considerable understatement of the real allocative problems.

5.2 YUGOSLAV EARNINGS DISPERSION, 1956–75

In this section, we detail various measures of inter-firm earnings dispersion in Yugoslavia between 1956 and 1975. Income differences between firms, measured at the sectoral and industrial level, and with adjustments for skill types and regions, are considered in the first part. Although theory would focus attention on dispersion in the incomes of a particular homogeneous labour type among firms in different product markets, data restrict us to these approximations. The resulting inferences are hopefully strengthened by international comparisons. In the second part, we detail dispersion within each sector and in the third, combine the findings for measures of overall dispersion by sector, firm size and skill type. We outline the scale and complexity of labour market misallocation in post-Reform Yugoslavia, and show that dispersion increased considerably when self-management was introduced.

We will first review briefly some historical material and deduce our prior hypotheses. Wages were effectively determined by the central authorities until 1958, although the system was administered by the unions. There was already some attempt to associate incomes and productivity when the net revenue system was first introduced in 1958, but it is hard to evaluate the consequences. The new system was gradually confirmed and extended over the period until 1961, when the short-lived reforms further strengthened enterprise autonomy. However, some guidelines were reintroduced in 1962 because of the wage explosion of the previous year, and these could have held back further pressures until the 1965 Reforms. The new market self-management system left firms with more at their disposal, and free to determine their own incomes until the 1974 Reforms. However, in practice the authorities were probably worried about income inequalities from the late 1960s, and may have used regulatory powers and moral suasion to control it from then, and certainly after the revival of central party authority in 1971. The actual changes between 1972 and 1974 were intended to impose social norms on income dispersion, and therefore would have acted to reduce differentials further.

Hence, one would expect income differentials, whether measured among sectors, skill groups or firms, to have been relatively narrow in 1958. Such dispersion as the planners actually permitted would probably have reflected particular labour scarcities. The gradual devolution of authority to individual cooperatives would have acted to widen differentials, with an initial peak in 1961 because of the first abortive reform, and especially after 1965. One would expect dispersion to have continued to widen prior to the early 1970s, given the general weakness of competitive pressures. However, from then the increased regulation of enterprise decisions, whether formally or informally, would have acted to narrow differentials. Of course, income dispersion would not be expected to alter greatly if the introduction of self-management did not affect resource allocation.

Finally, it is worth stressing that our data only concern the industrial sector, and provide no information on the overall distribution of income. In fact, as can be seen in Table B1, Yugoslavia is a relatively egalitarian country, particularly given its level of development. Indeed, the Gini coefficient, a measure of overall inequality, was only 0.32 in Yugoslavia in 1963, compared with 0.38 for the UK and US and 0.48 for France (UN, *Incomes in Post-War Europe*). Thus, we are not trying to suggest that Yugoslavia is an inegalitarian country, but rather that the nature of the inequalities follow a pattern that theory would predict, at least for the period following the introduction of self-management.

5.2.1 *Dispersion of unadjusted average incomes between sectors and industries, 1956–75*

We detail below the income differences, on average, measured between twenty-two Yugoslav sectors[3] and seventy-six industries (as defined in Chapter 4) over the period 1956–75. Ideally, one would like to use earnings for a given type of worker, adjusted to take account of differences in skill proportions and payments in each industry. However, Yugoslav sources do not offer information of this sort. In consequence, we outline dispersion of unadjusted average incomes[4] measured at the sectoral level, and then establish that a similar pattern of differentials held for each labour type, region, and job, and that the distribution across these sub-divisions remained

Table 5.1. *Proportion of sectors paying in different income ranges, 1956–75*

Earnings' range (% mean)	Proportion of sectors (%) 1956	1961	1965	1968	1972	1975
0–79	0	5	9	0	4.5	0
80–89	22	19	14	9	4.5	9
90–109	47	33	31	31	59	50
110–119	26	19	14	23	14	14
120–149	5	19	23	14	18	18
>150	0	5	9	23	0	9

Source: Table B2.

stable over the period. The level of income inequality is also measured at the industrial level and compared where possible with evidence from other economies. Dispersion will be measured by the coefficient of variation of the series, denoted V and defined as the standard deviation divided by the mean, and the range or ratio from highest to lowest income, denoted R. In general, the coefficient of variation, as a standardised indicator of variation, is the preferred measure but it proved to be sensitive to grouping so the ratio is sometimes used instead. In these cases, the text usually offers additional ratios which exclude outliers because this measure is sensitive to extreme observations.

Unadjusted earnings per worker by sector

Table B2 provides the average level of gross monthly earnings per person employed in each sector as a percentage of the unweighted mean income for that year over the period 1956–75, and the material is summarised in Table 5.1. Income dispersion between sectors was relatively narrow at the start of the period. The highest earnings, on average, were in heavy industries such as ship-building, coal-mining and metals (around 115% of the industrial mean) and the lowest in sectors such as building, wood and tobacco (around 85% of the mean). This picture did not alter greatly before 1961. In that year, electrical supply, oil and printing all began to pull away from the mean. Though these were apparently constrained from 1962 to 1965, differentials continued to rise because of the relative decline in incomes earned in the wood and textile sectors.

The 1965 Reforms heralded marked changes in differentials. The oil, electricity supply, non-ferrous metals, printing, ships, chemicals and mining exploration sectors all raised their average earnings well above the mean in a short period of time. Incomes in oil, on average, rose by 50% of the mean income in three years, and others by up to 30% in the same period. The highest earning sectors reached almost double the industrial average, while those at the bottom of the range fell to 75% of the mean. This was around half the earnings in the remaining successful sectors. However, the differentials began to narrow from both sides of the distribution after 1968, and especially from a relative decline in the earnings of the highest paid sectors. The movement was strengthened around 1972 but apparently reversed by 1975. The decline in dispersion was slower and less uniform than its previous increase.

The movement in dispersion at the sectoral level is measured more formally in Table B3. Three estimates are given for most years, computed from Table B2, Yugoslav sources for annual incomes and for average hourly pay from Wachtel (1973), and Yugoslav sources. Diagram 5.1 traces out the movement in the inter-sectoral coefficient of variation computed from Table B2, though all measures display similar changes over time. It can be seen that the pattern closely conforms to expectations, with striking increases in differentials around the time of economic reforms. The coefficient of variation increased by 50% between 1956 and 1961, and a further 50% between 1965 and 1967, after which it slowly declined, ending the period some 50% above the initial value. The ratio displayed similar movements: one can also see the sharp increase in dispersion after 1961 and 1965.

International comparisons will be useful in evaluating these changes. First, average wage dispersion between sectors was relatively stable over time in other countries. For example, Table B4 shows the annual coefficient of variation for twenty-one US sectors between 1955 and 1971 (derived from US, *Employment and Earnings*, 1973). It remained almost unchanged at around 19%, never altering by more than 0.9% in any year. Indeed the change over the whole period was less than 2% in total. Similar evidence for seven countries of Western Europe is shown in Table B5.[5] The table shows that the coefficient of variation of wages by sector in the sample never altered by more than 1% in any year over the period 1950–60, with little change generally over the entire decade. Thus, the

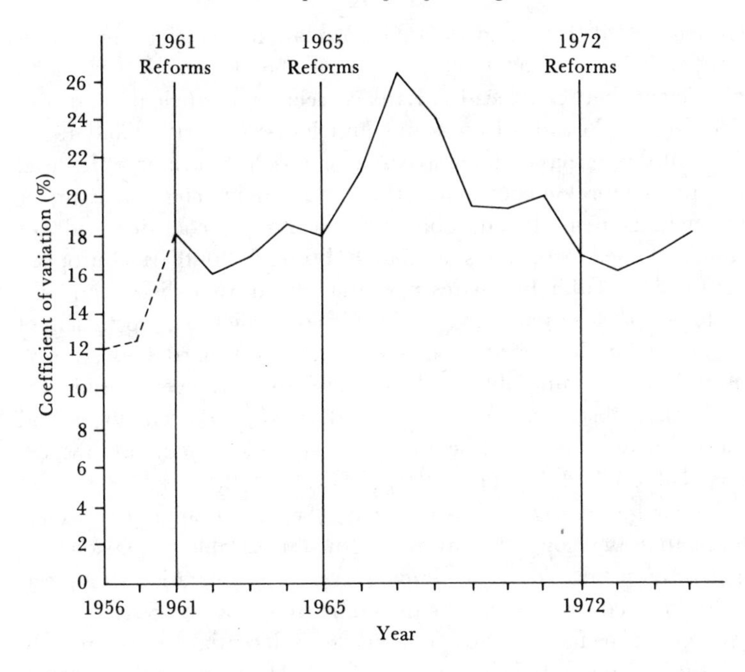

Diagram 5.1. Changes in sectoral income coefficient of variation over time, 1956–75

variability displayed by income differentials between sectors in Yugoslavia was unusual by international standards.

The changing measures of Yugoslav income dispersion were also associated with shifts in the sectoral ranking with respect to earnings, which also contrasts with the experience of other countries. The gradual liberalisation in Yugoslavia during the early 1960s favoured light at the expense of heavy industrial sectors. This was reversed to some extent by government intervention at the start of the 1970s. Thus, the rank correlation coefficient of sectoral incomes (from Table B2) was 0.759 between 1956 and 1975, but only 0.563 between 1965 and 1967, and 0.654 between 1967 and 1975. A good illustration of this is the relative position of coal miners over time. They declined from being sixth, on average, in 1956 to fourteenth in 1969, and rose again to reach fourth place in 1974. The reverse pattern can be observed for the printing sector. All this can be compared with the stability in rank orders portrayed for the US by

Cullen (1956). He found the rank correlation coefficient for eighty-four industries from 1899 to 1950 to be 0.66 with very high coefficients between decades. Rank correlation coefficients were also very high in Western European countries between 1950 and 1960.

Finally, international comparisons can help to evaluate the level of inter-sectoral income inequality attained in Yugoslavia under self-management. In addition to Table B5, we consider evidence from planned economies in Table B6 and Southern European countries in Table B7, to describe unadjusted wage dispersion for a wide sample of potentially comparable economies. The coefficient of variation for developed economies generally ranged between 7% and 11% for comparable levels of aggregation. In every case it was lower than observed in Yugoslavia at the peak, and normally around half, although large diverse economies such as Canada and the US (see Table B4) did display relatively higher differentials.

One might expect the Eastern bloc to be a more suitable reference point than developed countries, and in this sample dispersion was generally measured at a similar level of aggregation (nineteen industrial sectors), except for the GDR (ten) and the Soviet Union (twelve).[6] In fact, Yugoslav sectoral differentials were already relatively wide by 1958, during the Visible Hand era, and proceeded to outstrip the levels attained by its planned neighbours.[7] The dispersion measure for Eastern European countries may also be overstated by the inclusion of mining as can be seen from Table B6b. This table shows the sectoral average weekly earnings per worker as a percentage of the industrial mean in Bulgaria, Hungary and the Soviet Union. The pattern was rather different to that observed in Yugoslavia, with much of the observed inequality derived from the particular favour shown to miners.

The scale of income dispersion was rather closer to that observed in Southern European economies such as Spain (seventeen sectors) and Greece (twenty sectors), as can be seen in Table B7.[8] However, the Yugoslav coefficient of variation was generally somewhat larger, and at its peak significantly greater than observed for Greece. On the other hand Spain displayed very wide differentials, which is even harder to explain when the relatively egalitarian overall distribution of income is considered (Table B1). One can only speculate that the very wide dispersion at that time was associated with regional disparities and the operation of Franco's corporatist system.

Thus, there were relatively large changes in inter-sectoral earnings dispersion around the time that self-management was introduced in Yugoslavia and the levels attained were relatively high by international standards, whether in comparison with developed, centrally planned or other Mediterranean countries. Moreover, unlike experience elsewhere, the changes were associated with highly variable incomes and sectoral rank orders over time.

Inter-sectoral dispersion for skill and job types

The same pattern of broad income inequality over the period can be reproduced for each labour type, which indicates that the changes in unadjusted income dispersion were not caused by shifts in the proportion of the labour force in each sector in particular skill categories. The evidence on inter-sectoral income differentials by job goes on to suggest how severe these problems were in Yugoslavia after 1965.

Yugoslav sources categorise labour into eight groups, based on education or manual skills. Though these are clearly not homogeneous labour types, at this level of aggregation it seems reasonable to assume that most members of each group could apply for posts in a similar classification and different sector, but fail to obtain employment in a higher category of job, nor accept it in a lower one. The skill groups shown in Table B8 are:

1 = further education	white collar workers
2 = higher or technical education	
3 = secondary education	
4 = elementary education	
5 = highly skilled	blue collar workers
6 = skilled	
7 = semi-skilled	
8 = unskilled	

Table B8 shows the inter-sectoral coefficient of variation and range of gross average monthly earnings for each group and the whole labour force, and the movement for certain key skill groups is illustrated in Diagram 5.2. (The 1968 data derive from a different source, which may be inconsistent with the others so the values are bracketed.) Table B9 shows the correlation coefficient between the coefficient of variation for all groups of worker, and each particular one over the eight years. It can be seen that the value of the coefficient followed the movements of the aggregate for each skill

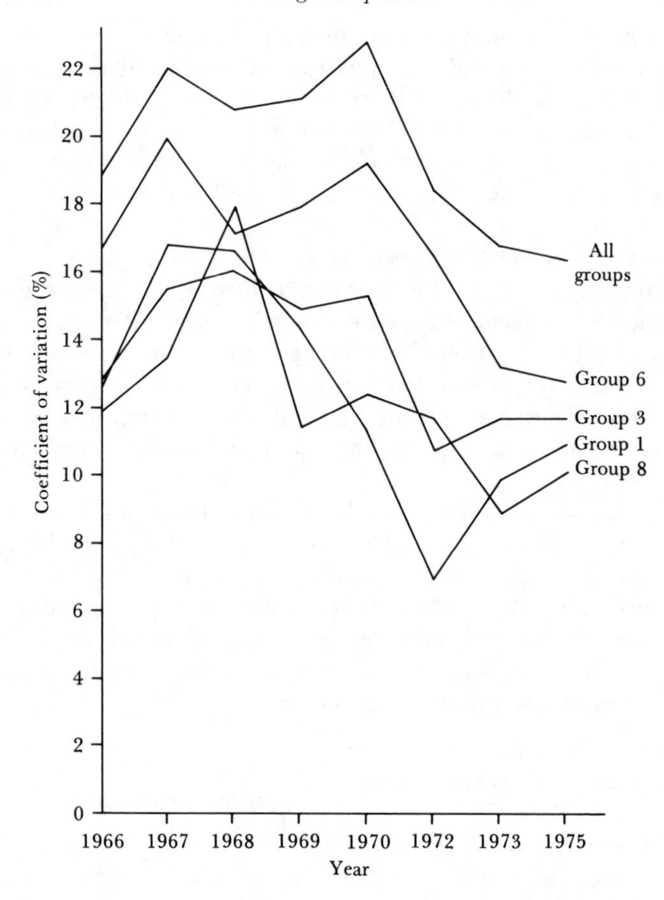

Diagram 5.2. Movement in coefficient of variation by key skill groups between sectors over time

type, and was very similar for groups 3, 5, and 6. Type 1 fitted less well because of an abnormal narrowing of the skill distribution schedule in 1972 (see below), while there was an unexplained decline in the dispersion for type 4 in 1969. These figures suggest that one cannot explain the rise in unadjusted earnings dispersion over the period by changes in either the labour force composition or the skill distribution schedules between sectors.

The measure of dispersion within each skill group was less than for all groups combined, but generally remained high by the standards of the unadjusted levels in many other countries (Tables B5, B6, B7). Both the upper and lower groups displayed significantly less inter-sectoral variations of income, and this can probably be explained by economic factors. There was a relative scarcity of management, and relatively higher turnover of unskilled workers in Yugoslavia, so there were likely to be effective labour markets for both types. The lower earning sectors would therefore have offered management and technicians a payment that did not differ too markedly from the average, since enterprise rules enforced competition for these posts. Similarly, unskilled workers had less attachment to the firm and less interest in self-management so they would be more likely to stay or quit according to the wages offered.

Sociological studies (Gorupic and Paj, 1970; Adizes, 1971; Koloja, 1964) have suggested that the controlling group in Yugoslav cooperatives are skilled workers and less qualified white collar employees. If these act as a majority coalition, and effectively hire the remaining labour types, the predicted inter-sectoral income dispersion would be most marked for these groups. Tables B8 and B9 are consistent with this argument, since the coefficient of variation for these groups was not greatly different to that of the unadjusted earnings dispersion. If correct, this suggests that the effects of introducing self-management can be measured by the gap between minimum and maximum coefficient of variation by skill type, which in the 1960s was around 6% or one half of the total.

It is interesting to note that skill differentials in Yugoslavia remained relatively narrow and stable over time during the period of market self-management. This is shown in Table B10, which provides the average earnings of each of the eight labour types in the industrial sector as a whole from 1965 to 1975 as a proportion of the incomes of the unskilled.

At the start of the period, Yugoslav skill differentials, on average, from top to bottom were relatively narrow at 2.6:1, but there was a major increase before 1961. This suggests that the gradual widening observed in inter-sectoral dispersion in the early years of the period could have partly been caused by enterprises using their autonomy to broaden income differences between skill types. However, the initial differentials were restored by 1963 and drifted only slightly upwards during the late 1960s, so one cannot relate the change in the overall dispersion after 1965 to changes in skill differentials. There was a further narrowing of the range after 1970 which may have been associated with the reduction of inter-sectoral dispersion at that time.

Table B10 also confirms the strong position of highly skilled workers in Yugoslavia. This group earned, on average, approximately twice as much as the unskilled, more than most white collar workers and around two-thirds of the income of college graduates. The changes in the skill distribution over time affected primarily these and the highest category, while the remainder faced stable relativities. Once again, these findings can be compared with international experience. Table B11 shows the skill differentials in Eastern and Western Europe (derived from *National Yearbooks* and UN, *Incomes in Post-War Europe*). Though there may be differences in categorisation, the figures suggest that Yugoslav differentials were narrow by Western standards, but wide in comparison with Eastern Europe. Even at peak, Yugoslavia did not reach a skill range as wide as that observed in relatively egalitarian market economies such as Sweden or the UK, and during the 1950s the range was about half that of Italy. The Eastern bloc data are hard to interpret since they ignore the bonuses which can be a large proportion of the incomes of the higher paid groups, so these countries may be less egalitarian than the table suggests. Even so, that seems likely to be more egalitarian than Yugoslavia. Yugoslav skilled workers were in a stronger position than anywhere apart from the US.

Differences in the definitions of skill groups and payments between countries mean that these comparisons must be interpreted cautiously. However, they do suggest that the relatively egalitarian distribution of income observed in Yugoslavia (see Table B1) can be partly attributed to the rather narrow skill differentials in the country, which may also have gone some way to offsetting the large inter-sectoral differences in the industrial sector.

There are also Yugoslav data on gross average monthly earnings per person in twenty-one sectors for particular jobs. This gives an important insight into labour market resource misallocation during the sixties since the jobs are sufficiently well defined for the assumption of skill and work condition homogeneity. Hence, marked differences in incomes must be explained by some constraint on labour mobility such as self-managed behaviour, and could not be sustained in a competitive market system.

Table B12 presents the coefficient of variation and range in earnings between the twenty-one sectors for ten job types in 1969 and 1973. Though there are data for more jobs, only these are reported since they are the only ones in which all sectors are represented. Dispersion was large on either measure, with the ratio varying from around 150% to 250% depending on the job. The coefficient of variation was generally as high as observed for unadjusted average earnings by sector, and there was considerable variability in the dispersion for each job over time. Indeed, the inter-sectoral coefficient of variation for particular jobs in Yugoslavia was generally larger than observed for overall wages in other countries. It seems unlikely that an inter-sectoral ratio, on average, from top to bottom of 253% in the incomes of telephone operators could emerge without some major institutional block to competitive forces in the labour market.

Inter-sectoral dispersion by regions

It is frequently pointed out that most Yugoslav problems have a regional element, and income differentials are no exception. Although we are discussing incomes on average by sector, it is possible to explain the changes in this way if higher paying sectors became increasingly concentrated in the developed republics, and vice versa. In fact, there is no evidence that the regional dimension adds insights to the particular problem under consideration.

Table B13 shows the coefficient of variation and income range between gross monthly average earnings per head for the twenty-one sectors measured for Yugoslavia as a whole, and for each of the eight constituent republics and autonomous provinces. Every region except Slovenia displayed at some time inter-sectoral income dispersion greater than for the country as a whole. Moreover, each followed the national pattern over time in the same way that each skill group followed all skill groups taken together. The income ratio peaked at 272% for Macedonia in 1969, and hovered around 200% or slightly over for most of the others. Table B14 gives the correlation coefficients between average earnings by sector in all Yugoslavia and each region. It shows that dispersion between sectors approximately reproduced itself in each region, and particularly for Croatia, Bosnia and Serbia. The weak association in Montenegro (1969) occurred because in that year incomes were high in mining but low in ships – a reversal of the norm. Finally, although Slovenia, the most developed area, had a markedly lower measure of dispersion (and therefore lower coefficient in Table B14),

Table 5.2. *Industrial coefficients of variation and proportion of industries paying in given income ranges, 1968–74*

Income range (% mean)	1968	1969	1970	1971	1972	1974
	Proportion of industries					
0–79	12	11	12	9	5	3
80–89	15	17	12	9	12	19
90–109	37	33	39	49	53	50
110–119	9	14	14	7	13	12
120–149	18	16	16	17	9	11
>150	9	9	7	9	8	5
Coefficient of variation (%)	25.7	23.2	30.1	28.8	26.2	23.5

Source: Table B15, B16.

regressions using all the republics indicated that there was no significant association between the level of development and the degree of income dispersion between sectors. Since inter-sectoral income differences on average for Yugoslavia as a whole were approximately reproduced for each republic in each year, the observed changes in the series cannot be associated with purely regional factors.

Unadjusted inter-industrial dispersion of incomes

Our final piece of evidence on income differences between productive groupings concerns dispersion measured at the industrial rather than sectoral level of aggregation. Table B15 shows the level of gross average monthly earnings per worker as a percentage of the mean for the twenty-two sectors divided into seventy-six industries between 1968 and 1974, and Table B16 the coefficient of variation and range for the sectoral and industrial classifications. The material on dispersion as well as industrial earnings by income range is summarised in Table 5.2.

The evidence of income disparities becomes stronger when one uses less aggregated data. The coefficient of variation between industries, described in Table B16, ranged between 23.2% and 30.1% over the period, compared with 16.9% to 23.7% for sectors. The ratio from top to bottom varied between 217% and 335%. Such differentials are very wide by international standards, as can be seen from Tables B5, B6 and B7. The effects of the 1972 Reforms can be observed in both the income ratio and dispersion figures of Table 5.2. The latter measure proved to be relatively less stable, because the steady increase in the proportion of industries paying in the 90–109% range around mean was offset by an increased deviation from the mean in those paying outside the range 80–119%. The proportion in each income range changed so much because the average income of an industry altered considerably from year to year. This variability is important, since only in a self-managed economy would one expect rapid adjustments to relative earnings as demand or cost changes altered the residual surplus. Even if there were similar dispersion in a capitalist economy, coming from, for example, union power, the initial variability would be reflected in profits, and only slowly filter through to wages.

Industrial earnings differentials were broadly based in 1968, with some 39% of industries paying outside the range 80–119% around the mean, and only 37% in the 90–109% range. These proportions were approximately maintained until 1970, but there was a large increase in the proportion of industries in the narrow 90–109% range around the mean in 1971, which came almost entirely from the middle range groups, 80–89% and 110–119% around the mean. There was little change in the percentage paying outside these ranges. After 1972, the share of the central group increased at the expense of the extremes, with the middle groups approximately restored to the previous proportions. This suggests that entry and moral suasion before 1972 may have primarily affected the moderately high or low payers, while the Reforms reduced the earnings in the very highest paid sectors and increased them in the lowest. Excluding the unquantifiable effects of moral suasion, this conforms to the arguments of the previous chapter in which entry was seen to occur primarily in the medium paying sectors without strong entry barriers, and exit was very rare.

Measurements of dispersion at the sectoral and industrial level displayed a different pattern over time; there was no narrowing trend between 1968 and 1971 at the industrial level. This suggests that employment may have been restructured over this period between higher and lower paid industries within the successful sectors, and their resulting relative decline on average could explain the reduction in dispersion at the more aggregated level. Thus, although industrial income dispersion showed no downward trend, the aggregation weights in each sector altered in favour of the lower earning industries, so sectoral dispersion appeared to be narrowing. The shift of labour from high to low marginal revenue product uses is, of course, predicted by self-management theory.

In summary, there were considerable changes in the pattern of Yugoslav income differentials by sector and industry between 1956 and 1975, and particularly around the times of economic reforms. Dispersion increased significantly on various measures, even when labour types, skill differentials, jobs and regions had been taken into account. The resulting differentials were wide by international standards. These changes were associated with considerable income variability in particular sectors or industries over time and in the sectoral rank order of earnings, which contradicts international experience. The apparent narrowing of dispersion towards the end of the period, measured at the sectoral level, could reflect adjustments towards Pareto efficiency, because of changing firm numbers in each market or moral suasion. All these pieces of evidence are generally consistent with our hypotheses from the first part of the book.

5.2.2 *Intra-sectoral dispersion, 1966–72*

In this sub-section on earnings differences within each sector, we are concerned to indicate the scale of income inequality which had emerged in Yugoslavia after 1965. The theory suggests that earnings should differ between firms in a sector because of differences in the efficiency of production or input costs. One would like to observe whether this emerged in Yugoslavia after 1965 with inter-firm data, but since they are not available the information is proxied by evidence on earnings in small groups of firms classified by firm size groups. Material for the industrial sector as a whole, relative to international experience, is considered before outlining income dispersion within each sector during the self-management era.

Income data are available from Yugoslav sources for each sector divided into size categories according to net product, capital employed or the labour force. In fact, the categorisation changes over time, so the series which follow are not strictly comparable in every year. In 1966, 1968 and 1972, the grouping is by net product (a); 1969 and 1971 are by capital employed (b); and 1970 by the number of workers employed (c). There are no data prior to 1966, so these tables indicate the degree of resource misallocation after 1965 rather than the changes when self-management was introduced.

For the first category (a), the groupings in the tables are:

1 = less than 15,000 dinar
2 = 15,000–50,000 dinar
3 = 50,001–150,000 dinar
4 = 150,001–500,000 dinar
5 = 500,001–1,500,000 dinar
6 = 1,500,001–5 million dinar
7 = 5 million–15 million dinar
8 = 15 million–50 million dinar
9 = 50 million–150 million dinar
10 = greater than 150 million dinar

For capital employed (b), the size categories are:

1 = less than 15,000 dinar
2 = 15,001–50,000 dinar
3 = 50,001–150,000 dinar
4 = 150,001–500,000 dinar
5 = 500,001–1,500,000 dinar
6 = 1,500,001–5 million dinar
7 = 5 million–15 million dinar
8 = 15 million–50 million dinar
9 = greater than 50 million dinar

For labour employment (c), the categories are:

1 = less than 15 workers
2 = 15–29 workers
3 = 30–60 workers
4 = 61–125 workers
5 = 126–250 workers
6 = 251–500 workers
7 = 501–1,000 workers
8 = 1,001–2,000 workers
9 = greater than 2,000 workers

The small number of Yugoslav firms (see Chapter 4) and the fineness of the categorisation mean that these groupings do provide a reasonable approximation to inter-firm data. Table B17 shows the number of enterprises in each grouping by sector in the year 1970, and the structure was not greatly different in the other years. There were 2,374 firms categorised into the twenty-two sectors and nine size groups, so allowing for empty categories the average number of firms in each division was fourteen. However, approximately 1,000 firms were in the three least concentrated sectors and a further 500 in the next two, so the average number of firms in the remaining divisions was only six. In fact, a majority of all the firm size groups contained fewer than five industries and around 15% contained only one.

The coefficient of variation for incomes by sector in each particular size group was always greater than observed between whole sectors (see Table B3). For example, in 1966 the lowest inter-sectoral dispersion was measured in size group 8, where the coefficient was 22.2%, and in 1972 the lowest observation was in size group 7, with a value of 26.6%. Therefore, it cannot be argued that inter-sectoral dispersion of average incomes was caused by differences in minimum efficient scale which was positively associated with average earnings. In fact, as for skill types and regions the pattern of inter-sectoral dispersion was approximately reproduced in each firm size group. Hence the correlation coefficient between unadjusted sectoral earnings and those for class group 8 was .71 in 1966, around .88 in 1969 and 1970, and .91 in 1972.

Our evidence on incomes at this level is contained in Tables B18 to B21. Table B18 shows earnings dispersion by firm size group for the industrial sector as a whole, 1966–72, and Tables B19 and B21 the intra-sectoral distribution of incomes for each of the twenty-two sectors over the same period. In Table B20, we present similar material for Western European economies in five or six size group classes for 1966 and 1972.

From Table B18, it can be seen that annual earnings per worker in the industrial sector as a whole varied considerably according to the size of establishment in which the worker was employed. Incomes were not in general positively associated with the scale of production in Yugoslavia; higher earnings were received at both the top and bottom of the distribution. The coefficient of variation was large, in excess of 30% in every year except 1969 when unadjusted for extreme values, and in excess of 17% until 1972 when these were excluded. The most important statistic, however, concerns the income variability of most size groups over time. Although there was some degree of stability in groups 6–8, this was probably the consequence of averaging across larger numbers of firms. The relative position of very large firms appears to have become rather worse, and that of smaller enterprises rather better over time. Given that the data were not comparable in every year, this can be observed by comparing the years of the constant definition (1966, 1968 and 1972). Size group 2 improved from 10% of the industrial mean in 1966 to 293% in 1972, and size group 3 increased from 69% in 1966 to 118% in 1968 and 96% in 1972.

The material on the Yugoslav industrial sector as a whole provides an interesting comparison with the situation in Western Europe. Table B20 shows similar data categorised by employment classes, though for fewer firm size groups, and is derived from EEC, *Social Statistics in Europe: Labour Costs in Industry* (1972, 1975). It can be seen that in Western Europe, incomes increased monotonically according to the size of the employing enterprise. Moreover, the level of dispersion itself was rather small. Almost every Western European but less than half of the Yugoslav observations were in the 80–120% range of the industrial mean. Finally, there was much less volatility of incomes by size class in Western Europe, though the relative position of the largest plants also improved. Thus once again the pattern of wage dispersion in Yugoslavia did not conform with that observed in other market economies, though the variability is consistent with predictions from labour management theory.

Turning to intra-sectoral differentials, in Table B19 we show dispersion of annual gross earnings per head within each of the twenty-two industrial sectors over the period 1966–72. Also provided are the number of non-empty firm size classes in each sector, denoted no. D. It can be seen that there were huge differences in the incomes paid, on average, to workers in different firms or groups of firms within a sector. The findings are summarised in Table 5.3. In 1966, only 4% of sectors displayed an income ratio among their ten firm size groups of less than 150%, and around two-thirds of sectors showed an income range in excess of 200%. Similarly, the income range between the nine firm size groups in 1970 was less than 150% in 18% of Yugoslav sectors but more than 200% in half of them. A majority of sectors displayed an internal income ratio from top to bottom in excess of 200% in four years of the six, and it exceeded 300% in a sizeable minority. The largest income ratio among firm size groups in a sector exceeded 250% in every year, 1,000% in four of the six years and 1,500% in one year. The smallest was never less

Table 5.3. *Proportion of sectors in intra-sectoral range groups, 1966–72*

Income range (% mean)		Years				
		(a)		(b)		(c)
	1966	1968	1972	1969	1971	1970
<149	4	5	18	35	23	18
150–199	32	35	41	25	18	32
200–299	45	20	27	21	27	27
>300	18	40	14	21	32	23

Source: Table B19.

than 123% and not less than 134% in two of the six years. Differentials were volatile over time, but using only net product categories one can see a reduction in intra-sector dispersion in 1972.

In Table B21 we offer further details about Yugoslav intra-sectoral dispersion, at its peak in 1968. The value of sectoral annual earnings, the rank order of the sector, the income range, the minimum and maximum observed income and, in brackets, the size group in which these values were found, are provided. If either category was the largest non-empty one, it is denoted by *, while the smallest is denoted by †. The table highlights the variability of incomes within each sector and the absence of any clear or consistent empirical pattern. Dispersion was not related to the average income of the sector and there was no significant association between either the relative level or the rank order of earnings and the observed income range within a sector. The correlation coefficient ranged from between −0.217 (1968, rank order) to 0.232 (1971, level of income). In general, the highest incomes in 1968 occurred in the largest firm size group (91% of sectors), and the minimum in the smallest (68% of sectors). However, as suggested by the aggregate data, this picture was not true in every year, and in fact in 1972 45% of sectors had maximum earnings in their largest firm size group, 18% in their smallest, and minimum earnings were only recorded in the smallest category in 32% of sectors.

There is virtually no international evidence on intra-sectoral wage dispersion, but some evidence is available for the UK mechanical engineering sector (derived from the Economics Development Committee for Mechanical Engineering: *Company Financial Results*, 1967–72). The coefficient of variation between thirty-three firms in this industry was 1.5%, with very few observations outside the range

80–120% of the industry mean and a ratio from top to bottom of around 130%.

To summarise, there was considerable dispersion in the incomes paid to Yugoslav workers in a given industrial sector after 1965. This could not arise if labour markets had been operating freely, and self-management theory would attribute it to differences in enterprise efficiency and costs. The income range within a sector reached more than 10:1 in several years, and generally exceeded 2:1 in most cases. One can find little evidence of similar differentials in other market economies. Moreover, even for the industrial sector as a whole we find that the Yugoslav distribution did not follow the normal international pattern, and all the evidence indicates that there was considerable volatility in the measures of dispersion over time.

5.2.3 *Overall income dispersion, 1965–72*

We have seen that relatively wide income differentials had emerged between and within sectors after 1965. As our final contribution, we report on how these differences affected the overall distribution of income among firms and skill types in Yugoslavia. We commence with the overall distribution of average earnings between firms in the manufacturing sector, as approximated by incomes in each firm size group and sector. We then consider the relative importance of sectoral and skill group differentials for average earnings, on the basis of the data in the first sub-section on incomes, to indicate the effects of self-management on the incentives to accumulate human capital in Yugoslavia.

Commencing with inter-firm differentials, in Table B22 we show gross annual earnings per head in each size group and sector for three years, 1966, 1968 and 1970. Table 5.4 in the text provides a summary of the evidence in the first two of these years, as well as for 1972, so one can discern if there is a pattern over time using consistent categories. The maximum observed ratio in this matrix exceeded 1,000% in every year, and reached 7,160% in 1966. When the most extreme values were excluded, the ratio generally fell between 650% and 750%, with the familiar inter-sectoral pattern displaying a non-systematic variation according to size category. This obscured the inter-sectoral dispersion, narrowing the gap between minimum earners in high paying sectors and maximum

Table 5.4. *Proportion of firm size groups in earnings ranges, 1966–72*

Range of incomes (% mean)	% Firm size groups 1966	1968	1972
0–50	6	10	3
51–80	30	27	22
81–120	43	41	48
121–200	17	18	20
>200	4	4	7

Sources: Table B22, IP.

ones in less well paid areas, and increased the overall range. For example, while the highest-paid group in textiles earned more than the lowest ones in oil, ships or printing in 1966, the overall ratio between these sectors increased to 450%.

As a result, the bulk of firm size groups paid within a relatively narrow range as can be seen in Table 5.4, though there remained very wide income differences among a significant minority of the divisions. Thus, between 10% and 14% of the groups paid outside the range 51–200% of the mean industrial income in any year, while between 41% and 48% of the groups paid within the range 81–120% of the mean. Combining the relatively large sectoral and intra-sectoral income dispersion indicates that many firm size groups actually paid within a quite narrow range, though the gap between rewards in the successful and unsuccessful cooperatives was very wide. This is consistent with expectations for a self-managed economy, where one might expect the profits or losses which would accrue to entrepreneurs in capitalism not to prove large in many cases, but to widen the observed income range considerably when distributed to labour.

One can also examine the average income differentials between the eight skill groups defined above in each sector to study the relative importance of skills and industry in determining Yugoslav incomes. In Table B23 we show the matrices of gross annual incomes per head by twenty-two sectors and eight skill groups for 1967 and 1973. These years were chosen to represent the peak and trough of overall dispersion.

In 1967, the inter-sectoral ratio from top to bottom was approximately 200% and the largest skill differential was around 2.7:1.

Thus, on average, sectors of employment were of comparable importance with general skills in determining incomes, which led to serious anomalies. For example, in their best paying sectors the highly skilled earned more than the average of the college graduates and of the technically trained group in every sector but their own. The unskilled earned more than the industrial average, more than skilled workers in a third of sectors and more than the minimum earnings of every category except the top two white collar groups and the highly skilled. The converse held for each group in their worst paying sector. Skilled workers earned only slightly more than the mean of the unskilled and the highly skilled approximately the mean of the skilled. The university-trained group earned less than the average of the technically educated, only slightly more than the mean of the highly skilled, and less than the highest income of skilled workers.

It is interesting to note that in 1967 the income gain for an individual, on average, in changing industrial sector from the mean to the highest paying industry always exceeded the benefits to improving skills into the next category of labour type. Although of course the whole problem in Yugoslavia is a block to the free mobility of labour between sectors as well as skills, the skewing of incentives is striking; even on average, Yugoslav workers could increase their earnings more by shifting employment between sectors than by accumulating human capital.

As one would expect, the situation was less serious in 1973. The overall ratio from top to bottom in the matrix had declined from around 5:1 in 1967 to 3.3:1 because the range between the sectors and the skill groups had both narrowed considerably. However, as can be seen in Table B23, many of the anomalies remained. For example, highly skilled workers in the best paid sector on average continued to earn more or about as much as the best paid group in three-quarters of Yugoslav sectors. College graduates in the least well paid sectors earned rather less than highly skilled workers in the best paid sectors. Given the considerable averaging in the data reported here, there is reason to believe that the distortion of incentives to accumulate human capital resulting from the firm and sector specific character of earnings in Yugoslavia would have continued beyond the 1974 Reforms.

Thus, an industry-skill classification of earnings indicates the emergence of striking income differentials and anomalies in Yugo-

Table 5.5. *Correlation coefficients between average earnings and capital intensity by sector, 1964–72*

1964	0.7387
1965	0.7706
1966	0.7619
1967	0.7856
1968	0.7866
1969	0.7538
1970	0.8124
1971	0.7833
1972	0.7383

Partial correlation coefficient for twenty-one observations in each year.

slavia during the period of market self-management. On average, workers in different firms received incomes that differed by a ratio, at peak, of more than 70:1 and normally in excess of 5:1. Indeed, some 10% of categories were usually paid, on average, outside the income range 4:1. Moreover, at the height of the Self-Management era in 1967, the most highly educated labour group in two-thirds of Yugoslav sectors could, on average, have increased their incomes by resigning to undertake skilled manual work in the best paying sector. The nature and extent of these differentials indicate that this type of income inequality could generally be a serious problem under self-management. This brings incomes policies to the forefront of the policy agenda in such systems.

5.3 INCOMES AND CAPITAL–LABOUR RATIOS

It has been argued in Chapter 2 that any factor which would permit the cooperative to increase its earnings would also lead to the choice of a more capital-intensive technique of production. In this section we briefly examine whether this non-causal association was observed in Yugoslavia during the Self-Management era, at the sectoral and industrial levels of aggregation.

The evidence at the sectoral level is summarised in Table 5.5, where the partial correlation coefficients between average earnings (unadjusted monthly gross earnings per person) and the capital–labour ratio are presented. They are derived from cross-section linear regressions for twenty-one sectors (excluding the film industry) for each of the years 1964–72. It can be seen that the relationship was generally rather close, with the coefficient reaching 0.81 in 1970. The pattern over time conformed with expectations in that the coefficient rose after 1964 and fell towards the end of the period, though never achieving a value below 0.73. The regressions themselves show the coefficient on capital intensity to be statistically significant at the 99% level in every year, though the $\bar{R}^2$ was very low. As previous material would suggest, the association remained robust whichever series on inter-sectoral earnings was employed, though the relationship was weaker (generally the coefficient was between 0.6 and 0.7) for regressions using earnings for a skill type or region.

There are no data on capital employed measured at the industrial level in published Yugoslav sources, so the exercise cannot be exactly repeated at a more disaggregated level. However, *Industrija Preduzecu* provides material on amortisation by industry for the same groups as earnings per head from 1970 to 1972. If one assumes that depreciation in Yugoslavia was a fixed proportion of capital (in fact the authorities did set the amortisation rate, but it varied somewhat between sectors), the association between earnings and amortisation per head can be used as an approximation. In fact, the correlation coefficient across seventy-five industries was 0.541 in 1970, 0.537 in 1971 and 0.493 in 1972. Therefore, there is some limited evidence for the predicted positive association at the industrial level.

There is nothing new in the discovery of an association between Yugoslav incomes and capital–labour ratios. Similar findings have been reported in the Yugoslav literature (see Horvat, 1971a) and by 'capital school' analysts such as Vanek and Jovicic (1975) and Staellerts (1981). Indeed, the association is actually predicted by capital school as well as self-management models, though from entirely different premises. The former group would argue that the relationship is causal, so that incomes include an implicit rent to capital which is distributed to labour (see Chapter 2 and Estrin and Bartlett, 1982). Self-management models view both variables as strictly endogenous, leading to the reduced form equations of the following chapter. Since there are problems of interpretation, which do not arise with the bulk of the information about income differentials or changing growth patterns, we do not offer further evidence on the relationship between earnings and capital–labour ratios in Yugoslavia.

5·4 YUGOSLAV INDUSTRIAL GROWTH, 1952–73

This section examines whether the pattern of Yugoslav industrial growth actually changed in the way suggested by the first part of this book. The theory suggests that cooperatives generate an artificial scarcity in the labour market, thereby raising earnings above their market clearing levels and distorting the choice of technique towards more capital-intensive and labour-productive methods. To examine whether such phenomena appeared in Yugoslavia after the introduction of self-management, the trend rate of growth of the relevant variables in the Visible Hand and Market Self-Management periods are compared, and labour market clearing in the latter era is examined. Once again, it must be remembered that the approach is entirely empirical so consistency between hypotheses and observations does not establish the predicted influence of labour management. The data are contained in Appendix C.

We commence by describing the changing choice of production technique for manufacturing industry as a whole over the two periods, 1952–65 and 1965–73, and in each industrial sector as defined in Chapter 4. We go on to suggest an explanation in terms of changing relative input prices from the evidence of an heuristic study of labour market clearing and the movements in real wages. The discovery of changing output growth rates between the periods in the work which follows is taken to indicate the effects of introducing regulated markets in 1965 rather than of self-management. In this, we follow the bulk of the literature (e.g. Horvat, 1971a, Milenkovitch, 1971; Moore, 1980; Sapir, 1980a), which suggests that Yugoslav industrial growth declined after the 1965 Reforms because the centralised accumulation of capital was abandoned. As Chapter 2 has shown, one cannot deduce general comparative results about the rate of growth under self-management, so we have nothing to test on the output data. Finally, lest our findings are biased despite the use of long-run trends because the periods under consideration are so short, we shall attempt to show where relevant that the results are insensitive to minor changes in period length.

5.4.1 *Choice of technique in the manufacturing sector*

In Tables C1 and C2 we show the level and annual rates of growth of industrial production, the capital stock, the labour force, capital–labour ratios and average factor productivities for each year from 1952 to 1973. One can see Yugoslavia's very successful record of economic development since the early 1950s, with industrial production growing at more than 10% per year on average (from the compounding annual average growth rates in Table C1), based on 9% annual increases in the real industrial capital stock and 5% increases in the industrial labour force. On average, labour productivity increased by 5% per year over the period, with modestly declining capital–output ratios. This very rapid pace of industrial development has been slowed considerably in more recent years (see Schrenk, Ardalan and El Tatawy, 1979; Tyson, 1980), and the standard Yugoslav measures of growth have been questioned by Moore (1980) (see Estrin and Bartlett, 1982, for a survey). Even so, these tables indicate why the 'Yugoslav experiment' (see Marschak, 1968) was so highly regarded during the 1960s and early 1970s.

One can see from the mean and coefficients of variation of each series in Table C2 that there were cycles in Yugoslav industrial growth. This issue has been considered more fully in Bajt (1971) and Horvat (1971b), so here we shall merely note that growth occurred around a declining mean with approximately constant amplitude but shortening time span. Output varied moderately over the cycle, with capital altering less and labour more than production. Labour productivity moved pro-cyclically with a marked variation, apparently because of the lag between output and employment. Hence periods of very fast output growth displayed a major acceleration in labour productivity (1957, 1960, 1964, 1969) and declines in output per man were associated with recessions (1954, 1967, 1973). The correlation coefficient between the two growth rates was .636; this is some preliminary evidence for Verdoorn's Law.

Table C3 permits a comparison of the trend growth rates for the industrial sector as a whole in the Visible Hand and Self-Management eras, denoted period 1 and period 2. Two estimates of the six growth rates in the two periods are given, annual compounding growth rates and the trend measure ($\hat{\beta}$ in the logarithmic time equation), with the second period also being described as a percentage of the first.

On compounding measures, the rate of growth of industrial production was very rapid in the Visible Hand period (approximately 13% per annum), based on large increases in both the labour force (7% per year), and the capital stock (10% per year). There was a modest rise in the capital-intensity of production, and both factor productivities increased over time. One gets the same general picture from the trend equations, the fits of which were very good. One can see that employment rather than labour productivity growth was the most important element in the rapid industrial development over the period, comprising some 7% of the 12% trend growth in output. Labour productivity provided the remaining 5%. There is further evidence of economies of scale in the fact that capital productivity was increasing despite the gradually rising capitalisation of the sector.

The table shows that there was a break in the industrial sector's rate and pattern of growth around 1965. On compounding measures, the rate of growth of industrial production declined to approximately half the previous level, while the coefficient of variation doubled. As has been noted, these effects will be attributed to the introduction of markets. The evidence in favour of the self-management hypothesis comes from the changing pattern of development: the failure of factor input growth rates, on average over the period, to decline in proportion with output. Compared to the Visible Hand era, the Self-Management period was characterised by an acceleration in the rate of growth of the capital stock, capital–labour ratio and labour productivity, but a deceleration in the rate of growth of employment.

On the compounding measures, the growth of the capital stock after 1965 only declined by 16% over the previous period; an acceleration relative to output of approximately 30%. Moreover, the variance in the growth of the capital stock, as measured by the coefficient of variation, fell to almost half the level which had been maintained during the period of investment planning. One has similar findings using the trend measures, and the conclusions are not significantly affected if one takes other years between 1964 and 1967 as the dividing year between periods. Thus, cooperatives consistently chose to invest relatively more than during the Visible Hand period, despite the more uncertain (see Adizes, 1971) and cyclical market environment. This appears to contradict the suggestion discussed in Chapter 1 that imperfect property rights would relatively reduce investment in a self-managed environment (see Furubotn and Pejovich, 1970). The rate of growth of employment, on the other hand, declined more than proportionately with output in the Self-Management period, though the scale may have been influenced by the labour shake-out during the post-Reform recession. A re-estimation of the trends in the second period to exclude 1965–7 shows that output growth declined to 68% and employment growth to 57% of their previous values. The table may therefore overstate the deceleration in the growth of employment after 1965. Even so, the rate of growth of capital-intensity virtually doubled in the second period, largely because of the relative acceleration in the growth of the capital stock, and the decline in the growth of labour productivity was significantly less marked than for output.

The changing choice of technique in the manufacturing sector as a whole is illustrated in Diagram 5.3 which plots the index of the capital stock against that of the labour force in each year, 1952–73. The most striking thing to note is the apparent change in underlying trend around the time that market self-management was introduced. The capital–labour ratio for the industrial sector was approximately constant from 1952–60, following the 45° line, though with some cyclical fluctuation, and it then increased moderately until 1964. Production increases were apparently generated by providing a declining labour force with more capital in the early years of self-management, so the line displayed a negative slope until 1967. Of course, the declining level of employment was in part due to the post-1965 Reform recession, but even after 1967 one can observe a new and much faster trend rate of growth of capital-intensity. At the aggregate level, after the introduction of market self-management the industrial sector was choosing more capital-intensive production techniques to generate relatively smaller annual increases in production, with a relative increase in the pace of growth of labour productivity but declining capital–output ratios compared to the Visible Hand era.

5.4.2 *Choice of technique by industrial sector*

One can observe similar changes in the pattern of growth in each of the nineteen individual industrial sectors for which there are

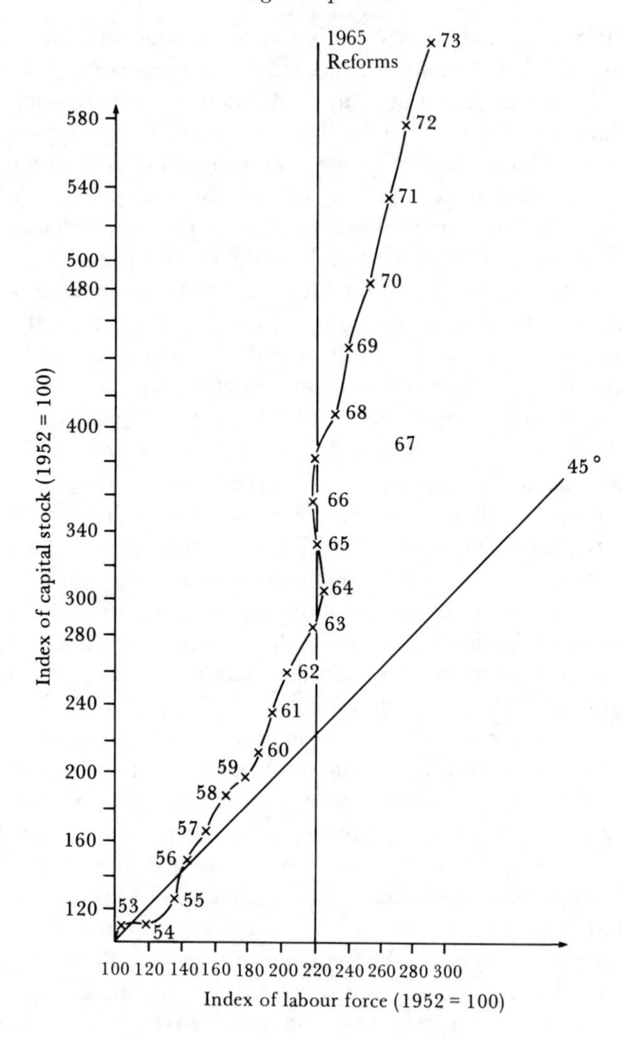

Diagram 5.3. Capital–labour ratios, 1952–74

appropriate data. Table C4 contains the average annual compounding rate of growth of physical production, the capital stock and employment in each period, as well as the mean and standard deviation of each growth rate series. As can be seen, on average the rate of growth of physical production declined by 55% after 1965, and also declined in each individual sector. The standard deviation of growth rates among sectors was lower in the Self-Management era, but the rank order was not greatly altered. The rank order correlation coefficient for rates of growth in the two periods was 0.697. Thus, the 1965 Reforms appear not to have led to a major restructuring of industrial development, though the differences between growth rates in the fastest and slowest growing branches were reduced.

Once again, the average rate of growth among the nineteen industrial sectors did not decline proportionately with output after 1965. In fact, capital accumulation actually accelerated in absolute terms in eleven of the branches, primarily those with hitherto low rates of capital growth. This acted to equalise growth rates in different sectors, and therefore to reduce variance of the series. However, on average, the rate of growth of employment declined more than proportionately with output after 1965. The rate of growth declined in every single sector, and employment actually fell in the coal and tobacco industries. But growth rates declined by a similar order of magnitude in each sector, so the standard deviation of the series was only slightly reduced. Since the mean declined to around a third of its previous level, the coefficient of variation therefore increased considerably in the second period.

These changes meant that the average rate of growth of the capital–labour ratio more than trebled between the two periods. During the Visible Hand era it declined absolutely in six of the industrial branches, while growth was generally modest in the remainder. Its rate of growth increased in all but four sectors after 1965; three of these having been the fastest growing industries during the Visible Hand period. Thus, one cannot argue that the capital–labour ratio increased at the aggregate level because employment was reduced in specific industries. It increased in most industrial sectors: those with sluggish employment growth, as well as those with rapid increases in the capital stock and production. The rate of growth of labour productivity can be deduced from the output and employment series. It declined less than proportionately with output, on average, to around 80% of its previous level after 1965. At the disaggregated level, the growth of labour productivity actually increased in eight of the nineteen sectors after 1965. This occurred in sectors with rapid capital growth (such as shipbuilding and chemicals) as well as those which reduced employment (such as tobacco).

Therefore, the sectoral data confirm and strengthen the results at the aggregate level. The reduction in output growth after 1965 was associated with a changing technique of production, which raised capital-intensity and labour productivity. This occurred primarily because the rate of growth of the capital stock accelerated after the Reforms, relative to output in every sector and absolutely in a few. The findings do not therefore depend on the relative decline in the rate of growth of employment, which was partly caused by the 1965–7 recession.

5.4.3 *Incomes and labour market clearing*

Finally, self-management theory suggests that in favourable conditions cooperatives will raise earnings above the market clearing level and generate unemployment. This change of relative input costs would explain our observed shifts in production technique. Below we attempt to examine this hypothesis with respect to changing trends within the industrial sector as a whole, and by comparing the rural and urban sectors. The latter exercise involves adapting our initial argument, which predicts behaviour in a developed country with an integrated labour market, to fit a less developed economy with dual labour markets.

We have already noted that the rate of Yugoslav industrial job creation was significantly reduced in the Self-Management era (see Table C3), and there is evidence of an ever-increasing excess supply of labour over the period. Table C5 shows the annual level of registered unemployment, 1964–73, as well as net migrations from Yugoslavia. The former data understate market slack because one could only register as unemployed in Yugoslavia after having been previously employed within the social sector. Thus the surplus agricultural labour force, estimated by the World Bank (1975) to comprise approximately one million workers, are excluded from consideration. It can be seen that registered unemployment rose steadily after the introduction of self-management except for a slight decline during the late 1960s boom. The stock of unemployed approximately doubled in nine years despite the relatively rapid pace of industrial development. One can obtain a further impression of the surplus labour force available for industrial employment by studying the net migration figures. The outflow was very large, summing to 1.2 million persons by 1973. In that year, around 17%

of the active population were either unemployed or working abroad. This represented more people than were actually employed in the entire Yugoslav industrial sector. Thus, there is considerable evidence of increasing manufacturing market slack in the Self-Management era.

To see whether this evidence is consistent with self-management theory, one must also investigate what was happening to real wages in the same period. Table C6 shows the index numbers for real earnings in the industrial sector from 1953 to 1973. It can be seen that incomes grew at an average rate, annually compounding, of 5.4% in the Visible Hand era and 5.1% under self-management. There was almost no change in the growth of real earnings for those in employment after 1965 despite the reduction of almost a half in the rate of output growth and the increasing labour market slack. Moreover, wage increases, which were highly volatile between years before 1965, actually became rather more stable after the introduction of self-management. Thus, the coefficient of variation of the series approximately halved from 148% to 92%, despite the greater uncertainty of the new market environment (see Adizes, 1971) made evident by the greater variability of output and employment. If one excludes the years after 1972, because the government may have been intervening informally in the setting of incomes, the annually compounding growth of earnings in the Self-Management period becomes 6%, which is somewhat above the level attained in the Visible Hand era.

In a relatively less developed economy, such as Yugoslavia, it seems likely that movements in the ratio of urban to rural wages would provide more significant evidence for the emergence of labour market monopoly power. Economic models of industrial development, such as Lewis (1954) and Rannis and Fei (1961), argue that there are distinct labour markets in the rural and urban sectors, with growth resulting from the gradual transfer of the surplus agricultural labour force to urban industrial employment. Industrial growth should occur at constant relative wages between the sectors. The transfer does not reduce agricultural output since there is a large agricultural labour pool. The introduction of self-management in the urban sector would reduce the rate of industrial employment creation, and therefore the rate of decrease of the excess labour supply. The monopoly power of cooperatives would be used to generate a relative increase in the rate of growth of industrial incomes despite the reserves of rural labour. This distortion of relative wages would shift the pattern of industrial development away from the relatively abundant to the relatively scarce factor. We have already noted that the rural sector offered a large pool of labour for industrial development in Yugoslavia, estimated by the World Bank (1975) to be approximately one million workers. We therefore consider movements in real wages in this wider context of dual labour markets.

Table C7 shows index numbers for proxies of real urban and rural incomes and their ratios from 1957 to 1971; there are no data for the years prior to 1957.[9] The movements are graphed in Diagram 5.4, which once again illustrates that there was a striking change in the ratio around the time of the 1965 Reforms, in the direction one would hypothesise from self-management theory. The ratio remained approximately constant through the Visible Hand era, though fluctuating from year to year, either because of government wage regulation or the presence from excess labour supply. Real urban wages were increasing until around 1960 and then slightly declined. Rural incomes remained virtually unchanged until 1962 and then increased. However, there was a dramatic movement in

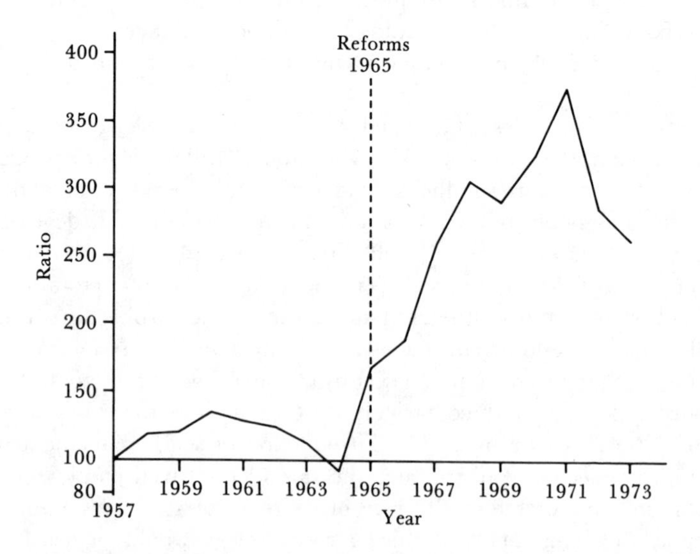

Diagram 5.4. The ratio of urban to rural wages, 1957–73

favour of urban real incomes after the introduction of self-management, which was due to rapid increases in urban wages themselves rather than declining rural ones. Even taking into the account the once and for all improvement in urban incomes following the restructuring of prices in 1965, growth continued very rapidly until 1970 though there was some decline after that date. In fact, rural wages also displayed a slight upward trend over the period, perhaps from technical innovation. This is consistent with our hypothesis that market pressures would have prevented rural wages from increasing faster than productivity. Enterprises in the urban sector became insensitive to the large surplus labour pool after the introduction of effective self-management, and so were able to increase their earnings.

In summary, as well as the widely noted change in the pace of growth (see Sapir, 1980a), the Yugoslav pattern of development altered considerably after 1965. The choice of technique in the industrial sector shifted towards more capital-intensive and labour-productive methods, measured at both aggregate and branch levels, which could be explained by a shift in relative inputs costs away from the employment of labour. This is precisely what did occur after 1965, with an acceleration in the rate of growth of industrial wages relative to the levels attained in the Visible Hand era, and of urban wages relative to the levels attained in the Visible Hand era, and of urban wages compared with rural ones. However, Yugoslavia was a relatively less developed economy in which capital is scarce and labour rather more abundant, so we are observing the results of the urban and industrial sectors managing to create an artificial scarcity on the labour market after 1965, precisely as would be predicted by self-management models.

5.5 SUMMARY

This chapter has provided evidence that the introduction of market self-management into Yugoslavia in 1965 affected decision-making in the manner predicted by economic theory. Our method has been to provide as many separate pieces of evidence as possible on the premise that, although no individual finding would be entirely convincing, one could paint a broad and detailed picture of Yugoslav allocation which could only be consistent with the self-management model. We conclude by summarising our major findings, and observing that they are not consistently explained by any other single hypothesis.

First, we observed a break in most of the data series in around 1965, which suggests that institutional changes did have a significant impact on economic behaviour. Differences in incomes paid between productive units increased considerably in a manner not consistent with international experience. Similarly, the choice of technique within the industrial sector became markedly more capital-intensive, and the ratio of urban to rural wages moved dramatically in favour of social sector workers. All these changes were measured at numerous different levels of aggregation and in various ways, gradually building a coherent overall picture consistent with the possibility that incomes become an enterprise-specific choice variable around 1965, which led to the suppression of effective labour market forces.

The strongest evidence that firms were able to choose their incomes regardless of labour market pressures after 1965 was probably the material on earnings dispersion for a given job by sector and by firm. It will be remembered that, even on average, workers in a given job faced an income ratio of 2.5:1, and the range from top to bottom for firms within a sector generally exceeded 10:1. The largest observed differential between firms actually reached 70:1, and some 10% of firms paid outside the range 4:1. Indeed, the sectoral dispersion, let alone the inter-firm one, proved to be of comparable importance to that of skills in determining workers' incomes. It is hard to explain the emergence of earnings differentials so rapidly, or which were so wide, without reference to the distribution of enormous 'pure profits' to the labour force as incomes. The data on the changing ratio of urban to rural wages were also important evidence. They showed that workers in the urban and industrial sectors were able to force up their incomes considerably after 1965, both by historical standards and with reference to the rural sector, despite the large and growing excess supply of labour. Self-management theory provides a model of just such an institutionalised labour market imperfection and the changing relative input costs could explain observed shifts in the choice of technique.

The only finding for which there is an explicit alternative explanation is the relationship between incomes and capital–labour ratios, and for this reason we present little evidence on the topic. In fact, our findings contradict the predictions of the 'property rights' school (e.g. Furubotn and Pejovich, 1970, see Chapter 1), which argues that the introduction of self-management would lead to under-investment in the capital stock. It will be remembered that the pace of Yugoslav investment both accelerated and stabilised relative to the previous investment planning at the Visible Hand era after 1965. However, it is possible that low or negative real interest rates were also partly responsible for the increasing capital-intensity of production. One would not wish to deny the relevance of capital market imperfections for allocative inefficiencies in Yugoslavia in 1965, but this chapter has also indicated the separate impact of self-management on the allocation of labour.

Appendix B: Yugoslav earnings dispersion

The data on Yugoslav incomes are almost entirely derived from *Statisticki Godisnak Jugoslavie* (SGJ) and *Industrija Preduzeca* (IP) in the relevant years, although some reference is also made to the material quoted by Wachtel (1973). Once again, we do not refer to the table numbers of the primary sources because they actually change from year to year. However, the material comes from the sections on the industrial sector and on incomes in SGJ, and on industrial enterprises in IP. All information on sectoral earnings, including with respect to skill groups, regions and job types, comes from SGJ, and the evidence on incomes by industry and by firm size groups is derived from IP. The numerous sources for the comparative material on wages in other countries are listed in the main text.

In general, total gross labour earnings for a given period divided by the number of enterprise members are used to represent average earnings. This approximates the income notion of the theory more closely than basic wages, because it includes the surplus and bonus payments in each sector, industry or firm size group, but means our study suffers somewhat from the effects of averaging. The official Yugoslav wage series show about the same rank order but have a lower variance, as can be seen in Table B3.

We attempt to show tables which are internally consistent in definition over time, but the series are not always comparable across sources. For example, inter-sectoral dispersion for each skill group can be compared with the overall distribution for all skills, but both series represent official Yugoslav wage data. The overall distribution measured in this way is therefore not based on the same series as for the unadjusted wage dispersion of Table B2. The same holds for the material on regional income dispersion. Finally, in certain years the film sector actually earns around five times the industrial average, which seriously distorts the dispersion measures. In consequence, this industry is generally excluded unless otherwise mentioned in the text.

High inequality Share of lowest 40% less than 12%					Moderate inequality Share of lowest 40% between 12% and 17%					Low inequality Share of lowest 40%, 17% and above				
Country (year)	Per capita GNP US$	Lowest 40%	Middle 40%	Top 20%	Country (year)	Per capita GNP US$	Lowest 40%	Middle 40%	Top 20%	Country (year)	Per capita GNP US$	Lowest 40%	Middle 40%	Top 20%
Income up to US $300														
Kenya (1969)	136	10.0	22.0	68.0	El Salvador (1969)	295	11.2	36.4	52.4	Chad (1958)	78	18.0	39.0	43.0
Sierra Leone (1968)	159	9.6	22.4	68.0	Turkey (1968)	282	9.3	29.9	60.8	Sri Lanka (1969)	95	17.0	37.0	46.0
Philippines (1971)	239	11.6	34.6	53.8	Burma (1958)	82	16.5	38.7	44.8	Niger (1960)	97	18.0	40.0	42.0
Iraq (1956)	200	6.8	25.2	68.0	Dahomey (1959)	87	15.5	34.5	50.0	Pakistan (1964)	100	17.5	37.5	30.0
Senegal (1960)	245	10.0	26.0	64.0	Tanzania (1967)	89	13.0	26.0	61.0	Uganda (1970)	126	17.1	35.8	47.1
Ivory Coast (1970)	247	10.8	32.1	57.1	India (1964)	99	16.0	32.0	52.0	Thailand (1970)	180	17.0	37.5	45.5
Rhodesia (1968)	252	8.2	22.8	69.0	Madagascar (1960)	120	13.5	25.5	61.0	Korea (1970)	235	18.0	37.0	45.0
Tunisia (1970)	255	11.4	53.6	55.0	Zambia (1959)	230	14.5	28.5	57.0	Taiwan (1964)	241	20.4	39.5	40.1
Honduras (1968)	265	6.5	28.5	65.0										
Ecuador (1970)	277	6.5	20.0	73.5										
Income US $300–750														
Malaysia (1970)	330	11.6	32.4	56.0	Dominican					Surinam (1962)	394	21.7	35.7	42.6
Colombia (1970)	358	9.0	30.0	61.0	Republic (1969)	323	12.2	30.3	57.5	Greece (1957)	500	21.0	29.5	49.5
Brazil (1970)	390	10.0	28.4	61.5	Iran (1968)	332	12.5	33.0	54.5	Yugoslavia (1968)	529	18.5	40.0	41.5
Peru (1971)	480	6.5	33.5	60.0	Guyana (1956)	550	14.0	40.3	45.7	Bulgaria (1962)	530	26.8	40.0	33.2
Gabon (1968)	497	8.8	23.7	67.5	Lebanon (1960)	508	13.0	26.0	61.0	Spain (1965)	750	17.6	36.7	45.7
Jamaica (1958)	510	8.2	30.3	61.5	Uruguay (1968)	618	16.5	35.5	48.0					
Costa Rica (1971)	521	11.5	30.0	58.5	Chile (1968)	744	13.0	30.2	56.8					
Mexico (1969)	645	10.5	25.5	64.0										
South Africa (1965)	669	6.2	35.8	58.0										
Panama (1969)	692	9.4	31.2	59.4										
Income above US $750														
Venezuela (1970)	1,004	7.9	27.1	65.0	Argentina (1970)	1,079	16.5	36.1	47.4	Poland (1964)	850	23.4	40.6	36.0
Finland (1962)	1,599	11.1	39.6	49.3	Puerto Rico (1968)	1,100	13.7	35.7	50.6	Japan (1963)	950	20.7	39.3	40.0
France (1962)	1,913	9.5	36.8	53.7	Netherlands (1967)	1,990	13.6	37.9	48.5	United Kingdom (1968)	2,015	18.8	42.2	39.0
					Norway (1968)	2,010	16.6	42.9	40.5	Hungary (1969)	1,140	24.0	42.5	33.5
					German Federal					Czechoslovakia (1964)	1,150	27.6	41.4	31.0
					Republic (1964)	2,144	15.4	31.7	52.9	Australia (1968)	2,509	20.0	41.2	38.8
					Denmark (1968)	2,563	13.6	38.8	47.6	Canada (1965)	2,920	20.0	39.8	40.2
					New Zealand (1969)	2,859	15.5	42.5	42.0	United States (1970)	4,850	19.7	41.5	38.8
					Sweden (1963)	2,949	14.0	42.0	44.0					

Source: Chenery, Ahluwalia, Bell, Duloy and Jolly (1974).

Table B2. *Inter-sectoral earnings (monthly, gross, per head) as % industrial mean*

Sector	1956	1958	1961	1962	1963	1964	1965	1966	1967	1968	1969	1970	1971	1972	1973	1974	1975
1. Electricity supply	115	107	129	131	136	144	160	151	163	166	154	154	149	138	136	136	140
2. Coal	111	113	100	99	107	100	111	92	92	100	94	95	104	99	111	119	113
3. Oil/Gas	109	116	151	143	135	149	133	157	180	185	143	144	168	145	153	154	164
4. Ferrous	106	116	123	116	116	122	121	116	99	112	108	110	111	114	113	116	110
5. Non-ferrous	114	114	108	113	111	117	118	125	123	132	114	116	109	103	110	116	120
6. Non-metals	99	101	89	101	89	93	91	89	90	93	90	91	92	92	90	90	93
7. Metals	109	108	112	113	111	105	102	100	98	111	104	102	101	100	98	99	101
8. Ships	122	120	119	123	133	124	126	129	138	157	146	144	141	140	132	125	124
9. Electronics	114	110	114	112	106	102	94	101	105	117	104	102	100	99	95	96	97
10. Chemicals	104	114	115	116	116	112	115	117	118	126	116	114	110	109	108	114	119
11. Building	84	79	85	80	84	83	86	87	96	104	96	98	102	102	96	96	95
12. Wood	88	83	96	81	79	81	79	75	77	86	83	88	88	90	89	90	93
13. Paper	109	115	107	113	113	100	99	96	97	102	101	104	98	96	99	109	109
14. Textiles	90	89	79	85	81	76	84	85	77	82	77	76	78	84	84	83	81
15. Leather	96	96	89	93	90	90	89	89	87	96	88	85	88	91	90	85	83
16. Rubber	87	109	103	101	104	100	98	99	104	104	94	92	94	78	93	93	92
17. Food	94	86	96	94	91	93	100	103	103	112	99	101	102	103	99	98	101
18. Printing	116	105	133	114	120	129	131	144	155	170	129	128	124	117	113	114	120
19. Tobacco	86	80	81	89	85	90	78	81	77	104	91	87	91	99	96	92	93
20. Films					(131)	(439)	(313)	(446)	(300)	(610)	(295)	(188)	(159)	(147)	(126)	(84)	(170)
21. Mining expl.			123		113	120	124	118	146	144	110	107	108	102	106	107	106
22. Other			100			107	108	105	114	114	100	106	109	110	99	96	102

Source: SGJ.

Table B3. *Inter-sectoral earnings: coefficient of variation (V) and ratio (R) (%)*

	Unadjusted earnings			Basic wages		
Year	*V*	*R*	*V*[a] (films)	*V*	*R*	Hourly earnings[b]
1956	12.1			11.8	152	12.0
1958	12.6			13.3	163	12.9
1961	18.3					
1962	16.0					
1963	17.0			16.7	172	14.8
1964	18.6	196	60.4	16.4	170	16.0
1965	18.0	203	41.6	18.1	183	19.0
1966	21.5	209	61.6	20.2	193	21.6
1967	26.5	234	41.2	22.4	219	
1968	24.2	226	76.2	20.3	203	22.0
1969	19.5	200	19.3	19.5	192	21.0
1970	19.3	203	24.0	19.8	197	
1971	20.0	215	21.5	18.9	200	
1972	17.0	173	17.0	15.8	174	
1973	16.4	182	16.5	16.4	182	
1974	17.1	186	17.1	17.1	184	
1975	18.5	202	21.4	17.2	196	

a Coefficient of variation, including the film sector.
b Derived from Wachtel (1973) and SGJ.
Sources: SGJ; Wachtel (1973).

Table B4. *US: coefficient of variation (V) for twenty-one sectors: average weekly earnings, 1955–71*

Year	*V*
1955	19.1
1956	19.0
1957	19.4
1958	19.9
1959	20.3
1960	20.0
1961	20.6
1962	20.6
1963	21.0
1964	20.8
1965	21.0
1966	20.6
1967	19.7
1968	19.0
1969	19.5
1970	19.2
1971	19.6

Source: US, *Employment and Earnings*, 1973.

Table B5. *Coefficient of variation (%) of earnings between industries in the West, 1950–64*

Country and number of industries	1950	1952	1953	1954	1956	1958	1959	1960	1964
88 industries									
Sweden[a]		18	17	17	17	16	17	17	
53 industries									
Canada[b]	16	18	18	18	19	20	20	21	
27 industries									
Germany[c]	14	16	16	17	17	17	16	15	
25 industries									
France[d]					19	18			
Sweden[b]		11.1							
20 industries									
Norway[d]	6	6	6	6	6	6	7		
France[b]				5					
17 industries									
Canada[d]				9			10	10	
UK[e]	7	7	7	7	8	8	8		
13 industries									
Belgium[d]				14					18
France[d]				13					12
Germany[d]				13					11
11 industries									
Norway[d]			9						12
Sweden[d]		13.6							11.8
UK[d]			10.7						6.5

a Annual earnings, all wage earners.
b Weekly earnings, all wage earners.
c Hourly earnings, all wage earners.
d Annual earnings, male earners.
e Hourly earnings, male earners.

Sources: OECD, *Wages and Labour Mobility*, 1965; UN, *Incomes in Post-War Europe*, 1967; French Quarterly Survey of Wages and Employment; Swedish Social Board Statistics; Reynolds and Taft (1956).

Table B6a. *Coefficient of variation (%) for inter-industry earnings in East Europe*

Country	1950	1955	1957	1960	1963	1964	1974
Bulgaria	17.4 (15.5)	15.9 (14.5)	12	15.2 (13.2)	15	14.9 (13.2)	
East Germany				13		13.9	
Hungary			7		7		13.6 (9.7)
Poland			15		14		
Soviet Union		20.1 (18)					
Yugoslavia			14		17	18.6	17.1

Sources: National Yearbooks: Bulgaria, GDR, Hungary, Poland, Soviet Union, Yugoslavia.

Table B6b. *Average weekly earnings as % industrial average in Eastern Europe*

	Bulgaria				Hungary	Soviet Union
	1950	1955	1960	1964	1974	1955
Energy	110	101	101	106	102	115
Mining	133	123	130	129	146	141
Ferrous	135	128	115	119	100	110
Non-ferrous	127	135	132	130	105	125
Metals	104	100	107	104	113	81
Chemicals	105	104	101	98	101	82
Building	110	106	107	105	98	87
Wood	110	104	105	104	91	83
Paper	99	92	94	93	97	81
Textiles	82	84	85	85	90	
Printing	96	94	94	90	100	71
Leather	108	95	97	94	85	
Food	84	87	88	90	96	72
Other building	87	89	91	86		
Electricity					97	
Handicraft	83	80	81	81	76	

Sources: National Yearbooks: Bulgaria, Hungary, Soviet Union.

Table B7. *Earnings dispersion between industries in Greece and Spain*

	Greece		Spain
	1970	1975	1975
$V(\%)$	16.7	17.1	34.6
$R(\%)$	187	194	320

Sources: National Yearbooks: Greece and Spain.

Table B8. *Inter-sectoral (21) coefficient of variation and range (%) for each skill group, 1966–75*

Coefficient of variation

Skill group	1966	1967	1968	1969	1970	1972	1973	1975
All groups	18.9	22.0	(20.8)	21.1	22.8	18.4	16.8	16.4
Group 1	12.6	16.8	(16.7)	14.4	11.5	7.0	9.9	10.9
2	11.4	15.0	(15.9)	12.1	13.1	10.5	12.5	10.9
3	12.7	15.5	(16.0)	14.9	15.3	10.7	11.7	11.7
4	12.7	15.6	(15.6)	13.8	18.0	16.8	13.5	9.9
5	16.0	19.1	(16.5)	17.7	18.3	13.6	12.3	13.4
6	16.7	19.9	(17.2)	17.9	19.2	16.5	13.2	12.8
7	13.6	17.2	(18.9)	13.7	17.7	13.8	15.2	12.2
8	11.9	13.5	(17.9)	11.4	12.4	11.7	8.9	10.1

Range

	Skill group								
Year	1	2	3	4	5	6	7	8	All
1967	175	179	172	173	199	200	179	167	202
1973	152	152	156	171	153	162	164	141	185

Source: SGJ.

Table B9. *Correlation coefficients between the coefficient of variation for all skill groups, and each group, over time*

	Skill group							
	1	2	3	4	5	6	7	8
r^2	0.610	0.670	0.900	0.700	0.956	0.959	0.736	0.840

Table B10. *Skill differentials in industry 1956–75: as % of earnings of the unskilled (=100%)*

Year	Skill group 1	2	3	4	5	6	7	8	Coefficient of variation
1956	264							100	35.7
1959	316							100	41.1
1961	330							100	43.3
1963	261							100	33.4
1966	272	219	163	120	187	135	113	100	36.4
1967	262	217	160	121	188	133	110	100	35.6
1969	270	211	158	120	187	130	113	100	36.2
1970	299	225	170	122	199	135	115	100	39.6
1972	276	214	160	117	187	132	112	100	37.2
1973	246	198	154	122	177	132	107	100	32.3
1975	264	207	160	123	184	136	114	100	34.1

Source: SGJ.

Table B11. *Skill differentials in European industry as % unskilled earnings (=100%)*

Country and year	Skill group 1		2		3		4	5	6	7	8
1965: Denmark	430		210				130		124		100
1964: France	554		280			155			146	122	100
1959: Italy	700		300			150			124	110	100
1963: Sweden	320		190			150			140		100
1960: UK	350		160			130			149	109	100
1960: Belgium	148	(142)		118							100
1960: Czechoslovakia	136	(130)		134							100
1960: East Germany	148			122							100
1960: Hungary	151	(151)									100
1960: Poland	205	(165)									100
1960: Rumania	168										100
1965: Germany	180		140			100			125	113	100
1965: Switzerland			170						130	120	100
1958: US	240				180				200	157	100

Source: UN, *Incomes in Post-War Europe*, 1967.

Table B12. *Inter-sectoral (21) coefficient of variation (V) and range (R) (%) for job type, 1969 and 1973*

Job type	1969		1973	
	V	*R*	*V*	*R*
Director	14.0	168	13.4	181
Technical director	13.7	165	19.1	208
Electrician	16.4	205	9.9	150
Administrative staff	21.5	217		
Boilermaker			13.2	170
Mechanic	15.8	176	17.5	199
Trainee mechanic			17.0	176
Telephone operator			15.2	253
Economic planner	15.5	167		
Builder	17.8	231		

Source: SGJ.

Table B13. *Inter-industry (21) earnings coefficient of variation (%) and range (%) by six republics and two autonomous provinces, 1962–74*

Coefficient of variation

Region	1962	1965	1967	1969	1972	1974
Yugoslavia	16.2	18.1	21.8	19.5	15.7	16.7
Bosnia (BiH)	23.3	19.5	30.4	18.0	14.8	15.0
Montenegro	16.9	21.7	22.0	22.8	18.4	19.0
Croatia	16.8	18.6	25.1	22.4	16.7	16.6
Macedonia	19.1	21.2	24.3	23.8	15.6	19.3
Slovenia	16.8	16.5	16.5	15.1	11.5	13.9
Serbia	19.6	16.2	23.8	18.7	20.7	17.6
Vojvodina		24.5	27.3	27.0	21.7	20.6
Kosovo		26.2	29.2	28.1	19.1	21.6

Range

Year	All	Bosnia	Monte.	Croatia	Maced.	Slov.	Serb.	Voj.	Kos.
1962	176	234	164	182	193	177	267		
1969	191	184	208	202	272	180	191	244	235

Source: SGJ.

Table B14. *Correlation coefficient of earnings in each republic, against all Yugoslavia's earnings: twenty-one sectors: 1962 and 1969*

	Correlation coefficient Year	
Republic	1962	1969
Bosnia (BiH)	0.954	0.845
Montenegro	0.726	0.522
Croatia	0.938	0.957
Macedonia	0.782	0.766
Slovenia	0.608	0.665
Serbia	0.888	0.844
Vojvodina		0.680
Kosovo		0.813

Table B15. *Earnings by industrial branch, 1968–74 (%)*

	1968	1969	1970	1971	1972	1974
1. *Electricity*	152	153	153	148	143	139
(1) Hydro	170	162	171	161	164	171
(2) Thermo	153	145	146	161	149	164
(3) Oil	149	151	151	143	138	127
2. *Coal*	191	94	98	101	100	114
(4) Collieries	90	93	96	100	97	113
(5) Coke/gas	118	124	144	141	157	131
3. *Oil*	169	159	151	160	160	157
(6) Production	141	160	132	151	170	155
(7) Refineries	175	158	158	163	148	214
4. *Ferrous*	102	109	111	106	110	114
(8) Mines	112	84	100	97	119	108
(9) Works	101	114	113	109	111	115
5. *Non-ferrous*	122	115	112	104	104	112
(10) Mines	112	96	98	98	96	110
(11) Factories	128	120	115	108	105	111
(12) Rolling mills	110	116	114	97	105	118
6. *Non-metals*	85	88	89	92	92	90
(13) Mines	77	80	75	74	79	84
(14) Salt	100	85	105	111	98	125
(15) Glass	87	88	91	94	96	94
(16) Lenses	86	98	104	104	96	80

(17) Ceramics	83	86	87	87	94	85
(18) Other	92	103	104	104	103	88
7. *Metals*	100	106	104	101	101	98
(19) Reproduction	91	95	97	100	100	97
(20) Structures	124	128	126	123	114	97
(21) Machinery	104	112	108	107	107	101
(22) Precision	106	115	110	104	97	95
(23) Rail vehicles	90	96	98	107	98	94
(24) Road vehicles	104	108	102	97	97	98
(25) Household	101	100	106	102	106	94
(26) Other	99	107	109	103	100	100.4
8. (27) *Ships*	143	144	141	142	142	133
9. *Electronics*	106	107	103	101	100	97
(28) Machinery	111	114	110	107	108	104
(29) Household	123	109	97	112	88	90
(30) Cables	120	120	116	120	107	98
(31) Radio	92	94	92	85	90	89
(32) Other	106	96	101	98	95	102
10. *Chemicals*	115	117	115	110	110	109
(33) Basic	108	115	116	108	107	111
(34) Fibres		109	95	97	110	115
(35) Drugs	150	145	146	129	128	104
(36) Other	111	114	111	109	108	
11. *Building*	94	95	90	103	103	94
(37) Quarries	83	87	85	90	92	90
(38) Bricks	81	82	71	93	93	85

Table B15. (*cont.*)

	1968	1969	1970	1971	1972	1974
(39) Cement	128	127	131	133	132	124
(40) Other	117	120	126	121	111	94
12. *Wood*	86	84	89	90	90	93
(41) Saw-mills	86	78	86	88	88	95
(42) Finished	85	89	91	91	92	91
(43) Chemical	91	100	91	101	96	90
13. *Paper*	93	101	104	97	98	107
(44) Reproduction	92	101	101	95	98	106
(45) Processing	95	100	112	102	99	109
14. *Textiles*	75	76	75	78	82	84
(46) Flax spinning/weaving	59	51	52	67	75	79
(47) Cotton spinning/weaving	75	75	75	77	82	88
(48) Wool spinning/weaving	74	76	78	78	82	82
(49) Silk spinning/weaving	74	82	84	91	91	93
(50) Other spinning/weaving	72	71	71	77	78	82
(51) Knitwear	75	73	74	75	79	77
(52) Under/Overwear	76	73	76	78	84	85
(53) Other	81	90	85	89	83	82
15. *Leather*	87	89	85	89	91	87
(54) Factories	90	102	93	90	95	94
(55) Footwear	85	83	80	87	89	85
(56) Moroccan	94	90	98	98	95	82

16. (57) *Rubber*	94	100	92	89	87	98
17. *Food*	103	101	105	105	103	99
(58) Grain	100	102	107	104	101	98
(59) Bakeries	128	121	114	112	110	103
(60) Canning	93	89	95	97	96	93
(61) Sugar	100	115	102	110	111	104
(62) Sweets	94	99	98	97	93	102
(63) Oil	108	117	115	121	119	101
(64) Spirits	127	114	125	121	117	105
(65) Starch	124	125	129	141	118	120
18. *Printing*	155	145	153	152	143	119
(66) Works	101	110	104	104	101	104
(67) Publishing	198	170	192	186	175	132
19. *Tobacco*	95	83	83	92	96	101
(68) Fermenting	80	68	76	88	94	95
(69) Cigarettes	108	98	89	96	99	112
20. (70) *Films*	558	294	363	297	435	125
21. (71) *Mining Exploration*	131	130	134	141	122	109
22. *Miscellaneous*	104	105	104	127	127	97
(72) Teaching	142	165	134	140	184	81
(73) Sports	89	104	94	103	103	95
(74) Musical	73	85	86	135	88	92
(75) Records	291	136	292	293	250	109
(76) Other	93	100	94	145	108	95

Source: IP.

Table B16. *Inter-industry coefficient of variation (V) and range for earnings (R), 1968–74*

	1968	1969	1970	1971	1972	1974
21 Sectors						
(no films)						
V (%)	23.7	21.8	21.8	21.6	19.6	16.9
R (%)	225	209	205	205	195	187
75 Industries						
(no films)						
V (%)	25.7	23.2	30.1	28.8	26.2	23.5
R (%)	335	332	367	277	236	217

Table B17. *Distribution of sectors by firm and size class 1970: by employment classes*

	No. in sector	No. of firms in class type 1	2	3	4	5	6	7	8	9
All industry	2,374	79	61	150	378	522	475	347	221	141
1. Electricity	84	1	1	7	9	22	15	18	9	2
2. Coal	47			3	4	9	10	8	3	10
3. Oil	5			1			1		1	2
4. Ferrous	13	1			1				1	10
5. Non-ferrous	26				1	1	1	7	11	5
6. Non-metal	85			6	17	20	20	8	9	5
7. Metals	331	3	4	2	44	80	76	48	39	35
8. Ships	20			1	3	5	4	2	2	3
9. Electronics	77		1	3	8	17	18	11	10	9
10. Chemicals	142	2	2	11	30	38	20	15	12	10
11. Building	233	5	6	29	71	61	40	16	3	2
12. Wood	254	2		7	41	63	55	51	28	7
13. Paper	40			1	3	7	7	12	6	4
14. Textiles	328		2	4	21	60	96	80	43	22
15. Leather	91		1	1	14	26	23	13	12	1
16. Rubber	15				2	2	3	2	3	3
17. Food	189	5	7	12	29	36	46	29	18	7
18. Printing	308	51	35	53	65	56	25	15	7	1
19. Tobacco	37	1		3	5	12	7	4	3	2
20. Films	16	7		4	3	1	1			
21. Mining exploration	14	1		1	3	2	2	3	1	1
22. Other	19			1	4	4	5	5		

Source: IP.

Table B18. *Annual earnings per worker for all industry by firm size class (as % industrial average) and coefficient of variation (V) (%)*

Year	Earnings as % mean, in size class										
	1	2	3	4	5	6	7	8	9	10	V
1966	73	10	69	79	71	81	91	99	112	115	37.3
1968	72	32	118	72	80	80	92	97	116		30.9
1969	145	169	159	124	93	85	93	95	107		26.6
1970	296	167	143	106	100	94	98	100	101		49.0
1971	146	191	225	166	13	92	93	97	102		50.9
1972	80	293	96	112	91	89	92	96	101	108	54.0

Coefficient of variation (V) for all industry without extreme value

	1966	1968	1969	1970	1971	1972
Adjusted V	20.6	17.6	24.2	23.4	32.0	10.2

Source: IP.

Table B19. *Summary of intra-sectoral earnings dispersion: coefficient of variation (V) (%), range (R) (%) and number of classes filled, 1966–72*

Sector	1966			1968			1969			1970			1971			1972		
	No. D[a]	*V*	*R*	No. D[a]	*V*	*R*	No. D[a]	*V*	*R*	No. D[a]	*V*	*R*	No. D[a]	*V*	*R*	No. D[a]	*V*	*R*
All	10	37.3	1,193	9	30.9	377	9	26.6	172	9	49.0	383	8	50.9	1,730	10	54.0	360
1. Electricity	7	29.0	264	6	37.6	501	5	44.6	360	9	28.3	388	6	72.7	1,110	9	30.6	220
2. Coal	6	21.5	181	5	17.7	161	5	19.2	152	7	22.5	197	6	16.5	162	8	17.5	179
3. Oil	3	29.2	179	1	—	—	1	—	—	4	32.8	195	3	20.6	143	6	18.4	173
4. Ferrous	6	31.7	208	5	14.3	135	1	—	—	4	37.8	227	3	58.2	304	5	16.7	154
5. Non-ferrous	7	39.7	225	5	25.9	179	3	27.8	167	6	22.5	173	3	9.1	119	5	16.7	154
6. Non-metal	6	16.0	167	6	16.9	165	5	13.6	132	7	5.5	118	5	114.0	131	8	43.5	273
7. Metals	9	56.1	(481)	7	30.4	280	8	5.0	115	9	92.5	614	8	28.8	289	9	33.2	280
8. Ships	6	23.9	216	6	17.4	169	5	12.6	1,391	7	55.2	365	5	65.7	377	7	30.2	316
9. Electronics	7	20.6	208	7	27.6	212	5	8.0	123	8	23.7	260	6	24.7	187	7	24.4	218
10. Chemicals	7	10.3	169	8	28.4	302	7	18.9	182	9	9.2	137	7	22.7	204	8	23.9	187
11. Building	7	26.4	186	8	38.9	504	9	46.6	600	9	18.2	194	8	36.9	447	8	37.6	386
12. Wood	7	14.7	134	7	48.0	607	6	47.6	781	8	31.8	212	6	39.8	228	7	7.4	125
13. Paper	6	21.0	174	6	19.8	184	5	12.7	136	7	19.6	186	3	11.2	125	7	25.9	217
14. Textiles	8	36.9	314	7	66.5	614	7	26.8	280	8	20.9	175	7	21.2	187	8	22.2	196
15. Leather	7	49.7	422	7	36.9	416	6	13.1	144	8	46.3	284	6	34.3	393	8	23.3	188
16. Rubber	6	26.4	202	5	19.3	175	4	21.0	171	6	14.6	140	5	62.7	364	5	9.2	127
17. Food	8	31.3	345	9	39.7	472	7	10.0	127	9	4.5	114	6	10.1	123	10	12.5	144
18. Printing	9	28.7	248	9	25.4	188	9	44.1	290	9	27.8	225	9	21.2	188	11	40.1	300
19. Tobacco	6	21.0	170	6	27.3	243	5	12.6	138	8	18.2	163	5	35.4	204	7	8.2	132
20. Films	6	38.2	240	5	—	260	7	16.7	168	5	54.0	473	8	60.9	562	6	36.7	277
21. Mining exploration	6	26.7	233	7	51.6	1,792	6	23.5	217	8	39.2	301	6	25.5	211	5	21.3	183
22. Other	5	35.8	292	4	30.9	222	4	33.7	207	5	49.4	294	5	31.3	237	5	21.9	172

a. No. D = Number of firm size classes filled in the sector.
Source: IP.

Table B20. *Hourly earnings per head in Western Europe, as % countries industrial mean 1966, and 1972, and coefficient of variation, by employment size class*

1966

Size class (no. of workers)	Germany	France	Italy	Holland	Belgium
10–49	98	96	91	14	90
50–99	97	93	93	94	93
100–199	96	94	96	96	94
200–499	97	98	99	99	99
500–999	99	105	104	104	106
>1,000	106	112	118	113	115
Coefficient of variation (%)	3.7	7.4	9.9	7.4	9.5

1972

Size class (no. of workers)	Germany	France	Italy	Holland	Belgium	UK (1973)
50–99	91	88	80	90	86	90
100–199	94	91	87	94	91	92
200–499	98	95	97	98	92	96
500–999	102	105	112	103	106	101
>1,000	115	121	123	115	121	121
Coefficient of variation (%)	9.2	13.6	17.4	9.5	13.8	12.2

Source: EEC, *Social Statistics: Labour Costs in Industry*, 1972 and 1975.

Table B21. *1968: earnings variation in and between sectors*

	Value earnings	Rank	Intra-sectoral range	Maximum earnings	Minimum earnings
1. Electricity	16,100	3	5.01	16,540(10)†	3,300(3)*
2. Coal	9.600	16	1.61	10,700(10)†	6,650(6)*
3. Oil	17,870	1	0.00	17,870(10)†	(17,870) *
4. Ferrous	10,800	9	1.35	10,950(10)†	8,100(6)
5. Non-ferrous	12,800	5	1.78	14,300(10)†	8,000(6)*
6. Non-metals	8,400	18	1.65	11,200(10)†	6,800(5)*
7. Metals	10,700	10	2.80	11,200(10)†	4,000(2)*
8. Ships	15,200	4	1.69	16,250(10)†	9,600(6)
9. Electronics	11,200	7	2.12	11,850(9)	5,600(2)*
10. Chemicals	12,200	6	2.91	13,100(10)†	4,500(2)†
11. Building	10,000	12	5.04	14,100(10)†	2,800(2)*
12. Wood	8,300	19	6.0	9,100(10)†	1,500(2)*
13. Paper	9,900	14	1.84	11,400(10)†	6,200(6)
14. Textiles	7,900	20	2.45	8,600(10)†	3,500(5)
15. Leather	9,200	17	4.2	10,400(10)†	2,500(2)*
16. Rubber	9,900	14	1.75	10,300(10)†	5,900(5)*
17. Food	10,700	10	4.72	11,800(10)†	2,500(3)
18. Printing	16,400	2	1.82	24,300(10)†	13,300(6)
19. Tobacco	10,000	12	2.43	11,200(10)†	4,600(5)*
20. {Film}	58,900		{26.00}	{689,300(10)†}	{26,500(7)}
21. {Mining exploration}	13,900		{17.90}	{23,300(5)}	{1,300(2)*}
22. Miscellaneous	11,200	7	2.1	11,400(9)†	5,400(6)*
Coefficient variation across sectors	24.6			31.7	55.6
Ratio across sectors	2.66			2.85	8.86

Note: Ratio from minimum to maximum: 16.2:1.
* Denotes that earnings were found to be in the largest non-empty category.
† Denotes that the observation was found in the smallest non-empty size group.
Source: IP.

Table B22. *Earnings by sector and firm size as % industrial mean*

1966

	Firm size									
Sector	1	2	3	4	5	6	7	8	9	10
1.	94	58			128	149	151	153	147	
2.					62	73	76	76	112	93
3.						89			158	153
4.	58				61	80		119	110	120
5.			62		46	64	89	108	139	134
6.				65	80	74	83	90	103	
7.		1	21	61	48	65	97	100	107	88
8.					65	101	116	128	128	140
9.				80	55	90	94	98	115	97
10.				80	93	99	113	115	126	135
11.	66			67	69	72	96	103	124	
12.	63			53	67	71	71	79	84	
13.	87				61	75	78	106	106	
14.	63			39	55	66	82	88	85	124
15.			36	57	44	81	85	91	152	
16.					52	63	85	103	104	98
17.	67		76	35	74	91	97	102	120	
18.	65	78	102	139	109	122	143	162	160	
19.				56	52	71	85	80	88	
20.			299		716	322	394	345	596	
21.				90	64	116	119	149	112	
22.				109	54	99	97	157		

Source: IP.

Table B22. (*cont.*)

1968

	Firm size								
Sector	1	2	3	4	5	6	7	8	9
1.		30			137	153	147	149	156
2.					63	74	79	78	101
3.									169
4.	101				76		79	101	104
5.					75	85	79	109	135
6.				64	76	77	88	82	106
7.	38			58	79	82	96	99	106
8.	108				91	117	123	126	154
9.	53			64	70	92	106	112	108
10.	43		128	79	95	97	119	111	124
11.		26	106	72	68	76	94	121	133
12.	14		15	71	68	74	75	84	86
13.	85				58	77	85	97	108
14.			203	33	54	59	75	78	81
15.	24			50	67	82	82	91	98
16.				56		89	90	82	97
17.	42	24	62	66	86	83	102	107	111
18.	220	236	173	136	125	126	144	162	229
19.				43	91	68	91	92	106
20.				25		619	622		
21.	12			220	89	120	140	127	139
22.					51	92	113	108	

Source: IP.

Table B22. (*cont.*)

1970

	Firm size								
Sector	1	2	3	4	5	6	7	8	9
1.	46	147	196	178	160	146	148	151	147
2.			120	61	87	97	78	72	101
3.			236			132		121	149
4.	188			829				106	110
5.				66	77	75	90	115	111
6.			89	94	79	88	83	90	88
7.	614	158	210	130	104	100	103	103	101
8.			342	94	112	113	127	151	142
9.		53	139	106	90	108	98	102	102
10.	88	107	111	117	119	108	118	121	106
11.	87	75	79	80	88	98	99	110	57
12.	177		118	89	88	84	88	88	84
13.			142	92	77	100	100	110	101
14.		117	67	71	71	70	77	75	72
15.		91	74	86	81	210	80	88	77
16.				93	67	88	68	85	94
17.	98	104	103	104	96	99	109	101	105
18.	271	221	170	130	134	121	158	175	199
19.	55		99	64	74	77	77	89	86
20.	793		542	281	458	168			
21.	169		293	97	207	147	130	119	126
22.			256	97	151	109	87		

Source: IP.

Table B23. *Earnings by sector and skill type, as % industrial mean*

1967

Sector	1	2	3	4	5	6	7	8
				Skill type				
1.	275	236	163	130	209	158	122	102
2.	195	176	121	86	138	105	83	68
3.	265	196	172	124	204	145	120	93
4.	190	159	117	89	134	110	92	81
5.	242	182	145	104	172	134	105	90
6.	202	164	112	82	144	102	87	73
7.	156	134	100	75	120	88	75	61
8.	229	184	128	103	168	127	100	84
9.	164	153	107	80	129	93	68	66
10.	225	163	126	91	138	109	91	79
11.	206	165	126	93	149	104	91	75
12.	182	154	109	81	105	84	70	73
13.	200	167	131	89	149	105	85	73
14.	166	147	98	79	120	79	69	65
15.	183	143	106	84	118	92	76	75
16.	199	166	121	98	157	110	88	83
17.	196	166	120	88	148	114	93	81
18.	224	198	131	111	174	123	82	78
19.	157	132	104	84	113	82	74	64
20.	242	183	143	98	156	131	92	87
21.								
22.	174	132	111	84	124	87	75	70

Maximum range between sectors = 202%.
Maximum range between skill types = 287%.
Maximum range = 450.8%.
Source: SGJ.

Table B23. (*cont.*)

1973

Sector	Skill type 1	2	3	4	5	6	7	8
1.	235	196	145	113	171	126	100	84
2.	203	165	124	89	137	108	91	80
3.	243	199	162	129	179	141	121	102
4.	181	149	112	93	130	106	94	88
5.	207	157	124	94	128	104	93	86
6.	203	156	111	91	125	98	91	83
7.	175	140	111	82	124	98	78	76
8.	184	144	116	97	130	118	113	91
9.	181	140	112	89	125	100	76	76
10.	199	145	130	111	126	109	92	85
11.	204	159	120	92	125	99	81	73
12.	160	155	111	89	117	92	78	77
13.	190	154	118	76	132	104	90	79
14.	187	158	105	91	126	86	76	73
15.	173	153	113	87	118	94	80	79
16.	182	131	107	76	121	97	82	79
17.	181	142	113	102	129	102	87	76
18.	179	162	130	105	146	117	79	76
19.	196	159	121	104	141	104	92	87
20.	199	193	140	110	140	126	114	91
21.								
22.	188	144	118	94	130	103	85	75

Maximum range between sectors = 185%.
Maximum range between skill types = 279%.
Maximum range = 332%.
Source: SGJ.

Appendix C: Yugoslav Industrial Growth

The tables in this appendix refer to the second part of Chapter 5 on Yugoslav industrial growth. The source for all this material was *Statisticki Godisnak Jugoslavie* (SGJ) for the relevant years. The aggregate and disaggregate growth information was all derived from the early sections of SGJ concerned with production, capital accumulation and employment. The series describe the manufacturing sector including mining, and all value data are in constant 1966 prices. The capital stock figures, valued at historic cost, are likely to be relatively reliable since they were collected by the Social Accounting Service as the basis for taxation before the late 1960s. The remaining material is from the employment and income sections of SGJ and Bartlett (1980).

Table C1. *Growth of key variables, 1952–73, index numbers: industry*

Year	Output (Q)	Capital (K)	Labour (L)	K/L	Q/L	K/Q	Q/K
1952	100	100	100	100	100	100	100
1953	115	106	105	101	110	92	109
1954	128	114	119	96	108	89	112
1955	148	128	135	96	110	87	115
1956	163	147	144	102	113	90	111
1957	191	165	155	106	123	86	116
1958	211	184	165	112	128	87	115
1959	243	195	179	109	135	81	123
1960	275	210	186	113	148	76	132
1961	292	234	193	121	152	80	125
1962	319	259	204	127	156	81	123
1963	373	283	221	129	168	76	132
1964	434	306	224	136	194	70	143
1965	466	333	223	150	209	71	141
1966	488	358	220	163	222	73	137
1967	491	381	223	172	221	77	130
1968	526	408	232	177	227	78	128
1969	588	448	241	186	244	76	132
1970	646	483	254	190	225	74	135
1971	716	535	267	201	268	75	133
1972	768	577	274	210	280	75	133
1973	809	625	292	214	277	77	130
Growth rate	10.4%	9.0%	5.24%	3.69%	4.97%	−1.26%	1.26%

Source: SGJ.

Table C2. *Annual growth rates of output (Q), Capital (K), Labour (L), K/L, Q/L, Q/K*

	$\dot{Q}/Q$	$\dot{L}/L$	$\dot{K}/K$	$\left(\frac{\dot{K/L}}{K/L}\right)$	$\left(\frac{\dot{Q/L}}{Q/L}\right)$	$\left(\frac{\dot{Q/K}}{Q/K}\right)$
1953/52	14.7	4.6	5.5	0.9	10.1	9.2
1954/53	11.6	13.7	8.0	−5.7	−2.1	3.6
1955/54	15.9	13.1	13.8	0.7	2.8	2.1
1956/55	9.4	6.7	13.4	6.7	2.7	−4.0
1957/56	17.4	8.3	12.2	3.9	9.1	5.2
1958/57	10.7	6.1	11.4	5.3	4.6	−0.7
1959/58	14.0	8.4	6.1	−2.3	5.6	7.9
1960/59	14.4	3.9	7.9	4.0	10.5	6.5
1961/60	6.2	3.7	11.1	7.4	2.5	−5.1
1962/61	8.9	6.1	10.9	4.8	2.8	−2.0
1963/62	16.7	8.4	9.4	1.0	8.3	7.3
1964/63	16.7	1.2	7.4	6.2	15.5	9.3
1965/64	7.4	−0.6	9.1	9.7	8.0	−1.7
1966/65	4.8	−1.05	7.8	8.9	5.9	−3.0
1967/66	0.8	0.9	6.5	5.6	0.1	−5.7
1968/67	6.8	4.1	7.3	3.2	2.7	−0.5
1969/68	11.9	4.2	9.0	4.8	7.7	2.9
1970/69	10.0	5.2	7.7	2.5	4.8	2.3
1971/70	10.8	5.1	11.1	6.0	5.7	−0.3
1972/71	7.2	2.8	7.7	4.9	2.3	−0.5
1973/72	5.3	6.3	8.4	2.1	−3.1	−3.1
Average growth rate	10.6	5.3	9.1	3.8	5.1	1.4
Coefficient of variation (%)	43.0	71.8	25.8	93.9	87.0	337.0

Source: SGJ.

Table C3. *Estimated growth rates of the variables by period*

Compounding annually (%)

	Q	K	L	K/L	Q/L	Q/K
All periods	10.4	9.0	5.24	3.69	4.97	1.26
Period 1	13.0	9.77	6.95	2.6	5.68	3.03
Period 2	7.14	8.24	2.96	5.14	4.05	−1.1
Period 2/period 1 (%)	55	84	43	198	71	—

Trend growth rates: estimated for two periods

Variable	$\hat{\alpha}$	$\hat{\beta}$	$\bar{R}^2$
$Q1$	8.75 (545.9)	0.1191 (58.99)	.9966
$Q2$	10.26 (376.7)	0.0753 (15.57)	.9679
$K1$	10.11 (659)	0.0967 (50.12)	.9952
$K2$	11.33 (1,172)	0.07999 (46.56)	.9963
$L1$	6.4 (237.5)	0.0688 (20.28)	.9716
$L2$	7.14 (385.78)	0.0364 (11.08)	.9383
$KL1$	3.71 (164.3)	0.0279 (9.81)	.8881
$KL2$	4.19 (355)	0.04355 (20.76)	.9817
$QL1$	2.352 (97.44)	0.05029 (16.54)	.9578
$QL2$	3.123 (194.26)	0.0389 (13.63)	.9585
$QK1$	−1.359 (−64.2)	0.0224 (8.39)	.8525
$QK2$	−1.069 (−55.87)	−0.0046 (−1.35)	.0945

Estimated equation: $\log \begin{pmatrix} \text{variable 1} \\ \text{or variable 2} \end{pmatrix} = \hat{\alpha} + \hat{\beta} \begin{pmatrix} \text{time 1} \\ \text{or time 2} \end{pmatrix} + \mu.$

The variables are suffixed to denote time period 1 (1952–64) or time period 2 (1964–73).

Trend growth rates: period 2/period 1 (%)

Q	K	L	K/L	Q/L	Q/K
63.2	82.7	52.9	156	77.3	—

Table C4. *Annual average growth rates by sector in the two periods (compounding annual averages)*

Sector	Index of physical production		Employment (000s)		Capital stock (m. dinar 1966 prices)		Capital–labour ratio (m. dinar/000)	
	1952–65	1965–73	1952–65	1965–73	1952–65	1965–73	1952–65	1965–73
1. Electricity	14.3	10.5	4.7	2.8	13.8	8.6	8.5	5.7
2. Coal	6.3	0.1	1.9	−3.9	7.5	4.5	5.1	8.5
3. Oil	19.2	9.9	6.9	6.5	11.5	14.0	4.7	6.8
4. Ferrous metals	9.2	6.8	3.4	2.3	10.4	7.1	6.8	4.7
5. Non-ferrous metals	13.2	8.0	6.0	2.6	10.6	6.3	4.7	3.5
6. Non-metals	13.0	7.2	9.7	1.5	7.1	7.7	−2.4	6.2
7. Metals	13.7	5.5	9.1	3.1	8.2	7.6	−0.6	4.4
8. Ships	10.6*	10.5	4.1*	2.4	4.8	7.7	0.2	5.2
9. Electronics	21.5	9.1	14.0	3.8	15.7	11.6	1.7	7.4
10. Chemicals	19.8	13.2	11.8	5.1	13.2	9.0	1.5	3.9
11. Building	8.4	7.5	5.5	0.0	5.9	8.4	0.1	8.4
12. Wood	10.4	5.1	6.6	1.3	6.8	8.3	0.3	6.9
13. Paper	17.8	8.0	9.9	3.1	16.3	6.8	6.4	3.6
14. Textiles	10.3	5.1	7.7	3.5	7.6	8.1	−0.1	4.6
15. Leather	11.5	3.5	7.8	3.8	8.0	9.3	0.2	5.2
16. Rubber	13.5	8.3	11.4	5.4	8.5	9.6	−2.1	4.0
17. Food	13.4*	6.8	7.7*	3.9	6.7	7.9	−1.4	3.8
18. Printing	10.6†	7.0	8.0†	2.9	8.2	10.1	0.9	7.0
19. Tobacco	6.3	0.6	5.4	−3.1	5.1	8.2	−0.1	11.5
Mean	12.79	6.98	7.45	2.47	9.26	8.46	1.81	5.86
Standard deviation	4.31	3.25	3.06	2.58	3.43	2.01	3.21	2.09
Coefficient of variation (%)	34	47	41	104	37	24	177	36

* 1956–65

† 1954–65.

Source: SGJ.

Table C5. *Unemployment and net migration, 1964–73*

	1964	1965	1966	1967	1968	1969	1970	1971	1972	1973
(000s)										
1. Unemployed	228	267	265	291	327	316	290	290	334	400
2. Net migration	0.10	20	26	27	57	124	240	674	—	—
3. As % active population	2.68	3.12	3.07	3.35	3.75	3.6	3.28	3.2	3.7	4.42

Source: SGJ.

Table C6. *Growth of real earnings, 1952–73*

	Real earnings	Growth of earnings
1952	100	
1953	94	−6.0
1954	105	5.0
1955	99	−6.0
1956	100	1.0
1957	122	22.0
1958	117	−4.1
1959	140	19.7
1960	148	5.7
1961	151	2.0
1962	150	−0.7
1963	169	12.7
1964	194	14.8
1965	199	2.6
1966	226	13.6
1967	238	5.3
1968	248	4.2
1969	265	6.9
1970	283	6.8
1971	301	6.4
1972	302	0.3
1973	295	−2.3

Growth rate

All periods	5.28%	coefficient of variation = 148%
1952–64	5.44%	coefficient of variation = 177%
1965–73	5.10%	coefficient of variation = 92%

Source: SGJ.

Table C7. *Real incomes in the urban and rural sectors, 1957–73*

	Urban real incomes	Rural real incomes	Relative incomes $\left\{\frac{\text{urban}}{\text{rural}}\right\}$
1957	100	100	100
1958	107.1	92.3	116.1
1959	131.8	112.6	117.1
1960	138.0	103.5	133.3
1961	127.8	101.0	126.5
1962	122.1	98.6	123.8
1963	125.3	113.2	110.7
1964	113.1	123.1	91.9
1965	137.2	82.4	166.5
1966	170.9	92.4	184.9
1967	225.3	86.6	260.0
1968	265.8	86.5	307.3
1969	280.7	96.6	290.6
1970	304.2	93.2	326.6
1971	317.6	84.9	374.4
1972	282.5	98.7	286.3
1973	257.4	98.0	262.6

Urban real incomes are average real urban incomes per worker per year. Rural real incomes are rural real incomes per worker from all sources.

Source: Bartlett (1980).

6

An explanation of Yugoslav income differentials

6.1 INTRODUCTION

In this chapter, we examine whether Yugoslav income differentials, measured at the sectoral level, can be explained by the factors hypothesised in self-management models. This takes us one stage beyond the largely empirical evidence amassed in the previous chapters, in that we attempt to associate the observed pattern of endogenous variables with the exogenous variables predicted by the theory. In the following section, we develop a model of the determinants of equilibrium cooperative earnings in the long run, while the econometric methods and data to be used are outlined in the third. The results of estimating the model on Yugoslav cross-sectional data for each year 1964–75 and in cross-section time series pools are reported in the fourth section,[1] and the final section summarises our conclusions.

The econometric modelling which follows draws heavily on the other elements of this study. The development of an estimable model, and in particular the appropriate technical assumptions and functional forms, is based on our theoretical work, and the null hypothesis is drawn from the institutional material. The findings in Chapter 4 lead us to stress monopoly power, and Yugoslav income distribution is described in great detail in Chapter 5. However, our work remains restricted by the availability of data on exogenous variables; the previous chapters offer a richer description of allocative inefficiencies in Yugoslavia after the introduction of self-management than we here attempt to explain.

The four general sources of income dispersion under self-management can be deduced intuitively, and the same factors would cause profit dispersion under imperfectly competitive capitalism. Consider a competitive two factor economy (capital and homogeneous labour) in which cooperatives choose inputs and outputs given prices and technology to maximise incomes. Every enterprise is assumed to attain a long-run equilibrium in which the value marginal product of each input equals its price. We have seen that a unique market clearing interest rate would ensure efficiency in the allocation of capital, while entry and exit of firms would lead to product price changes until a unique payment for labour had emerged. In this case of full competitive equilibrium, the only source of income differentials would be differences in productive efficiency, with residual surpluses accruing to intra-marginal firms as earnings. However, we have also noted that the Yugoslav capital market was severely imperfect, with enterprises self-financing a considerable proportion of investment and facing different interest rates on borrowed funds. Dispersion in capital costs, whether internal to the firm or from the market, would lead to differences in the desired capital stock, labour value marginal products and incomes. Moreover, enterprise entry and exit was shown to be inadequate in this period for the continuous attainment of Pareto efficiency. Thus, one would expect changes in demand to lead to the emergence of income differentials, which would be positively associated with relative product prices. Finally, in the imperfectly competitive Yugoslav environment, differences in the market structure faced by firms would map into income differentials, with earnings positively associated with the degree of monopoly power. Therefore, in this chapter we will investigate the relationship between average earnings, measured at the sectoral level, and the exogenous factors suggested by self-management theory; the shape of production technology, capital costs, relative prices and industrial concentration.

The study which follows is a self-contained test of the empirical relevance of self-management theory in Yugoslavia. Unfortunately, we cannot compare our explanation with that offered by other approaches because the various models are non-nested. In fact, several other studies of Yugoslav income differentials have been made, including Wachtel (1973), Vanek and Jovicic (1975) and Rivera-Batiz (1980). Wachtel uses a competitive market framework and estimates earnings against labour productivity as a proxy for marginal products. The latter authors examine empirically the capital school hypothesis (see Chapter 1) which stresses the predicted impact of capital–labour ratios. However, our estimating equation is the reduced form of a cooperative long-run optimisation problem in which the set of independent variables as well as the functional form are fully specified. This means that it would be incorrect to include arbitrarily the exogenous variables of less complete models. Thus, we cannot test their statistical significance in our framework. We only attempt in this chapter to show that self-management models can offer a plausible explanation of Yugoslav income differentials.

6.2 THE MODELS

In this section, long-run equilibrium earnings are specified as a function of the exogenous variables faced by cooperatives operating in competitive and imperfectly competitive markets. These estimating equations are derived as the reduced form of the enterprise optimisation problem with particular technical assumptions under each market structure. We use the same notation as in Chapter 2 (see Table 2.1).[2]

Before proceeding we must specify the appropriate functional form with which to describe production technology. It will be remembered that equilibrium output is only unique in the long run under competition if returns to scale decline from an initial value exceeding unity as production increases. This rules out the use of homogeneous production functions, such as Cobb-Douglas, since they have the property of invariant returns to scale. Since we intend to concentrate entirely on earnings, we should also take advantage of the potential separation of output from income determination outlined in Chapter 2. Homotheticity, the assumption $\lambda_L = 0$, ensures that competitive output is determined solely by the returns to scale constraint, and is independent of relative costs or demand. At the same time, incomes depend on all the parameters to the system, with product price acting as the proxy for implicit labour costs.

The variable returns to scale Cobb-Douglas function,

$$qe^{\theta q} = AL^{\alpha}K^{\beta}, \qquad (6.1)$$

displays all these desired properties and will be the basis of our empirical work. It is derived from Zellner and Revankar (1969) and is homothetic but non-homogeneous. In fact, returns to scale diminish with output with,

$$\lambda = \frac{\alpha + \beta}{1 + \theta q},$$

so that $\lambda(0) > 1$ if we assume $\alpha + \beta$ exceeds unity. The function is strictly concave in each factor and has a unit elasticity of substitution. On this basis, we can solve the enterprise optimisation problem for earnings under competition and imperfect competition.

6.2.1 *The competitive case*

The competitive firm must choose equilibrium output, capital stock and membership, given product price, capital costs and technology to maximise earnings. The long-run optimisation problem is therefore;

$$y = \frac{pq - rK}{L}, \tag{6.2}$$

$$qe^{\theta q} = AL^{\alpha}K^{\beta}, \tag{6.1}$$

$$pf_L = \frac{p\alpha q}{(1 + \theta q)L} = \frac{pq - rK}{L}, \tag{6.3}$$

$$pf_K = \frac{p\beta q}{(1 + \theta q)K} = r. \tag{6.4}$$

The equation system can be solved for equilibrium values of output and the factor inputs, which are substituted back to give the maximum value of earnings in terms of the parameters.

$$q^* = \frac{\alpha + \beta - 1}{\theta}, \tag{6.5}$$

$$K^* = pr^{-1}\left(\frac{\beta}{\alpha + \beta}\right)\theta^{-1}(\alpha + \beta - 1), \tag{6.6}$$

$$L^* = A^{-1/\alpha}p^{-\beta/\alpha}r^{\beta/\alpha}\theta^{(\beta-1)/\alpha}\left(\frac{\beta}{\alpha + \beta}\right)^{-\beta/\alpha}(\alpha + \beta - 1)^{(1-\beta)/\alpha}e^{(\alpha+\beta-1)/\alpha}, \tag{6.7}$$

$$y^* = A^{1/\alpha}p^{(\alpha+\beta)/\alpha}r^{-\beta/\alpha}\theta^{(1-\beta-\alpha)/\alpha}\left(\frac{\alpha}{\alpha + \beta}\right) \times \left[\frac{\beta}{\alpha + \beta}\right]^{\beta/\alpha}(\alpha + \beta - 1)^{(\alpha+\beta-1)/\alpha}e^{(\alpha+\beta-1)/\alpha}. \tag{6.8}$$

Thus, as we would expect, equilibrium output is chosen independently of efficiency (A) and prices at the point of minimum efficient scale where $\lambda = (\alpha + \beta)/(1 + \theta q) = 1$. The optimal capital stock depends on equilibrium output and the ratio of product price to capital costs, while employment and the capital–labour ratio also depend on efficiency. Equilibrium earnings are a function of all the independent variables. The comparative statics of the system are:

change in price:

$$\frac{\partial q^*}{\partial p} = 0, \frac{\partial L^*}{\partial p} < 0, \frac{\partial K^*}{\partial p} > 0, \frac{\partial y^*}{\partial p} > 0; \tag{6.9}$$

change in the interest rate:

$$\frac{\partial q^*}{\partial r} = 0, \frac{\partial L^*}{\partial r} > 0, \frac{\partial K^*}{\partial r} < 0, \frac{\partial y^*}{\partial r} < 0; \tag{6.10}$$

change in 'efficiency' (A):

$$\frac{\partial q^*}{\partial A} = 0, \frac{\partial L^*}{\partial A} < 0, \frac{\partial K^*}{\partial A} = 0, \frac{\partial y^*}{\partial A} > 0; \tag{6.11}$$

change in θ:

$$\frac{\partial q^*}{\partial \theta} = 0, \frac{\partial L^*}{\partial \theta} \gtrless 0, \frac{\partial K^*}{\partial \theta} < 0, \frac{\partial y^*}{\partial \theta} < 0. \tag{6.12}$$

The only new findings here concern the relationship between the endogenous variables and the two technological parameters, A and θ, both of which influence average earnings. One would expect incomes to increase with productive efficiency but it is interesting to note that in our formulation earnings are also a positive function of minimum efficient scale.[3] In the following section, equation (6.8) will be adapted to become our estimating equation for the competitive case.

6.2.2 *The imperfectly competitive case*

The cooperative now faces a known demand curve, $p = p(q, \Delta)$, with $p_q < 0$ and Δ a shift parameter, $p_\Delta > 0$. Using the superscript m, the monopolistic optimisation problem is to choose inputs, output and product price, given the parameters including the demand curve. Thus,

$$y^m = \frac{p(q, \Delta)q - rK}{L}, \tag{6.13}$$

$$p = p(q, \Delta), \tag{6.14}$$

$$qe^{\theta q} = AL^{\alpha}K^{\beta}, \tag{6.1}$$

$$(p + qp_q)\frac{\alpha q}{1 + \theta q} = pq - rK, \tag{6.15}$$

$$(p + qp_q)\frac{\beta q}{1 + \theta q} = rK. \tag{6.16}$$

One approach to solving this system could be to specify a demand relationship and to solve for earnings in terms of the full parameter set. Instead, we solve in terms of a new variable denoted M, the ratio of marginal revenue to price, which will be related to concentration ratios in the following section.

Therefore, defining

$$M = \frac{p + qp_q}{p} \tag{6.17}$$

and rearranging terms in the system (6.1), (6.13)–(6.17) yields

$$q^{m*} = \frac{M(\alpha + \beta - 1) - 1}{\theta}, \tag{6.18}$$

$$K^{m*} = pr^{-1}[M(\alpha + \beta) - 1]\theta^{-1}\frac{\beta}{\alpha + \beta}, \tag{6.19}$$

$$L^{m*} = A^{-1/\alpha}p^{-\beta/\alpha}r^{\beta/\alpha}[M(\alpha + \beta) - 1]^{(1-\beta)/\alpha} \times \theta^{(\beta-1)/\alpha}\left[\frac{\beta}{\alpha + \beta}\right]^{-\beta/\alpha} e^{[M(\alpha+\beta)-1]/\alpha}, \tag{6.20}$$

$$y^{m*} = A^{1/\alpha}p^{(\alpha+\beta)/\alpha}r^{-\beta/\alpha}[M(\alpha + \beta) + 1]^{(\alpha+\beta-1)/\alpha} \times \theta^{(1-\alpha-\beta)/\alpha}\left(\frac{\alpha}{\alpha + \beta}\right)\left[\frac{\beta}{\alpha + \beta}\right]^{\beta/\alpha} e^{[M(\alpha+\beta)-1]/\alpha}. \tag{6.21}$$

Equation (6.21) will form the basis for our econometric work in the imperfectly competitive case. As one would expect, equilibrium output is chosen to ensure that returns to scale equal the ratio of price to marginal revenue ($\lambda = 1/M$), and the remaining choices are the same as under competition except in that respect. Therefore, the comparative statics under monopoly are the same as under competition (see equations (6.10)–(6.12)) except that a parallel upward shift in the demand curve, or a decline in M, leads to:

$$\frac{\partial q^{m*}}{\partial \Delta} > 0; \frac{\partial L^{m*}}{\partial \Delta} \gtrless 0; \frac{\partial K^{m*}}{\partial \Delta} > 0; \frac{\partial y^{m*}}{\partial \Delta} > 0. \qquad (6.22)$$

6.3 METHODS OF ESTIMATION

Equations (6.8) and (6.21) specify the value of equilibrium average earnings in competition and monopoly in terms of up to five independent variables. In this section, we outline the assumptions needed to make these equations estimable, and to relate the right hand side variables to actual data. We also outline the null hypothesis of the model, which will be estimated on sectoral data.

The Cobb-Douglas factor weights are assumed to sum to more than unity so that a unique determinate equilibrium exists, and to be invariant among firms allowing the earnings equations to be estimated in log-linear form. However, both the 'efficiency' parameter, A, and the 'scale' parameter, θ, are permitted to vary among the cooperatives. This treats enterprise efficiency conventionally, but studies on capitalist firms have generally regarded θ as being invariant as well, facilitating the use of the less cumbersome Cobb-Douglas form. Its inclusion as an independent variable in our equations reflects the fact that cooperatives produce under more restrictive conditions than their capitalist counterparts. If θ were invariant, every cooperative would choose the same level of output under competition, and any differences would have to arise from dispersion in the ratio of marginal revenue to price. Thus, unlike any of the other independent variables, the scale parameter has no direct analogue with the determinants of profit under capitalism. The nature of the relationship between earnings and the shape of technology can be clarified by considering capitalist behaviour. Given input prices, the variable returns to scale production function generates a U-shaped long-run average cost curve. Residual efficiency (A) determines average costs at each level of output, or the height of the curve, and the scale parameter fixes the slope and the minimum point given the factor weights. Therefore, A and θ jointly determine both output and surplus per unit under capitalism if product price is given. Each can vary among firms when one or the other parameter is assumed to be constant. However, the determinants are separable under self-management, with the scale parameter fixing equilibrium output and residual efficiency the surplus per unit of production. While both parameters could be associated with residual surpluses in either system, the assumption of constant θ implies inter-firm differences in both profits and output under capitalism, but only earnings under self-management.

We do not require θ to be an independent variable for cooperatives to produce different quantities under imperfect competition; output will still vary according to the ratio of price to marginal revenue. Hence the simple Cobb-Douglas production function could be the appropriate form for estimation provided we satisfy $\alpha+\beta>1$. Therefore, if there is evidence that the environment is imperfectly competitive, one can go on to test the significance of the variable returns to scale formulation.

The scale parameter, θ, will be proxied by equilibrium output, so substituting equations (6.5) into (6.8) and (6.18) into (6.21) yields:

$$\ln Y_i = \frac{\alpha+\beta}{\alpha}\ln P_i + \frac{1}{\alpha}\ln A_i - \frac{\beta}{\alpha}\ln R_i + \frac{\alpha+\beta-1}{\alpha}\ln Q_i + \mathrm{CNST}_1, \qquad (6.23)^4$$

$$(\ln Y^m)_i = \frac{\alpha+\beta}{\alpha}\ln P_i + \frac{1}{\alpha}\ln A_i - \frac{\beta}{\alpha}\ln R_i + \frac{\alpha+\beta-1}{\alpha}\ln Q_i - \frac{\alpha+\beta}{\alpha}M_i + \mathrm{CNST}_2. \qquad (6.24)^5$$

Estimating equations are distinguished by the use of capital letters to denote the variables. The natural logarithm of a variable is denoted by ln and the subscript i indicates each observation. Denoting rate of change with the prefix D, one can also derive:

$$D\ln Y_i^m = \frac{\alpha+\beta}{\alpha}D\ln P_i + \frac{1}{\alpha}\;D\ln A_i - \frac{\beta}{\alpha}D\ln P_i + \frac{\alpha+\beta-1}{\alpha}D\ln Q_i + \mathrm{CNST}_1, \qquad (6.25)$$

$$(D \ln Y^m)_i = \frac{\alpha + \beta}{\alpha} D \ln P_i + \frac{1}{\alpha} D \ln A_i - \frac{\beta}{\alpha} D \ln R_i + \frac{\alpha + \beta - 1}{\alpha} D \ln Q_i + \frac{\alpha + \beta}{\alpha} DM_i + \text{CNST}_2. \quad (6.26)$$

These equations will be the basis of our econometric work, and the formulation has attractive properties for hypothesis testing. The competitive and monopolistic equations are identical with the exception of the variable M_i and the value of the constant. Thus, one can discern the effect of industrial structure on incomes by testing whether the ratio of marginal revenue to price, M_i, should be excluded from equations (6.24) or (6.26). If one accepts the statistical relevance of monopoly power, one can go on to test the assumption that returns to scale vary with output via the exclusion of the scale parameter.

The model will be estimated on Yugoslav inter-sectoral data, with the relevant sources and tables contained in Appendix D. The fact that the data are grouped leaves ordinary least squares (OLS) estimation procedures unbiased, though the disturbance will be heteroskedastic because the groups are of uneven size (see Chapter 4 on the number of firms in each sector). There will also be a loss of efficiency because the values of independent variables are not the same in each grouping, so the $\bar{R}^2$ may be higher than for the underlying sample (see Kmenta, 1971).

Three of the independent variables – prices, capital costs and the scale parameter – can be obtained directly from Yugoslav sources. However, the ratio of marginal revenue to price and residual efficiency by sector are unobservable. We will therefore relate the former variable to market concentration, and use three different series to proxy for the effects of residual efficiency. These imperfections of the data will severely limit the precision with which the findings can be interpreted, and particularly bring into question any attempt to deduce the true structural parameters from the estimators of the reduced form.

Following Hitiris (1978), let k firms in an industry of $n+k$ producers operate as a cartel, fixing the product price so that the n enterprises take it as a parameter. The rest of the cartel produces to satisfy any remaining demand. Denoting demand functions by D, supply functions by S and subscripting according to the group of firms, the demand curve of the k firms is $D_{n+k} - S_n$. The elasticity of demand for each group is denoted Σ^d and the elasticity of supply Σ^s. Then

$$-\Sigma_k^d = \frac{\partial D_k}{\partial p}\frac{p}{D_k} = \frac{\partial D_{n+k}}{\partial p}\frac{p}{D_k} - \frac{\partial S_n}{\partial p}\frac{p}{D_k}, \tag{6.27}$$

$$\Sigma_k^d = \Sigma_{n+k}^d \frac{D}{D_k} - \Sigma_n^s \frac{S_n}{D_k}$$

$$= \frac{\Sigma_{n+k}^d}{Z} - \Sigma_n^s \frac{S_n}{D_k}, \tag{6.28}$$

where the concentration ratio D_k/D is denoted by Z. Then M, the ratio of marginal revenue to price, equals $(1 - 1/\Sigma_{k}^d)$ or,

$$M = 1 - \frac{Z}{\Sigma_{n+k}^d} + \frac{Z}{(Z-1)\Sigma_n^s}. \tag{6.29}$$

Since the elasticity of supply of the n firms is assumed to be infinite,

$$M = 1 - \frac{Z}{\Sigma_{n+k}^d} \tag{6.30}$$

where $\partial M/\partial Z < 0$. We shall assume the elasticity of demand to be invariant between sectors for reasons of data availability,[6] so the imperfectly competitive estimating equation becomes:

$$(\ln Y^m)_i = \gamma_0 + \gamma_1 \ln P_i + \gamma_2 \ln A_i + \gamma_3 \ln R_i + \gamma_4 \ln Q_i + \gamma_5 \text{ MONI}, \tag{6.31}$$

where MONI denotes the concentration ratio. One can relate the γ's to the αs and βs of the previous formulation with reference to equations (6.24) and (6.30).[7]

A number of problems limit the rigour with which equation (6.31) can be applied and interpreted. Our data require the arbitrary association of k with four firms, and the only reliable information for the Self-Management era concerns the year 1966 (see Chapter 4). Therefore, the series cannot be used in rate of change equations and will become increasingly unreliable in the latter part of the period. More generally, concentration ratios have serious flaws as measures of market power (see Hannah and Kay, 1977) and the relationship between M and MONI may actually be non-linear, with discontinuities as firms collude to joint profit maximising output at points which differ between sectors. This will cause a large increase in the price-marginal revenue ratio, after which increases in concentration will not generate higher incomes. The numerous imperfections in our proxy for M_i mean that we will not regard statistically significant differences in the coefficients γ_1 and γ_5, both of which should equal $(\alpha+\beta)/\alpha$, as evidence against the model. The estimating equation may be a tightly specified reduced form, but data imperfections necessitate a more casual interpretation of certain parameters.

The second unobservable independent variable is efficiency, and three distinct approaches have been followed in our econometric work to approximate its effects on incomes: employing measures of labour productivity, adjusted labour productivity and Farrell efficiency. We commence by using labour productivity to proxy for sectoral efficiency in factor usage, but the regressions are necessarily biased because output per head is an endogenous variable in our structural equation system. Therefore, the findings are only reported in the following section for general interest, and as a basis for adjustments to eliminate the elements of simultaneity.

Labour productivity is only directly related to joint factor productivity (A) when $\alpha=1$ and $\beta=0$. However, one can derive the relationship between equilibrium labour productivity, denoted QL, and the other independent variables with reference to the full optimisation problem (equations (6.1)–(6.4) or (6.13)–(6.18)). Thus, in the imperfectly competitive case:[8]

$$(\ln QL^m)_i = \frac{\beta}{\alpha}\ln P_i + \frac{1}{\alpha}\ln A_i - \frac{\beta}{\alpha}\ln R_i - \frac{(\alpha+\beta-1)}{\alpha}\ln Q_i - \frac{\alpha+\beta}{\alpha}M_i + \left[\frac{\beta}{\alpha}\ln\frac{\beta}{\alpha+\beta} - \frac{1}{\alpha}\right]. \tag{6.32}$$

This can be estimated jointly with an earnings equation which employs labour productivity as a proxy for A using a repeated least squares procedure. One cannot employ two stage least squares on a reduced form of the two equations because residual efficiency variable is unobservable but labour productivity in the earnings equation is adjusted through the procedure to represent residual efficiency plus a random error.

The method is to estimate the labour productivity equation without the independent variable, A, and partition it as a dependent variable in the earnings equation into predicted labour productivity, residual efficiency and an error term. This is a version of Jorgensen and Brundy's (1971) repeated least squares procedure. For example, in the competitive case the equation system is:

$$\ln QL_i = \hat{\beta}_0 + \hat{\beta}_1 \ln P_i + \hat{\beta}_2 \ln R_i + \hat{\beta}_3 \ln Q_i + \mu_2, \tag{6.33}$$
$$\ln Y_i = \hat{\beta}_4 + \hat{\beta}_5 \ln P_i + \hat{\beta}_6 \ln QL_i + \hat{\beta}_7 \ln R_i + \hat{\beta}_8 \ln Q_i + \mu_1.$$

The first equation generates predicted values of labour productivity ($\ln \hat{QL}$) and the residual of the equation equals efficiency (A) and a random error (μ), if there is no collinearity among the independent variables. Thus, the earnings equation can be estimated with labour productivity partitioned as

$$\ln QL_i = \ln \hat{QL}_i + \ln A_i + \mu_2, \tag{6.34}$$

so one actually observes

$$\ln Y_i = \hat{\beta}_4 + \hat{\beta}_5 \ln P_i + \hat{\beta}_6 (\ln \hat{QL}_i + \ln A_i) + \hat{\beta}_7 \ln R_i + \hat{\beta}_8 \ln Q_i + \mu_3, \tag{6.35}$$

or

$$\ln Y_i = \hat{\beta}_9 + \hat{\beta}_{10} \ln P_i + \hat{\beta}_{11} \ln QL_i + \hat{\beta}_{12} \ln R_i + \hat{\beta}_{13} \ln Q_i + \mu_3, \tag{6.36}$$

where
$$\hat{\beta}_9 = \hat{\beta}_4 + \hat{\beta}_0\hat{\beta}_6, \quad \hat{\beta}_{10} = \hat{\beta}_5 + \hat{\beta}_6\hat{\beta}_1,$$
$$\hat{\beta}_{11} = \hat{\beta}_6, \quad \hat{\beta}_{12} = \hat{\beta}_7 + \hat{\beta}_6\hat{\beta}_2,$$
$$\hat{\beta}_{13} = \hat{\beta}_8 + \hat{\beta}_6\hat{\beta}_8 \tag{6.37}$$

Of course, the same procedure can be used in the imperfectly competitive case, when the concentration ratio must be added to both equations. The process eliminates the simultaneous equation bias in using labour productivity as an independent variable in the earnings equation, provided residual efficiency is uncorrelated with the remaining variables. However, the labour productivity equation is always biased because a variable has been omitted, so the $\bar{R}^2$ and t-statistics will be biased downwards.

Our final approach will be to measure factor efficiency in an independent way, using the method developed by Farrell (1957). Therefore, we construct sectoral isoquants and measure the technical efficiency of production relative to a calculated 'efficient' sector. The idea is that this will measure the volume of output produced for the bundle of inputs with an appropriate adjustment for the differences in the technique of production. However, though the measure is unlikely to be associated with the other independent variables, it does suffer from problems which could distort the estimation. In the first place, constant returns were assumed to calculate the Farrell measure of efficiency. Chapter 2 suggests that this would be appropriate under competition, but that monopolistic firms might produce with increasing returns, which means our series would be inaccurate. The measure is also normalised to the most efficient sectors rather than the origin, and, being relative, it may be less closely associated with income levels. Moreover, it is calculated in values for both output and capital so, though these are evaluated in constant 1966 prices, it may be associated with demand. Finally, the measure is constructed at the sectoral level. Though a conventional grouping of data for such measures as labour productivity, to calculate Farrell efficiency on sectoral data implies the strong assumption that either production functions differ between sectors or relative prices are constant within each sector. For all these reasons, one must interpret any findings based on the Farrell measure of efficiency cautiously and with reference to the results from our other proxies for residual efficiency. These numerous problems with the data series and proxies employed, as well as the fact that the model is estimated at the sectoral rather than enterprise level, suggest a very liberal interpretation of the estimated parameters if treated as implicit functions of the Cobb-Douglas weights.

Finally, a model of decentralised planning would provide the most appropriate alternative hypothesis to that embedded in our self-management equations. Suppose that the 1965 Reforms did not actually introduce operational market self-management. Chapter 3 indicates as the most likely alternative the possibility that the reforms had no effect at all on resource allocation. Hence, choices would have continued to follow the pattern of the Visible Hand era. Evidence for such an outcome would include the considerable degree of government interference and regulation throughout the period (see Horvat, 1971a; Sirc, 1979) as well as the continued authority of the Communist Party, at the regional if not the federal level. In these circumstances, wages would be determined by the authorities to satisfy political and distributional criteria, and one would not expect any systematic association with the independent variables of our equations. Planners would set product and factor prices for accumulative purposes, and scale and concentration according to perceived development needs. Efficiency would be largely determined at the enterprise level, and would not be associated with the sectoral wage structure. Therefore, our alternative hypothesis is that allocation continued to be based on Visible Hand mechanisms after 1965, in which case our equation and all the independent variables would be statistically insignificant. The procedure will be to test the alternative hypothesis, before proceeding to the secondary hypotheses concerning the industrial structure and the shape of technology.

6.4 ESTIMATING THE MODELS

In the three parts of this section, we report on the findings from estimating the model using each of the proxies for residual efficiency: labour productivity, adjusted labour productivity and Farrell efficiency measures. In each case we test for the significance of concentration and then the scale parameter. The data cover nineteen sectors for each year 1964–72. We commence with cross-section regressions to see how the fit of the model changed as the effectiveness of Yugoslav self-management altered. One would expect the fit to improve after 1965, but to decline towards the end of the estimation period. The estimated parameters prove to be relatively stable over time which justifies pooling the data set across years to increase the degrees of freedom for hypothesis testing. Lags are included since the model otherwise assumes that the firms have attained long-run equilibrium by the end of each year. Data sources and results are contained in Appendix D.

6.4.1 *Labour productivity as proxy for residual efficiency*

We have seen that earnings equations which include labour productivity on the right hand will suffer from simultaneous equation bias, and should not be used as a formal test of our model. However, the annual cross-section regressions reported in Table D1 do represent an interesting ad hoc study of the determinants of Yugoslav income differentials, along the lines of Wachtel (1973).

Generally, the equations provided very good fits, which followed the expected historical pattern. The best explanation was for 1967, when the five independent variables explained over 90% of income dispersion. The coefficient on labour productivity was significant at the 99% level in every year, and every significant variable displayed the right sign and stable values over time. The size and significance of the estimator on concentration peaked in the year to which the series referred. The equations suggest that the main determinants of incomes in Yugoslavia were labour productivity, concentration and output price; neither the rate of interest nor the scale parameter were even weakly significant in any year. Therefore, Table D1 provides fairly strong support for a descriptive hypothesis linking Yugoslav incomes to efficiency, market concentration and demand patterns. The remainder of this chapter examines whether we can draw more robust conclusions from better specifications of the model.

6.4.2 *Adjusted labour productivity as proxy for residual efficiency*

The estimation procedure described in equations (6.32)–(6.37) adjusts labour productivity in the earnings equations to eliminate simultaneous equation bias. However, the labour productivity equations themselves are biased because residual efficiency has been omitted as an independent variable. The results of the nine annual cross-section regressions for the labour productivity and earnings equations in their most general form, and excluding concentration and then scale, are reported in Tables D2–D7. Table D2 shows the estimates of the imperfectly competitive labour productivity equations, from which are deduced residuals *QE*1 for the earnings equations reported in Table D3. Similarly, Table D4 shows the estimates of the competitive labour productivity equation, which generate a residual *E*1 for the earnings equations of Table D5. Finally, the scale parameter was omitted from the imperfectly competitive equation to estimate the labour productivity equations reported in Table D6 and the residual *QE* for the earnings equations of Table D7.

Not surprisingly, the three formulations of the labour productivity equations reported in Tables D2, D4 and D6 for the most part provided poor fits. In fact, none of the equations provided significant explanations of the dependent variables until 1969, although the fits become relatively good after that date. Thus, the time pattern of the explanation approximately conformed with historical expectations, although the effects of self-management were not discerned until later than expected. Moreover, the estimated coefficients proved to be relatively stable across years. There is also support for the imperfectly competitive equation form in the later years, despite the limited available degrees of freedom. Table D2 shows that every independent variable except concentration was significant in some year, and the signs all conformed with expectations apart from the coefficient on relative prices, which was negative. A comparison of Tables D2 and D4 indicates the effects of excluding industrial concentration; the $\bar{R}^2$s are lower in every year and one cannot accept the competitive form on the basis of F-tests. Similarly, a comparison of Tables D2 and D6 indicates that one cannot generally accept the exclusion of the scale parameter from the imperfectly competitive labour productivity equations.

Our main interest is with the earnings equations reported in Tables D3, D5 and D7. The findings from the most general functional form, including concentration and scale, are reported in Table D3. The fit of the equation improved considerably at the time of the 1965 Reforms, reached a peak in 1967 and worsened to some extent in the early 1970s. This pattern over time satisfies expectations and conforms with the deductions from the empirical evidence of the previous chapter. The estimated coefficients were generally stable across years, which supports the pooling of the data set for more stringent hypothesis testing. But even on the small cross-section data set, the explanation offered by the model in any year was extremely good. The $\bar{R}^2$ reached almost 0.92 in 1967 and exceeded 0.7 in every year of the self-management era. In 1969 and 1970, every independent variable was significant at the 99% level, and all displayed the predicted signs except for output price. In the central period 1965–71, there were four years in which at least four of the independent variables were significant, and in all but one year at least three coefficients were significant. Adjusted labour productivity and industrial concentration were both, in general, significant in every year with relatively stable coefficients over time. Four of the five significant estimates of the interest rate coefficient displayed the predicted negative sign while the coefficient on the scale parameter, which was significant in four years, was always estimated to be positive. However, although the price coefficient was also significant in four of the nine years, it was always estimated to have a negative sign.

One can again make preliminary tests on the functional form by comparing the regressions in Table D3 with those in Tables D5 and D7. As one would expect given the general significance of the concentration ratio, a comparison of the equations in Tables D3 and D5 confirms the relevance of market structure in Yugoslavia for most years. Excluding the concentration ratio reduces the $\bar{R}^2$ in every year prior to 1969, and F-tests reject the alternative hypothesis of competition. It is interesting to note how the historical pattern of the explanation in Table D5 is skewed towards the later end of the estimation period when the concentration variable, which refers primarily to the earlier years, is excluded. A comparison of the regressions in Tables D3 and D7 shows that the data do not, in general, support the homogeneous formulation for production technology, especially in the years when the scale parameter was statistically significant. Thus, the annual cross-section earnings equations provide support for the self-management model and indicate the relevance of both monopoly power and variable returns to scale technology in explaining Yugoslav incomes.

These findings are not, however, consistent with a strict interpretation of the model, which leads us to investigate further the possible impact of institutional factors on our equations. For example, although the Cobb-Douglas weight, α, was estimated from the coefficient on labour productivity to be around 2.6, the capital weight, β, was estimated to be negative. The three different ways of deducing β, from the coefficients on product prices, the interest rate and scale, gave similar values in most cases, each being around -1.2. This indicates that the restriction $\alpha + \beta > 1$ was generally satisfied, but a strict interpretation of the model also implies that the marginal product of capital was negative. This could be a perfectly reasonable conclusion given the large investments into the industrial sector over the period (see Chapter 5) and measurement problems. Alternatively, one could again note that limitations in the estimation procedure and proxies employed mean that the structural parameters deduced from our reduced form must be interpreted very liberally. But even given these points, we will demonstrate that government regulation of the market mechanism could have been an explicit source of downward bias in the value of certain estimators.

Yugoslav markets remained highly regulated after 1965 despite the devolution of decision-making authority to the enterprise level. This meant that the series used in our equations inadequately reflected the true relative scarcities of the model, leading to downward bias on the estimated coefficients. For example, some 70% of product prices were controlled to ensure that they would vary less than otherwise in a free market. Similarly, the nominal interest rates could have reflected planners' and bankers' preferences as well as marginal capital costs by sector. Finally, the Yugoslav industrial sector had inherited some large inefficient plants from the planning era (see Horvat, 1971a; Milenkovitch, 1971), in which incomes were low and maintained by subsidy. This means that our proxy for scale may not only reflect dispersion in production technology characteristics. In certain cases, the binary association between incomes and scale could therefore be negative, biasing the estimated coefficient downwards, though this effect might decline over time as inefficient plants became a decreasing proportion of the total. Thus, the peculiarities of the Yugoslav market environment offer a further reason why the structure of the model cannot be inferred reliably from the earnings equation coefficients.[9]

Table D8 is included to indicate the possible effects of institutional factors on our data set. It shows the partial correlation coefficient matrix for the six variables in 1967.[10] The observed pattern offers some support for our arguments, though of course one cannot deduce strong conclusions about multiple regressions from binary associations. There is a close relationship between incomes and efficiency, and incomes and concentration, which probably underlies the findings of our regressions. However, there is a negative association between income and both the price series, with the predictable cross effects on the other variables. This is consistent with the idea that efficient concentrated sectors which paid high incomes actually faced lower prices and higher nominal interest rates. The associations with concentration were sufficiently close to indicate a possible interest rate policy against monopolistic sectors. In such a scenario, the authorities would levy relatively higher capital charges on the rather small proportions of funds that these more successful sectors required to borrow for their capital accumulation. Thus, there may have been an implicit capital tax system operating in Yugoslavia after 1965; offering cheaper nominal funds to low-paying sectors and charging high prices for capital to the more solvent ones. One could construct a similar story from the correlation matrix about price controls, which also appear to have operated in the direction of income redistribution. As expected, there was a slight negative association between incomes and scale, which was reversed in the later years of the period. Finally, it is interesting to note that concentration and scale were inversely related, as our model predicts when comparing output in competitive and monopolistic markets.

The impact of institutional factors might be less in rate of change regressions if the authorities chose to adjust prices, and enterprises their scale of operations, in the predicted manner over time. Against that, there is the limitation that the concentration variable must be omitted from rate of change equations, which will necessarily worsen the fit, and that difference equations generally provide inferior explanations. Tables D9 and D10 report the findings for rate of change of labour productivity and earnings equations respectively in each year, 1964/5 to 1971/2. The labour productivity equation fit was relatively good in most years. The $\bar{R}^2$ ranged between 0.3 in 1969/70 to 0.9 in 1967/68, and it was generally higher than for the static equations (Tables D2, D4 and D6). Both the scale parameter and interest rate coefficients were significant in most years, with the expected signs, but the coefficient on relative prices was always negative, though rarely significant.

The eight annual rate of change of earnings equations are reported in Table D10. The fit varied enormously from year to year, and none of the independent variables were significant in three years, when the $\bar{R}^2$ was negligible. However, the equation offered a reasonable explanation of the annual sectoral income change in the remaining years, and particularly in 1964/5, 1966/7 and 1969/70. In fact, the $\bar{R}^2$ reached a peak of 0.82 in 1966/7, when every coefficient except the interest rate was significant with the predicted sign. The coefficient on prices was always positive, and significant in four years, while that on the interest rate showed a negative coefficient in the two years when it was significant. The scale parameter provided much of the explanation in the years of good fit, with significant positive coefficients of higher absolute value than observed in the static runs. Finally, changes in adjusted labour productivity were of less importance in the rate of change case, being only significant twice, but on each occasion the estimated coefficient was very similar to that in the static runs.

Thus, the self-management model was able to explain the rate of change of incomes by sector in a majority of years. This was despite the smallness of the data set employed in each year, which left only fourteen degrees of freedom, and the fact that one parameter, industrial concentration, had to be omitted although it may well have been significant. The consistency in the estimation of the adjusted labour productivity coefficient, and therefore the Cobb-Douglas weight α, in the static and dynamic forms of the equation was also encouraging. Finally, the relatively higher estimated coefficients on prices, capital costs and scale suggest that, although severely regulated, the Yugoslav economy was being permitted to adjust over time according to the pressure from market forces.

One might expect that firms would adjust to new long-run equilibria gradually, so the equations should include lags on the independent variables. In fact, the inclusion of lag structures generally proved to be unsatisfactory, presumably because of the small size of the data set and the short time span of the estimation period. In the rate of change case, one could not accept the inclusion of a lagging procedure in any year.[11] The consequences of placing a one year lag on each of the endogenous variables in the full static earnings equation (Table D3) are reported in Table D11. The lagged version of the equation generally fitted slightly worse than the unlagged one, except in 1971 when the dependent variable could be related to a better fitting configuration of independent variables. The estimated coefficients, their patterns of significance and the time path of the explanation were hardly altered by the inclusion of lags.

The estimated coefficients in the annual cross-section regressions were generally stable over time, which supports the pooling of the data set across years to increase degrees of freedom for hypothesis testing. Indeed, one cannot accept the hypothesis that the significant estimated coefficients were significantly different between years, and among various sub-divisions of the data span.[12] The three versions of the earnings equation on the full data set are reported in Table D12.[13] As can be seen, the imperfectly competitive earnings equation was estimated to be:

$$\begin{aligned} \ln Y_i = & \underset{(5.64)}{-0.166} - \underset{(3.32)}{0.089} \ln P_i + \underset{(17.00)}{0.361}\, QE_i + \underset{(1.19)}{0.025} \ln R_i \\ & + \underset{(1.45)}{0.017} \ln Q_i + \underset{(5.86)}{0.003}\, \text{MONI}, \\ & \bar{R}^2 = 0.704. \end{aligned} \tag{6.38}$$

Therefore, we cannot accept the null hypothesis that incomes were set via a decentralised planning mechanism. The self-management model actually explained some 70% of the sectoral dispersion in earnings over the period, a rather better explanation than offered by other models (see Vanek and Jovicic, 1975; Rivera-Batiz, 1980). The most important determinants of income differentials were residual efficiency and industrial concentration, and relative prices also had a significant though perverse effect. In fact, as discussed above the signs on the relative price and interest rate coefficients reflected the impact of government regulation of the market mechanism, and may even be evidence of a deliberate redistributive policy to counter the effects of self-management on incomes.

Our secondary hypotheses can be tested with reference to the other regressions reported in Table D12. A comparison of the competitive and imperfectly competitive equation forms shows that, on the basis of F- and t-tests, we cannot accept the exclusion of the concentration variable. Thus, even when all the other potential determinants suggested by economic theory have been taken into account, one still finds a significant association between market power and personal incomes in Yugoslavia.[14] Given the severely imperfect industrial structure described in Chapter 4, this is strong evidence that the self-management effects as described in Chapter 2 were operational in Yugoslavia after the 1965 Reforms. It is also interesting to note that, though the coefficient on the scale parameter was not statistically significant, one cannot accept its exclusion from the imperfectly competitive equation. This indicates the relevance of a variable returns to scale production function for the Yugoslav industrial sector, which may prove important in future empirical research.

6.4.3 *The Farrell measure as proxy for residual efficiency*

We finally report the results from a set of similar earnings equations in which the Farrell efficiency measure is used to proxy residual efficiency. The findings are included to strengthen our case for the effects of self-management via the diversification of evidence, and particularly for those who might query the repeated least squares procedure. In fact, the regressions provide a similar explanation of Yugoslav income dispersion, though the fit is generally worse than for adjusted labour productivity. This can be attributed to the drawbacks of the efficiency measure itself as well as some newly introduced collinearity problems.

To avoid unnecessary repetition, we proceed directly to test our hypotheses on the full cross-section time series data set.[15] Table D13 reports the results of regressing the three formulations of the earnings equation. The most general form of the equation was estimated to be:

$$\begin{aligned} \ln Y_i = & -\underset{(2.22)}{0.106} - \underset{(1.41)}{0.060} \ln P_i + \underset{(4.57)}{0.253} \ln A_i + \underset{(1.12)}{0.037} \ln R_i \\ & + \underset{(0.36)}{0.007} \ln Q_i + \underset{(2.30)}{0.002}\,\mathrm{MONI}, \\ & \bar{R}^2 = 0.277. \end{aligned} \tag{6.39}$$

Once again, on the basis of an F-test we cannot accept the null hypothesis that the incomes are unrelated to the independent variables. The fit was rather worse than for adjusted labour productivity (see equation (6.38)), but the explanation is essentially the same; earnings were primarily determined by residual efficiency and industrial concentration in both equations. The only additional significant variable in equation (6.38) was relative prices, but that had a perverse sign. Indeed, the estimated coefficients were similar in the two equations, though one cannot accept that the coefficient on residual efficiency was the same for both proxies. It can be seen from Table D13 that the data do not support the exclusion of the concentration ratio, which again confirms the relevance of market imperfections. However, the Farrell efficiency regressions did not support the variable returns to scale formulation of production technology, and tests accepted the exclusion of the scale parameter.

Thus, this data series offered similar conclusions about the effects of self-management upon incomes, though the findings were relatively weaker and less precise than when labour productivity was used. This was to be expected given the measurement problems discussed above, but can also probably be attributed to collinearity. The adjustments to labour productivity through the repeated least squares procedure eliminated associations with the other independent variables but, as Table D14 shows, the Farrell measure was collinear with the rest of the parameter set except scale. It is therefore possible that the negative association between efficiency and prices, and efficiency and the interest rate, acted to reduce the significance of the two price variables. Finally, Table D14 suggests that the Yugoslav industrial sector did not suffer from organisational slack, in that the Farrell measure of efficiency was positively correlated with industrial concentration.

6.5 SUMMARY

This chapter contains various pieces of evidence for the relevance of self-management models in explaining Yugoslav income differentials after the 1965 Reforms. Our estimating equations, derived as the reduced form of the cooperative optimisation problem under perfect and imperfect competition, provide good explanations of Yugoslav inter-sectoral income differences in most years and over the entire period, as well as over time. Despite the shortcomings of the data series and the estimation procedures, which led to the diverse ways of estimating the model, the broad consistency of the findings builds a convincing case for the operation of self-management forces.

We commenced by establishing that heuristic equations linking earnings with labour productivity, demand and industrial concentration provided good fits on annual cross-section data, offering better explanations of income differentials than most comparable equations in the literature (e.g. Wachtel, 1973; Vanek and Jovicic, 1975; Staellerts, 1981). We then proceeded to more formal tests of the model as a whole, and with respect to particular issues of specification. We could not accept the alternative hypothesis of decentralised planning after 1965 using either adjusted labour productivity or Farrell efficiency measures as proxies for residual efficiency. Moreover, the equations confirmed the predicted effects of monopoly power on incomes, and the more convincing labour productivity runs also indicated the relevance of variable returns to scale technology. These secondary hypotheses were, in general, confirmed by the annual cross-section regressions. The best equations actually explained around 70% of inter-sectoral income dispersion during the self-management era, and even more in certain years. The pattern of explanation over time conformed with expectations and the model also offered a reasonable explanation for the rate of change of incomes despite serious data restrictions. However, lag structures never proved to be significant in any of the specifications.

The most convincing aspect of our findings is their broad consistency across regressions with respect to the alternative hypothesis and the independent effects of monopoly power. We could not accept the alternative hypothesis on annual cross-section time series or rate of change data sets using any of the proxies for residual efficiency. The same holds for the competitive equation form. But the complexities of the Yugoslav environment still created considerable problems for any strict interpretation of our findings. The values of certain coefficients were estimated to be very small, which would suggest that the Yugoslav marginal product of capital could have been negative. We are not directly concerned with this issue, but it was worth noting that institutional factors could have been the source of downward bias in the estimation of these parameters. In fact, the observed pattern of collinearity generally supported the view that government interference was hindering some of the free market mechanisms described by the theory. Indeed, the authorities may have been deliberately intervening to counter some of the more serious self-management effects via interest rate and price controls. There is strong evidence in favour of the self-management model, but the Yugoslav system was too complex to justify any belief in structural parameters deduced from the coefficients of our marginalist reduced form equations.

Appendix D: Earnings dispersion equations

In this appendix, we report on the various estimates of the models explaining equilibrium earnings. The data series employed in the regressions were:

i. Earnings (Y): this was gross average monthly incomes per person employed by sector, derived from Table B2.

ii. Relative prices (P): the price variable was constructed by dividing the value of output in nominal terms by that in real terms, with the series based back to 1956. The data were derived from the sections on output and the industrial sector in SGJ.

iii. The rate of interest (R): this describes the cost of capital as a percentage of borrowed financial capital (excluding working capital) at historic cost. It therefore reflects the average cost of fixed capital in each sector, taking account both of differences in the scale of internal financing and of varying interest rate changes. The material was derived from the industrial section of SGJ.

iv. Scale (Q): this is the median firm size by sector, deduced from the firm size groups by net product in IP (see Appendix B).

v. Residual efficiency (A): labour productivity is value added per person in constant 1966 prices per sector, as in Appendix C. The Farrell measure was derived from the construction of points on isoquants for each sector in every year. One then compared each observation to the deduced 'efficient' locus.

vi. Industrial concentration (MONI): these are the four firm concentration ratios for 1966, contained in Table A4.

Table D1. $\ln Y$ on $\ln P$, $\ln A$, $\ln R$, $\ln Q$, MONI*

Year	CNST	$\ln P$	$\ln A$	$\ln R$	$\ln Q$	MONI	$\bar{R}^2$	F
1964	4.193	0.150	0.280	−0.022	0.00028	0.0024	.6633	8.09
	(5.45)	(1.04)	(4.89)	(0.46)	(0.10)	(1.84)		
1965	4.265	0.162	0.347	0.022	−0.013	0.0023	.7526	11.95
	(6.69)	(1.38)	(6.04)	(0.52)	(0.39)	(1.98)		
1966	4.749	0.125	0.352	−0.056	−0.0028	0.0029	.8650	24.07
	(13.82)	(2.25)	(8.41)	(0.86)	(0.10)	(2.58)		
1967	4.666	0.129	0.435	−0.0023	−0.022	0.0016	.9169	40.72
	(14.99)	(2.58)	(12.15)	(0.05)	(0.84)	(1.60)		
1968	5.004	0.0927	0.382	0.0287	−0.016	0.00098	.9022	34.22
	(15.30)	(1.85)	(10.58)	(0.49)	(0.66)	(0.95)		
1969	5.273	0.096	0.354	0.0137	−0.021	0.0008	.8174	17.11
	(9.59)	(1.32)	(6.59)	(0.14)	(0.69)	(0.64)		
1970	5.334	0.113	0.370	0.0263	−0.031	0.0005	.8436	20.42
	(11.92)	(1.89)	(7.34)	(0.37)	(1.08)	(0.41)		
1971	4.999	0.168	0.391	0.076	−0.027	0.0004	.7186	10.20
	(7.25)	(1.91)	(5.62)	(0.84)	(0.79)	(0.24)		
1972	5.755	0.097	0.322	0.0845	−0.026	−0.0005	.7552	12.10
	(10.44)	(1.39)	(6.48)	(1.38)	(0.96)	(0.41)		

* Note that, as defined in the text, CNST is the constant term, $\ln Y$ the log of average earnings, $\ln P$ the log of prices, $\ln A$ the log of residual efficiency, $\ln Q$ the log of the scale parameter and MONI the four firm concentration ratio.

There were nineteen observations in every year. The acceptance region for the t-statistic (shown in brackets below the coefficient) at the 5% level of significance is in excess of 2.093. The acceptance region for the F-statistic at the 5% level of

Table D2. $\ln A$ on $\ln P$, $\ln R$, $\ln Q$, MONI $\Rightarrow QE1$

Year	CNST	$\ln P$	$\ln R$	$\ln Q$	MONI	$\bar{R}^2$	F
1964	3.676	−0.150	0.126	−0.035	0.0056	−.0134	0.94
	(1.07)	(0.22)	(0.56)	(0.26)	(0.97)		
1965	5.045	−0.504	−0.017	0.502	0.0054	.0331	1.15
	(1.91)	(0.95)	(0.08)	(0.33)	(1.06)		
1966	4.401	−0.458	−0.203	0.143	0.0087	.1081	1.55
	(2.37)	(1.37)	(0.49)	(0.83)	(1.28)		
1967	4.364	−0.428	−0.0097	0.101	0.0061	.0646	1.31
	(2.18)	(1.21)	(0.03)	(0.52)	(0.86)		
1968	4.914	−0.525	−0.309	0.171	0.00897	.1874	2.04
	(2.41)	(1.53)	(0.73)	(1.02)	(1.23)		
1969	6.927	−0.717	−0.833	0.221	0.00867	.4358	4.48
	(3.45)	(2.35)	(1.92)	(1.60)	(1.49)		
1970	6.086	−0.668	−0.697	0.277	0.00808	.4962	5.43
	(3.51)	(2.56)	(2.14)	(2.08)	(1.41)		
1971	6.861	−0.712	−0.618	0.193	0.00674	.5072	5.63
	(3.59)	(2.56)	(2.03)	(1.59)	(1.16)		
1972	7.103	−0.753	−0.377	0.159	0.00492	.3853	3.82
	(3.11)	(2.39)	(1.20)	(1.17)	(0.77)		

There were nineteen observations in every year. The acceptance region for the *t*-statistic at the 5% level of significance is in excess of 1.729. The acceptance region for the *F*-statistic level of significance is in excess of 3.18.

Table D3. $\ln Y$ on $\ln P$, $QE1$, $\ln R$, $\ln Q$, MONI

Year	CNST	$\ln P$	$QE1$	$\ln R$	$\ln Q$	MONI	$\bar{R}^2$	F
1964	5.223	0.108	0.280	0.0132	0.0039	0.0039	.6633	9.09
	(7.06)	(0.75)	(4.89)	(0.27)	(0.33)	(3.16)		
1965	6.014	−0.0128	0.347	0.0163	0.0046	0.0042	.7526	11.95
	(10.60)	(0.11)	(0.39)	(6.04)	(0.14)	(3.76)		
1966	6.297	−0.0363	0.352	−0.128	0.0477	0.00597	.8650	24.07
	(21.69)	(0.70)	(8.41)	(1.97)	(1.77)	(5.60)		
1967	6.566	−0.575	0.435	−0.0066	0.0221	0.0042	.9169	40.72
	(24.41)	(1.21)	(12.15)	(0.13)	(0.86)	(4.43)		
1968	6.880	−0.108	0.382	−0.089	0.0497	0.00441	.9022	34.22
	(25.02)	(2.32)	(10.58)	(1.56)	(2.20)	(4.49)		
1969	7.728	−0.158	0.354	−0.281	0.0575	0.00388	.8174	17.11
	(19.12)	(2.57)	(6.59)	(3.23)	(2.07)	(3.31)		
1970	7.583	−0.134	0.270	−0.231	0.0714	0.0035	.8436	20.42
	(23.23)	(2.74)	(7.34)	(3.77)	(2.85)	(3.22)		
1971	7.683	−0.111	0.391	−0.166	0.0483	0.00301	.7186	10.20
	(15.43)	(1.53)	(5.62)	(2.10)	(1.52)	(1.98)		
1972	8.04	−0.145	0.322	−0.0367	0.0257	0.0011	.7552	12.10
	(18.95)	(2.48)	(6.48)	(0.63)	(1.01)	(0.91)		

There were nineteen observations in every year. The acceptance region for the t-statistic at the 5% level of significance is in excess of 1.729. The acceptance region for the F-statistic at the 5% level of significance is in excess of 3.11.

Table D4. $\ln A$ on $\ln P$, $\ln R$, $\ln Q \Rightarrow \ln El$

Year	CNST	$\ln P$	$\ln R$	$\ln Q$	$\bar{R}^2$	F
1964	5.781	−0.507	0.205	−0.055	−.0089	0.947
	(2.17)	(0.90)	(0.99)	(0.41)		
1965	6.899	−0.777	0.016	0.019	.0258	1.159
	(3.485)	(1.68)	(0.08)	(0.13)		
1966	5.404	−0.572	0.151	0.0598	.0705	1.455
	(3.148)	(1.75)	(0.47)	(0.37)		
1967	5.36	−0.544	0.196	0.032	.0811	1.529
	(3.30)	(1.68)	(0.69)	(0.18)		
1968	6.078	−0.727	0.256	0.121	.1592	2.14
	(3.31)	(2.37)	(0.77)	(0.73)		
1969	8.38	−0.982	−0.562	0.186	.3905	4.844
	(4.59)	(3.81)	(1.38)	(1.32)		
1970	7.609	−0.897	0.477	0.222	.4626	6.164
	(5.42)	(4.25)	(1.61)	(1.69)		
1971	8.282	−0.929	−0.457	0.163	.4961	6.908
	(5.59)	(4.47)	(1.67)	(1.35)		
1972	−8.197	−0.910	−0.280	0.136	.4023	5.038
	(4.66)	(3.87)	(0.988)	(1.04)		

There were nineteen observations in every year. The acceptance region for the t-statistic at the 5% level of significance is in excess of 1.729. The acceptance region for the F-statistic at the 5% level of significance is in excess of 3.34.

Table D5. $\ln Y$ on $\ln P$, $\ln El$, $\ln R$, $\ln Q$

Year	CNST	$\ln P$	$\ln El$	$\ln R$	$\ln Q$	$\bar{R}^2$	F
1964	6.699	−0.142	0.306	0.068	−0.023	.6063	7.93
	(10.81)	(1.09)	(5.11)	(1.42)	(0.75)		
1965	7.433	−0.222	0.378	0.041	−0.019	.7013	11.56
	(15.96)	(2.04)	(6.22)	(0.90)	(0.53)		
1966	6.986	−0.115	0.387	0.116	−0.0097	.8103	20.22
	(22.40)	(1.94)	(8.24)	(2.02)	(0.33)		
1967	7.255	−0.138	0.448	0.136	−0.0256	.9076	45.2
	(35.34)	(2.98)	(12.17)	(3.36)	(1.04)		
1968	7.452	−0.207	0.391	0.075	0.0249	.9029	42.85
	(30.68)	(5.11)	(11.50)	(1.72)	(1.14)		
1969	8.377	−0.277	0.367	−0.160	0.042	.8251	22.23
	(24.22)	(5.67)	(7.51)	(2.07)	(1.56)		
1970	8.235	−0.233	0.377	−0.137	0.048	.8529	27.09
	(33.18)	(6.23)	(8.26)	(2.62)	(2.07)		
1971	8.318	−0.207	0.396	−0.0942	0.035	.7376	13.65
	(22.59)	(4.02)	(6.17)	(1.39)	(1.16)		
1972	8.282	−0.180	0.318	−0.015	0.021	.7698	16.05
	(25.81)	(4.20)	(6.74)	(0.29)	(0.85)		

There were nineteen observations in every year. The acceptance region for the t-statistic at the 5% level of significance is in excess of 1.729. The acceptance region for the F-statistic at the 5% level of significance is in excess of 3.18.

Table D8. *Partial correlation coefficients, 1967*

	1	2	3	4	5	6
1 ln Y	1					
2 ln P	−.3316	1				
3 ln QE	.8255	0	1			
4 ln R	.2814	−.1673	0	1		
5 ln Q	−.1552	.4537	0	.1766	1	
6 MONI	.5003	−.5512	0	.5503	−.3871	1

Table D9. $\ln DA$ on $\ln DP$, $\ln DR$, $\ln DQ$

Year	CNST	$\ln DP$	$\ln DR$	$\ln DQ$	$\bar{R}^2$	F
1964/5	0.015	0.050	0.011	−0.016	−.1442	0.244
	(1.13)	(0.65)	(0.30)	(0.36)		
1965/6	0.029	−0.123	0.005	0.696	.5007	7.018
	(1.66)	(1.72)	(0.21)	(3.40)		
1966/7	0.048	−0.220	−0.136	0.373	.2995	3.57
	(2.78)	(1.84)	(1.86)	(2.09)		
1967/8	0.010	−0.003	−0.06	0.911	.9004	55.24
	(0.91)	(0.20)	(1.57)	(9.95)		
1968/9	3.510	−0.483	0.181	−0.077	.3853	4.76
	(19.54)	(2.79)	(0.37)	(0.05)		
1969/70	0.023	−0.183	−0.120	0.381	.2659	3.18
	(0.58)	(1.01)	(1.41)	(1.29)		
1970/1	0.142	−0.325	0.205	0.136	.3014	3.59
	(2.93)	(2.17)	(2.60)	(0.89)		
1971/2	0.011	−0.143	−0.102	0.909	.8536	35.98
	(0.52)	(1.55)	(2.21)	(6.51)		

There were nineteen observations for each equation. The acceptance region for the t-statistic at the 5% level of significance is in excess of 1.729. The acceptance region for the F-statistic at the 5% level of significance is in excess of 3.18.

Table D10. *Rate of change of earnings equation* $\ln DY$ on $\ln DP$, $\ln DE$, $\ln DR$, $\ln DQ$

Year	CNST	$\ln DP$	$\ln DE$	$\ln DR$	$\ln DQ$	$\bar{R}^2$	F
1964/5	0.322	0.153	−0.147	−0.068	0.137	.4164	4.21
	(25.84)	(2.16)	(0.62)	(2.02)	(3.34)		
1965/6	0.287	0.041	0.462	0.021	0.240	.0201	1.09
	(13.61)	(0.48)	(1.49)	(0.72)	(0.98)		
1966/7	0.108	0.379	0.464	−0.501	0.620	.8210	21.64
	(11.61)	(5.91)	(3.35)	(0.13)	(6.44)		
1967/8	0.073	0.321	0.144	−0.113	0.187	−.0483	0.79
	(3.74)	(1.40)	(0.31)	(1.58)	(1.14)		
1968/9	0.120	0.153	−0.007	0.072	0.029	.3156	3.08
	(8.51)	(1.12)	(0.33)	(1.87)	(0.25)		
1969/70	0.109	0.197	0.339	0.018	0.290	.3271	3.19
	(5.11)	(2.06)	(2.48)	(0.39)	(1.84)		
1970/1	0.114	0.202	0.459	−0.097	0.284	−.0574	0.76
	(1.51)	(0.86)	(1.14)	(0.79)	(1.18)		
1971/2	0.088	0.234	0.077	−0.101	0.424	.2565	2.55
	(4.18)	(2.45)	(0.29)	(2.13)	(2.95)		

There were nineteen observations for each equation. The acceptance region for the t-statistic at the 5% level of significance is in excess of 1.729. The acceptance region for the F-statistic at the 5% level of significance is in excess of 3.18.

Table D11. $\ln Y$ on CNST, $\ln P$, $\ln QE$, $\ln R$, $\ln Q$, MONI: *1 year lag*

Year	CNST	$\ln P$	$\ln QE$	$\ln R$	$\ln Q$	MONI	$\bar{R}^2$	F
1965	6.558	−0.089	0.302	0.054	−0.018	0.003	.6864	8.87
	(8.29)	(0.57)	(4.92)	(1.05)	(0.58)	(2.34)		
1966	6.340	−0.039	0.390	−0.001	0.021	0.005	.8846	28.58
	(15.64)	(0.48)	(9.50)	(0.03)	(0.89)	(5.75)		
1967	6.715	−0.056	0.443	−0.107	0.020	0.005	.9012	33.83
	(23.86)	(1.11)	(10.93)	(1.71)	(0.75)	(5.05)		
1968	6.617	−0.052	0.383	0.004	0.023	0.004	.8622	23.51
	(20.84)	(0.93)	(0.07)	(0.07)	(0.75)	(3.49)		
1969	7.050	−0.082	0.340	−0.191	0.052	0.005	.8316	18.78
	(20.48)	(1.42)	(7.54)	(2.67)	(1.84)	(4.31)		
1970	8.053	−0.179	0.354	−0.297	0.060	0.003	.8424	20.28
	(22.13)	(3.25)	(7.32)	(3.79)	(2.41)	(3.01)		
1971	7.528	−0.104	0.417	−0.142	0.060	0.003	.7676	12.89
	(18.45)	(1.71)	(6.63)	(1.86)	(1.86)	(1.90)	(2.22)	
1972	7.885	−0.096	0.339	−0.151	0.032	0.003	.7412	11.31
	(19.43)	(1.63)	(5.98)	(2.34)	(1.23)	(1.99)		

There were nineteen observations for each equation. The acceptance region for the t-statistic at the 5% level of significance is in excess of 1.729. The acceptance region for the F-statistic at the 5% level of significance is in excess of 3.11.

Table D12. *Adjusted labour productivity cross-section time series runs*

CNST	$\ln P$	$\ln E1$	$\ln QE$	$\ln QE1$	$\ln R$	$\ln Q$	MONI	$\bar{R}^2$	F
−0.166	−0.089			0.361	0.025	0.017	0.003	.7042	81.92
(5.64)	(3.32)			(17.00)	(1.19)	(1.45)	(5.86)		
0	−0.169	0.369			0.065	0.003		.7022	101.2
(0)	(7.35)	(17.86)			(3.33)	(0.22)			
−0.157	−0.082		−0.352		0.278		0.003	.6984	99.40
(5.41)	(3.09)		(16.77)		(1.33)		(5.63)		

There were 171 observations for each regression. The acceptance region for the t-statistic (shown in brackets below the coefficient) at the 5% level of significance is in excess of 1.645. The acceptance region for the t-statistic at the 2.5% level of significance is in excess of 1.96. The acceptance region for the F-statistic at the 5% level of significance is in excess of 2.21 for the middle equation and 2.37 for the remainder.

Table D13. *Farrell cross-section time series runs*

CNST	ln P	ln A	ln R	ln Q	MONI	$\bar{R}^2$	F
−0.106	−0.060	0.253	0.037	0.007	0.002	.2773	14.04
(2.22)	(1.41)	(4.57)	(1.12)	(0.36)	(2.30)		
0	−0.103	0.290	0.062	−0.003		.2587	15.83
(0)	(2.68)	(5.38)	(2.01)	(0.18)			
−0.102	−0.057	0.256	0.038		0.002	.2811	17.62
(2.20)	(1.37)	(4.66)	(1.18)		(2.28)		

There were 171 observations for each year. The acceptance region for the t-statistic at the 5% level of significance is in excess of 1.645. The acceptance region for the t-statistic at the 2.5% level of significance is in excess of 1.96. The acceptance region for the F-statistic at the 5% level of significance is in excess of 2.21 for the middle equation and 2.37 for the remainder.

Table D14. *Partial correlation coefficients: Farrell cross-section time series data*

	$\ln Y$	$\ln P$	$\ln A$	$\ln R$	$\ln Q$	MONI
$\ln Y$	1					
$\ln P$	−.3611	1				
$\ln A$	.4572	−.3311	1			
$\ln R$	.2162	−.2205	.0926	1		
$\ln Q$	−.1012	.3191	−.0512	−.0345	1	
MONI	−.4316	−.5949	.3923	.3837	−.3309	1

7

Conclusions

The Yugoslavs have continuously experimented with institutional arrangements at the most fundamental level, arguably at no small cost to themselves in terms of development and growth. In the space of less than thirty years, the country has moved from the strict command principle via enterprise self-management with both decentralised planning and markets to a contractual planning system which acts with markets to link autonomous self-governing units within each cooperative. These reforms have stimulated widespread public interest, not least because they represent attempts to ensure that the economic system satisfies predetermined social and political goals, and in particular self-managing socialism.

The Yugoslavs' resourcefulness has also been a boon to students of comparative economic systems, who are rarely offered actual experiences of changes to the allocative mechanism. The resulting interest has spawned a large literature which fully describes the development of institutions and measures economic performance in various dimensions. However, few have explicitly based their work on economic models, and this was a central element in our study. One of our aims has been to investigate whether self-management theory, appropriately formulated for the Yugoslav environment, could provide a better understanding of how the Yugoslav economy actually operated between 1965 and 1974. Our findings have provided strong support for such a view, as well as being interesting in their own right.

Self-management models indicated that there might be interrelated inefficiencies in Yugoslav labour and product markets. These would be attributable to the relative weakness of labour market forces and the imperfections of the industrial structure. This analysis pointed us to descriptions of the Yugoslav market structure, the pattern of income differentials and the choice of technique over time. We found competitive pressures in Yugoslavia to be relatively weak, though, except in severely non-competitive sectors, such entry as there was took place in search of earnings. Income dispersion was shown to have widened considerably when market self-management was introduced, and the choice of technique to have become more capital-intensive and labour productive. We also confirmed the emergence of predicted associations between endogenous variables, such as incomes, concentration, capital-intensity and labour productivity. Finally, a formal model explaining inter-sectoral earnings differentials in terms of self-management theory was tested. This proved to offer a good explanation, and established the impact of product as well as labour market imperfections on Yugoslav earnings. These diverse strands of evidence were linked together by the theory in the first part of the book. Taken together, they indicated that self-management theory can help in understanding Yugoslav resource allocation between 1965 and 1974.

We shall conclude by considering some of the broader implications of the study. On the methodological front, the case for the more frequent use of formal models and hypothesis testing in comparative economics has hopefully been strengthened. Institutional and descriptive material has generally been more common in this area, but formal methods also have an important role to play. They can provide powerful insights into the operation of the economy, and lead to the discovery of hitherto unrecognised elements of economic behaviour. By defining an appropriate analytic framework, they can also permit conclusions beyond the initial scope of the study to be drawn. For example, our empirical work was guided by and vindicated the assumption that Yugoslavia is best described by models of imperfectly competitive self-management. Most Yugoslav analysts have stressed capital market imperfections as the main cause of allocative inefficiency, but our findings strongly indicate a role for imperfections in the labour market as well. Hence, policies based on the former view, such as taxing enterprises according to their capital stock, may prove to be severely inadequate. Similarly, our study points to the negative impact of monopoly power on resource allocation, a phenomenon generally understated or ignored in the Yugoslav literature. This suggests that the Yugoslavs might consider more stringent anti-trust legislation, and perhaps also encourage competitive forces via entry and exit. One could also use imperfectly competitive self-management models to simulate the effects of policy prescriptions, such as the role of planning agreements in reducing income differentials or of tax schemes to stimulate employment.

Finally, we must be careful not to draw misleading inferences from this study about either the Yugoslav economy or self-management itself. Some precise answers about the Yugoslav system have been generated, but only by restricting attention to very specific questions. For example, we have exclusively considered issues of static allocative efficiency, though Yugoslavia is a relatively less developed economy with severe regional disparities and macroeconomic imbalances. This means that, whatever else one might think of our findings, they cannot be a major element in an overall assessment of Yugoslav economic performance. In this we are limited by the state of the art in self-management theory, which currently only provides testable hypotheses about allocative issues. An obvious further step for researchers is therefore to develop and test more sophisticated self-management models, looking at the potentially more interesting questions of growth, capital accumulation, incentives and welfare. Similarly, our analysis has been too narrow to draw general conclusions about self-management as an economic system. It will be remembered that we did not consider any of the areas in which self-management might be expected to have had a beneficial impact, such as with respect to private motivation, productivity and communal welfare. Our study has certainly provided evidence for the existence of some expected negative effects. But the Yugoslavs' persistence with the system indicates that these may have been outweighted in practice by the perceived social benefits.

Notes

1. INTRODUCTION

1 Vanek (1970) forcefully argues that a self-managed economy will be relatively more competitive than its capitalist counterpart because each enterprise will generally be smaller.
2 Unsurprisingly, since it assumes away any link between allocative inefficiencies and self-management, this view is widely prevalent in Yugoslavia (e.g. Bajt, 1982).
3 See Estrin and Bartlett (1982) for a full survey of the 'capital school' approach and findings.

2. THE THEORY OF A SELF-MANAGED ECONOMY

1 Such firms will also be referred to as workers' cooperatives and labour-managed firms. Some authors (e.g. Vanek, 1975) try to draw a distinction between different types of self-managed firms according to the source of investment funds or degree of effective participation, but these are not relevant for our purposes. Other literature tends to focus discussion on the ownership aspect and non-economic decision-making (e.g. Hunnius, Garson and Case, 1973, Zwerdling, 1979).
2 Extensions to the case of heterogeneous labour and unequal distribution are conceptually simple but analytically cumbersome, and therefore not considered. Vanek (1970) and Ireland and Law (1982) show that equivalent results go through unaltered by the generalisation if a distribution schedule is chosen in advance.
3 See Jones (1974) on the British experience and Vanek (1971) for a critique of such enterprises.
4 They do produce different enterprise equilibrium configurations, and sometimes comparative static responses in the short-run, but these either cannot be discerned or will not be considered empirically.
5 The distinction between the 'uprovljanje' and 'rukovanje' systems.
6 We will point out in the text the occasions where our results cannot be extended from the restrictive to the general case.
7 Thus, at least around the enterprise equilibrium, it is assumed that the

Hessian of second order derivatives is negative semi-definite to fulfil the second order conditions for maximisation. Our analysis therefore only deals with necessary conditions, and assumes that sufficient conditions are satisfied. The reason for the unusual assumption of concavity only around the equilibrium, rather than throughout the range, is explained in the following section.

8 Since $\pi = pq - rK - wL$, $w + \frac{\pi}{L} = \frac{pq - rk}{L} = y$.

9 Thus, if $q = f(L, K)$, $\frac{\partial q}{\partial L} = f_L$, $\frac{\partial^2 q}{\partial L^2} = f_{LL}$, $\frac{\partial^2 q}{\partial K \partial L} = f_{KL}$, etc.

If $p = p(q, \Delta)$, $\frac{\partial p}{\partial q} = p_q$, $\frac{\partial p}{\partial \Delta} = p_\Delta$, etc.

10 $\frac{\partial R}{L} = \frac{\partial F}{\partial L}$ when $\frac{p}{L}\left(f_L - \frac{q}{L}\right) = \frac{-rK}{L^2}$ or $y = pf_L$.

This is the basis of the diagrammatic representation in Domar (1966) and Meade (1972).

11 We know $y = w + \pi/L$, and with every parameter and choice variable the same in each enterprise type, $y = w$ if $\pi = 0$.

12 Domar (1966), Vanek (1970) and Meade (1972) have stressed that the actual perversity of the short-run supply function, as distinct from sluggishness relative to capitalist counterparts, depends on the technical assumptions of the model. Although self-managed firms always respond less than comparable capitalist firms to changes in parameters, the production response to product price may be positive if there are multiple outputs, in which case resources will be shifted to the relatively more profitable commodity in the context of declining overall membership, or more than one variable input, when complementarity between factors may lead to an increase in employment. However, even in these cases earnings remain a function of the parameter set.

13 Thus Domar (1966) imposed a labour supply constraint within the collective, and Vanek (1970) and Meade (1972) looked to market level constraints. More recently, Ireland and Law (1978) studied an internal incentive scheme, and Bonin (1980) a short-time working scheme.

14 The perverse supply response can be eliminated under certain assumptions in a utility maximising framework: see Robinson (1967), Law (1977), Berman (1977), Estrin (1979).

15 Indeed, the concentration on short-run comparative statics in the theoretical literature may go some way towards explaining the widespread dissatisfaction with these models expressed by applied workers in this field (e.g. Jan Vanek, 1972; McCain, 1973). Researchers into actual cooperative behaviour have generally denied that such firms actually do reduce membership as cost or demand conditions improve. This may also explain why income maximising models have rarely provided the basis for empirical work on Yugoslav or Western cooperatives.

16 The long-run model discussed below is outlined in more detail in Estrin (1982a) and Estrin (1982b), and we only here refer to the aspects relevant for our later empirical work.

17 Domar (1966), Ireland and Law (1982) point out that these expressions describe the relative rates at which factor marginal products decline along a ray in capital–labour space, which is an alternative to the description provided below. Vanek (1970) relates the long-run supply curve to a 'locus of maximum physical efficiency' in capital–labour space, along which returns to scale equal unity. This is similar to the approach developed in the following sections, except that Vanek fails to identify the determinants of the slope of this locus, and therefore the conditions for positive supply responses. However, the results which follow can be regarded as a reinterpretation of existing material in the literature which permits an extension of the analysis.

18 Returns to scale are normally described as varying with output along a ray in capital–labour space (denoted $\lambda_{\bar{q}}$). It can be shown that second order conditions imply that $\lambda_{\bar{q}} < 0$ at the equilibrium, which drives the comparative static responses under capitalism. However, output responses under self-management also depend on how returns to scale vary with employment for a given level of output (and therefore, implicitly, capital) λ_L, and how they vary with output for a given level of employment, λ_q. This explains the unconventional parameterisation of production technology in equation (2.6).

19 As before, the results for technical advance which increase output for a given bundle of inputs are formally equivalent to these for an increase in product price.

20 For example, the assumption of homogeneity or homotheticity make the choice of technique independent of product price.

21 It should be noted that analytic or empirical work based on the assumption of homogeneous technology, such as Vanek and Jovicic (1975) and Jones and Backus (1977) cannot therefore be derived from income maximising micro-economic models.

22 This links to the interpretation of cooperative behaviour in the long run provided by Ireland and Law (1982).

23 It should be noted that the model could also permit the indirect estimation of the slope of the long-run cooperative supply curve by estimating production functions to determine the sign of the λ_L parameter. Data constraints mean that this line of argument will not be followed in the later chapters.

24 Since earnings equal the marginal value product of labour, these will not be equal unless workers of a given skill group earn the same in different sectors. Thus any change in parameters means that the Pareto conditions for the efficient allocation of labour are not satisfied.

25 It has been seen that the actual change in employment depends on λ_L as well as λ_q, so we cannot be sure that labour will be transferred in this way. Even so, the point remains that employment responses by existing firms *cannot* restore Pareto efficiency in the allocation of labour.

26 Interested readers are referred to Vanek (1970) and Meade (1974) for a

more detailed analysis. The method employed in this section is outlined more fully in Estrin (1982b).

27 $e = -p/qp_q$.

28 This is because the second order conditions require the revenue function, not the production function, to be locally concave, and the demand curve is downward sloping.

29 Uniqueness is derived from the monotonic shape of the functions, and comparability by the shape of the returns to scale function and the assumption that the ratio of price to marginal revenue equals unity when output equals zero. In fact, the monopolist can produce with either homogeneous technology (when λ is horizontal) or constant elasticity demand functions (when E is horizontal).

30 This situation would be approximated by the introduction of import controls in a country which had hitherto been small and open, and only had a single domestic producer of the product in question.

31 The analogous rearrangement in the competitive capitalist firm is

$$\lambda^{c*} = 1 - \frac{\pi^{c*}}{p^* q^*}.$$

32 The output response to an interest rate change continues to depend solely on λ_L since only the returns to scale function is affected, via the direct impact of relative factor costs on the desired capital–labour ratio.

33 If capital is rationed according to economic criteria, it merely slows the adjustment of enterprises to their long-run equilibrium positions.

3. THE YUGOSLAV ENVIRONMENT

1 Other economies, such as Peru and Algeria, have experimented with self-management in certain sectors or for short periods (see, for example, Clegg, 1971, and Vanek, 1975) and most developed economies contain some producer cooperatives (see, for example, Jones, 1974 for the UK) but Yugoslavia remains the only system-wide experiment of long duration.

2 The main ethnic groups are Serbs (41.7%), Croats (23.4%), Slovenes (8.8%), Macedonians (5.3%) and Montenegrins (2.8%), with minorities of Hungarians who live in the northern plains of Serbia (Vojvodina) and ethnic Moslems who live in the South (Kosovo). The six republics are Serbia, Croatia, Slovenia, Macedonia, Bosnia and Montenegro, each of which approximately contain their ethnic group except for Bosnia, which is mixed Serb and Croat. The two autonomous provinces for Hungarians and Moslems are in Serbia. The main languages are Serbo-Croat (which some nationalistic groups argue is two languages), Slovenian, Macedonian and Albanian; Slovenia and Croatia employ the Roman alphabet, while the remainder use cyrillic characters. The bulk of the North is Catholic (Slovenia, Croatia, Northern Serbia), while the southern groups are Serbian Orthodox or Muslim (World Bank, 1975).

3 'Yugoslavia' means the nation of the Southern Slavs.

4 The Communist Party changed its name to the League of Communists in 1952.
5 For data on inter-regional differences in the level of development, see Gregory (1973), World Bank (1975). The topic is considered in the discussion on underdevelopment below.
6 For example, some Western research accepts the official view that central planning was necessary for reconstruction after the war, and was successfully implemented until 1948, although it had outlived its usefulness after that date. However, there is some evidence to the contrary, which suggests that the plan was over-ambitious, inconsistent and relatively unsuccessful before 1948 (Waterson, 1962).
7 It is probably the poverty of the area, as much as the nationalist yearnings of the indigenous Albanians, which has contributed to the recent unrest in Kosovo. This is the sense in which economic and regional issues become inextricably linked in Yugoslavia.
8 The Yugoslav 'model' has caused considerable interest in other countries which are trying to remain socialist yet escape from Soviet influence, including Czechoslovakia before the invasion in 1968 and, most recently, China.
9 Some studies, for example Vanek (1973), Tyson (1980) and Sapir (1980a), are in the same general spirit as this work.
10 Marschak (1968) refers to post-war Yugoslavia as a 'laboratory'. In this section we outline the conditions under which the social 'experiments' were conducted.
11 Apart from the general legacies discussed above, the operation of the centrally planned system between 1946 and 1952 is not of central relevance to our study.
12 The title is derived from Neuberger (1970).
13 It is important to stress that the hiring of non-members as workers is illegal, although there are apprenticeships.
14 The Collective can use the Assets, and retain the income from them, but cannot freely dispose of them. See Furubotn and Pejovich (1972), Stephen (1979).
15 In 1960, some 77% of members of Councils, and their committees, were manual workers, though the largest proportion, an absolute majority (55%), were skilled workers. The representative shares were 67.5% for manual workers and 51% for skilled in 1970 (World Bank, 1975).
16 At various times he was appointed by the Commune, (Local Authority) Kormora (Economic Chambers) Workers' Council, or some combination of the three.
17 The Yugoslav distinction between 'upravljanje' and 'rubovanje'.
18 See Koloja (1964) on this point.
19 Thus, it operated as a wage bonus to a centrally determined income system.
20 In the early years, the relatively weak impact of self-management committees probably arose as much from the inexperience of the work force, in industrial work itself as much as self-management, than external constraints. In this context, it is worth remembering that

self-management was introduced from above, and appears to have aroused mainly indifference, or even hostility, at the grass roots.

4. YUGOSLAV INDUSTRIAL STRUCTURE

1 All references to tables in a particular appendix are denoted by the relevant letter and number, such as Table A1 for the first table in Appendix A.
2 There are no data in published Yugoslav sources on the number of small firms operating in the highly restricted private sector.
3 The coefficient of variation is the standard deviation divided by the mean.
4 The percentage of industry sales, capital assets or employment accounted for by the largest four producers.
5 The actual procedure is far more complicated since no one 'owns' Yugoslav self-managed firms. Thus, these 'mergers' are only semi-formal and take place through complex contractual arrangements on pricing, earnings and so forth.
6 There is no information which would permit an explanation of the inconsistency between the series; presumably, in addition to double counting, enterprises are actually defined differently in the three sources.

5. SOME CONSEQUENCES OF SELF-MANAGEMENT

1 Some of this material has already appeared in Estrin (1981).
2 Some of this material was published in Estrin (1982c).
3 Incomes in the film industry proved to be an extreme observation and were therefore omitted from measures of dispersion unless otherwise stated.
4 Defined as the total wage bill divided by the labour force in each sector or industry.
5 The table is constructed from data in the OECD, *Wages and Labour Mobility*; UN, *Incomes in Post-War Europe*; French Ministry of Labour Quarterly Survey of Wages and Employment; Swedish Social Board Statistics; and Reynolds and Taft (1956).
6 The data were derived from the relevant *Statistical Yearbooks* for each country.
7 Except for the Soviet Union, where size and regional elements were important, and Bulgaria, where dispersion was rapidly declining.
8 The data were derived from the relevant *Statistical Yearbooks.*
9 Urban incomes are proxied by the average net personal receipts per annum in the social sector, which includes non-industrial and non-urban activities such as collective farms. Rural incomes are proxied by the average annual incomes from private land holdings per household, divided by three on the assumption that each agricultural household contains three adult equivalents. They are deflated by indices of producer prices and actually derived from Bartlett (1980). There is no consistent information prior to 1957.

6. AN EXPLANATION OF YUGOSLAV INCOME DIFFERENTIALS

1 Some preliminary findings from a related model are reported in Estrin (1979).
2 In fact, some entirely new notation is introduced where relevant in this chapter.
3 Minimum efficient scale increases as θ declines.

4 $$\text{CNST}_1 = \frac{\beta}{\alpha}\ln\left(\frac{\alpha}{\alpha+\beta}\right) + \ln\left(\frac{\alpha}{\alpha+\beta}\right) - \frac{\alpha+\beta-1}{\alpha}.$$

5 $$\text{CNST}_2 = \frac{\beta}{\alpha}\ln\left(\frac{\beta}{\alpha+\beta}\right) + \ln\left(\frac{\alpha}{\alpha+\beta}\right) + \frac{1}{\alpha}.$$

6 The assumption is made because we do not have data to calculate demand elasticities and it implies that the equations are estimated with an omitted variable. In consequence, the estimator on the constraint will be biased and inconsistent, though if the omitted variable is orthogonal to the remaining independent variables, their estimators will be unbiased. The elasticity of demand by sector should have no obvious association with the other independent variables. However, estimators of the variance of the remaining coefficients will be biased upwards, so significance tests will be relatively conservative.
7 $\gamma_0 = \text{CNST}_2 - (\alpha+\beta)/\alpha(\Sigma+1)$; $\gamma_1 = (\alpha+\beta)/\alpha$; $\gamma_2 = 1/\alpha$; $\gamma_3 = -\beta/\alpha$; $\gamma_4 = (\alpha+\beta-1)/\alpha$; $\gamma_5 = (\alpha+\beta)/\alpha$. The Cobb-Douglas factor weights are over-identified.
8 The competitive equation is the same except for the exclusion of M_i and a different constant.
9 The perverse sign of relative prices may be due to problems with data series, which measured prices relative to a Visible Hand base year. The Reforms in 1961 and 1965 involved relative price restructuring, and this could explain the negative association with incomes if the authorities had hitherto favoured efficient and concentrated sectors in price setting. Thus, although relative prices did increase in some sectors such as building or printing because of demand, the effect could have been swamped by price reductions in concentrated, efficient sectors, such as oil, and price increases in poorly paid industries, such as textiles.
10 The regressions fitted best in this year, but the structure of correlation coefficients was relatively stable over time, except for the scale parameter.
11 One, two and three year lags on each and all the independent variables were all statistically insignificant and F-tests supported their exclusion from the equations.
12 Dividing the period into two halves and into three sub-periods; 1964–6, 1966–70 and 1970–2.
13 The earnings, price and rate of interest series were adjusted to eliminate any trend due to inflation. The remaining series were in constant 1966 prices.

14 As for annual cross-section runs, the inclusion of lags did not improve the fit for the whole data set.

15 Estrin (1979) reports the results from annual cross-section regressions on this data set. The explanation had the familiar pattern over time, but the $\bar{R}^2$ only reached .44 in any one year. In general, one cannot accept the exclusion of the concentration ratio, but does accept the exclusion of the scale parameter. The rate of change of earnings equations provided good fits in some years, with an $\bar{R}^2$ of .8 in 1966/7 and all the variables except the interest rate being significant and displaying the predicted sign.

Bibliography

The bibliography referring solely to Yugoslavia is contained in a separate reference section.

Arrow, K. J. (1963) *Social Choice and Individual Values*, 2nd edn, Wiley, New York.

Atkinson, A. B. (1973) 'Worker Management and the Modern Industrial Enterprise', *Quarterly Journal of Economics*, Vol. 87, pp. 375–92.

Bajt, A. (1971) 'Investment Cycles in European Socialist Economies: A Review Article', *Journal of Economic Literature*, Vol. 9, pp. 53–63.

(1982) 'The Girl in Illyria', Paper presented to the Second International Conference on the Economics of Self-Management, forthcoming, *Economic Analysis and Workers Management.*

Balassa, B. and T. J. Bertrand (1970) 'Growth Performance of Eastern European Countries', *American Economic Review*, Papers and Proceedings, Vol. 60, pp. 314–20.

Barkai, H. (1977) *Growth Patterns of the Kibbutz Economy*, North-Holland, New York.

Bartlett, W. J. (1979) *Economic Development, Institutional Reform and Unemployment in Yugoslavia, 1945–1975*, PhD Thesis, Liverpool University.

(1980) 'A Structural Model of Unemployment in Yugoslavia – An Alternative to the Institutional Hypothesis', mimeo, University of Southampton.

Berman, M. D. (1977) 'Short Run Efficiency in the Labour Managed Firm', *Journal of Comparative Economics*, Vol 1, pp. 304–14.

Bonin, J. P. (1980) 'Optimal Membership and Contractual Employment in a Cooperative with Implications for Output Supply in an Uncertain Environment', mimeo, Birkbeck College.

(1982) 'Optimal Employment Policies for a Multiperiod Labour Managed Socialist Cooperative', forthcoming, *Jahrbuck für Wirstschaft Osteuropas.*

Cable, J. and F. Fitzroy (1980) 'Productivity, Efficiency, Incentives and Employee Participation: Some Preliminary Results for West Germany', *Kyklos*, Vol. 33, pp. 100–21.

Cave, M. and P. Hare (1981) *Alternative Approaches to Economic Planning*, Macmillan, London.

Chenery, H., M. S. Ahluwalia, G. L. G. Bell, J. H. Duloy and R. Jolly (1974) *Redistribution with Growth*, Oxford University Press, Oxford.

Clayre, A. (ed.) (1980) *The Political Economy of Cooperation and Participation*, Oxford University Press, Oxford.

Clegg, I. (1971) *Workers' Self-Management in Algeria*, Allen Lane, London.

Cowling, K. and M. Waterson (1976) 'Price-Cost Margins and Market Structure', *Economica*, Vol. 43, pp. 267–74.

Coyne, J., B. Chiplin and L. Sirc (1977) *Can Workers Manage?*, Hobart Paper 77, Institute of Economic Affairs, London.

Cullen, J. (1956) 'The Inter-Industry Wages Structure 1899–1950', *American Economic Review*, Vol. 46, pp. 353–69.

Dirlam, J. B. (1968) 'Problems of Market Power and Public Policy in Yugoslavia', in *Economic Concentration*, US Senate, Sub-committee on Anti-Trust and Monopoly, Committee on the Judiciary, 90th Cong., 2nd Session, Part 7, pp. 3758–85.

Domar, E. (1966) 'The Soviet Collective Farm as a Producer Co-Operative', *American Economic Review*, Vol. 56, pp. 734–57.

Drèze, J. H. (1974) 'The Pure Theory of Labour-Managed and Participatory Economies Part 1: Certainty', Centre for Operations Research and Econometrics, Université Catholique de Louvain Discussion Paper No. 7422.

(1976) 'Some Theory of Labour-Management and Participation', *Econometrica*, Vol. 44, No. 6, pp. 1125–39.

Drutter, I. (1964) *Seller Concentration of Some Industrial Products in 1959 and 1962*, Zagreb, reported in Dirlam (1968).

Dubravcic, D. (1970) 'Labour as Entrepreneurial Input: An Essay in the Theory of the Producer Co-Operative Economy', *Economica*, Vol. 37, pp. 297–310.

EEC, *Social Statistics in Europe: Labour Costs in Industry*, 1972 and 1975.

Estrin, S. (1979) 'An Explanation of Earnings Variation in the Yugoslav Self-Managed Economy', *Economic Analysis and Workers' Management*, Vol. 13, pp. 175–99.

(1981) 'Income Dispersion in a Self-Managed Economy', *Economica*, Vol. 48, pp. 181–94.

(1982a) 'Long Run Responses Under Self-Management', Cornell University Department of Economics Working Paper No. 272, forthcoming, *Journal of Comparative Economics*.

(1982b) 'Self-Managed and Capitalist Behaviour in Alternative Market Structures', Cornell University Department of Economics Working Paper No. 273.

(1982c) 'The Effects of Self-Management on Yugoslav Industrial Growth', *Soviet Studies*, Vol. 34, pp. 69–85.

Estrin, S. and W. J. Bartlett (1982) 'The Effects of Enterprise Self-Management in Yugoslavia: An Empirical Survey', in Jones and Svejnar (eds.) (1982).

Estrin, S. and P. M. Holmes (1983) *French Planning in Theory and Practice*, forthcoming, George Allen and Unwin, London.

Farrell, M. J. (1957) 'The Measurement of Productive Efficiency', *Journal of the Royal Statistical Society* (A), Vol. 120, pp. 253–81.

Ferguson, C. E. and S. C. Maurice (1972) 'Factor Usage by a Labour-Managed Firm in a Socialist Economy', *Economica*, Vol. 39, pp. 18–31.

Furubotn, E. G. (1976) 'The Long Run Analysis of the Labour-Managed Firm: An Alternative Interpretation', *American Economic Review*, Vol. 66, pp. 104–23.

Furubotn, E. G. and S. Pejovich (1970) 'Property Rights and Behaviour of the Firm in a Socialist State: The Example of Yugoslavia', *Zeitschrift für Nationalökonomie*, pp. 431–54.

(1972) 'Property Rights and Economic Theory: A Survey of Recent Literature', *Journal of Economic Literature*, Vol. 10, pp. 1137–63.

Galenson, W. and A. Fox (1967) 'Earnings and Employment in Eastern Europe', *Quarterly Journal of Economics*, Vol. 81, pp. 220–40.

Hannah, L. and J. A. Kay (1977) *Concentration in Modern Industry*, Macmillan, London.

Hare, P. G. (1977) 'Economic Reforms in Hungary: Problems and Prospects', *Cambridge Journal of Economics*, Vol. 1, pp. 317–33.

Hitiris, T. (1978) 'Effective Protection and Economic Performance in U.K. Manufacturing Industry 1963 and 1968', *Economic Journal*, Vol. 88, pp. 107–120.

Horvat, B. (1971a) 'Yugoslav Economic Policy in the Post-War Period', *American Economic Review*, Vol. 61 (supplement), pp. 71–169.

(1971b) 'Business Cycles in Yugoslavia', *Eastern European Economics*, Vol. 9, pp. 1–259.

Hunnius, G., G. D. Garson and J. Case (1973) *Workers Control: A Reader on Labour and Social Change*, Vintage Books, Random House, New York.

Ireland, N. J. (1981) 'The Labour-Managed Firm and Disutility from Supplying Factor Services', *Economic Analysis and Workers' Management*, Vol. 15, pp. 21–43.

Ireland, N. J. and P. J. Law (1978) 'An Enterprise Incentive Fund for Labour Mobility in a Cooperative Economy', *Economica*, Vol. 45, pp. 143–51.

(1982) *Economic Analysis of Labour-Managed Enterprises*, Croom Helm, London.

Itchiishi, T. (1980) 'Management Versus Ownership, 1', mimeo, University of Iowa.

(1981) 'A Social Coalitional Equilibrium Existence Lemma', *Econometrica*, Vol. 49, No. 2, pp. 369–79.

Jones, D. C. (1974) 'The Economics of British Producer Co-Operatives', Unpublished PhD Dissertation, Cornell University.

Jones, D. C. and D. K. Backus (1977) 'British Producer Cooperatives in the Footwear Industry: An Empirical Evaluation of the Theory of Financing', *Economic Journal*, Vol. 87, pp. 488–510.

Jones, D. C. and J. Svejnar (eds.) (1982) *Participatory and Self-Managed Firms: Evaluating Economic Performance*, Lexington Books, Lexington, Massachusetts.

Jorgensen, D. W. and J. M. Brundy (1971) 'Efficient Estimation of Simultaneous Equations by Instrumental Variables', *Review of Economics and Statistics*, Vol. 53, pp. 207–25.

Kmenta, J. (1971) *Elements of Econometrics*, Macmillan, London.

Law, P. J. (1977) 'The Illyrian Firm and Fellner's Union-Management Model', *Journal of Economic Studies*, Vol. 4, pp. 29–37.

Lewis, A. (1954), 'Development with Unlimited Supplies of Labour', *The Manchester School*, Vol. 22, pp. 139–92.

Manne, H. G. (1975) *The Economics of Legal Relationships*, West Publishing, New York.

Marschak, T. (1968) 'Centralised Versus Decentralised Resource Allocation', *Quarterly Journal of Economics*, Vol. 82, pp. 561–87.

Massé, P. (1965) 'The French Plan and Economic Theory', *Econometrica*, Vol. 33, No. 2, pp. 265–76.

McCain, R. (1973) 'Critical Notes on Illyrian Economics', *Kyklos*, Vol. 26, pp. 380–6.

Meade, J. E. (1970) *The Theory of Indicative Planning*, Manchester University Press, Manchester.

(1972) 'TheTheory of Labour-Managed Firms and of Profit Sharing', *Economic Journal* (Special Issue in honour of E. A. G. Robinson), pp. 402–28.

(1974) 'Labour-Managed Firms in Conditions of Imperfect Competition', *Economic Journal*, Vol. 84, pp. 817–25.

OECD, *Wages and Labour Mobility*, 1965.

Pearce, I. F. (1977) 'Participation and Income Distribution', in D. F. Heathfield (ed.), *The Economics of Co-Determination*, Macmillan, London.

Rannis, G. and J. C. H. Fei (1961) 'A Theory of Economic Development', *American Economic Review*, Vol. 51, pp. 533–65.

Reynolds, L. G. and C. H. Taft (1956) *The Evolution of Wage Structures*, Yale University Press, New Haven.

Rivera-Batiz, F. L. (1980) 'The Capital Market in Yugoslavia: A Theoretical and Empirical Note', *Quarterly Journal of Economics*, Vol. 44, pp. 179–84.

Robinson, J. (1967) 'The Soviet Collective Farm as a Producer Co-operative', *American Economic Review*, Vol. 57, pp. 222–3.

Sapir, A. (1980a) 'Economic Growth and Factor Substitution: Whatever Happened to the Yugoslav Miracle?', *Economic Journal*, Vol. 90, pp. 294–313.

(1980b) 'A Growth Model for a Tenured Labour-Managed Firm', *Quarterly Journal of Economics*, Vol. 95, pp. 387–402.

Sawyer, M. C. and S. Aaronovitch (1975) 'The Concentration of British Manufacturing', *Lloyds Bank Review*, January, pp. 14–23.

Scherer, F. M. (1980) *Industrial Market Structure and Economic Performance*, 2nd edn, Rand McNally, Chicago.

Sen, A. K. (1966) 'Labour Allocation in a Co-Operative Enterprise', *Review of Economic Studies*, Vol. 33, pp. 361–71.

Smith, S. C. (1982) 'The Maximising Behaviour of a Labour-Managed Firm: A (Testable) Reformulation', mimeo, Cornell University.

Staellerts, R. (1981) 'The Effects of Capital Intensity on Income in Yugoslav Industry', *Economic Analysis and Workers' Management*, Vol. 15, pp. 501–16.

Starrett, D. A. (1977) 'Measuring Returns to Scale in the Aggregate and the Scale Effect of Public Goods', *Econometrica*, Vol. 45, No. 6, pp. 1439–55.

Stephen, F. H. (1978) 'Bank Credit and Investment by the Yugoslav Firm', *Economic Analysis and Workers' Management*, Vol. 12, pp. 221–40.

(1979) 'Property Rights and the Labour-Managed Firm in the Long Run', *Economic Analysis and Workers' Management*, Vol. 13, pp. 149–66.

(1980) 'Bank Credit and the Labour-Managed Firm: Comment', *American Economic Review*, Vol. 70, pp. 796–9.

Thomas, H. and C. Logan (1982) *Mondragon: An Economic Analysis*, George Allen and Unwin, London.

Tyson, L. D'A. (1977a) 'A Permanent Income Hypothesis for the Yugoslav Firm', *Economica*, Vol. 44, pp. 393–408.

UN, *Incomes In Post-War Europe*, 1967.

US, *Employment and Earnings*, 1973.

Vanek, J. (1969) 'Decentralisation Under Workers' Management: A Theoretical Appraisal', *American Economic Review*, Vol. 59, pp. 1006–14.

(1970) *The General Theory of Labour-Managed Market Economies*, Cornell University Press, Ithaca, New York.

(1971) *The Participatory Economy: An Evolutionary Hypothesis and a Development Strategy*, Cornell University Press, Ithaca, New York.

(1973) 'The Yugoslav Economy Viewed Through the Theory of Labour-Management', *World Development*, Vol. 1, No. 9, reprinted in Vanek (1977).

(1975) *Self-Management: Economic Liberation of Man*, Penguin, London.

(1977) *The Labour-Managed Economy*, Cornell University Press, Ithaca, New York.

Vanek, J. and M. Jovicic (1975) 'The Capital Market and Income Distribution in Yugoslavia', *Quarterly Journal of Economics*, Vol. 89, pp. 432–43.

Ward, B. M. (1958) 'The Firm in Illyria: Market Syndicalism', *American Economic Review*, Vol. 48, pp. 566–89.

Wiles, P. J. (1962) *The Political Economy of Communism*, Basil Blackwell, Oxford.

Zellner, A. and N. S. Revankar (1969) 'Generalised Production Functions', *Review of Economic Studies*, Vol. 36, pp. 241–9.

Zwerdling, D. (1979) *Workplace Democracy*, Harper Colophon, Harper and Row, New York.

Yugoslav bibliography

Absees, Soviet and East European Abstract Series, 1974–1978.

Adizes, I. (1971) *Industrial Democracy: Yugoslav Style*, Free Press, New York.

Amacher, R. C. (1972) *Yugoslavia's Foreign Trade*, Praeger, New York.

Auty, P. (1974) *Tito*, revised edn, Penguin, London.

Bajt, A. (1967a) 'Decentralised Decision-Making in the Yugoslav Economy', *Economics of Planning*, Vol. 7, pp. 73–85.

(1967b) 'Yugoslav Economic Reforms, Monetary and Production Mechanisms', *Economics of Planning*, Vol. 7, pp. 201–18.

(1971) 'Investment Cycles in European Socialist Economies: A Review Article', *Journal of Economic Literature*, Vol. 9, pp. 53–63.

Bićanić, R. (1973) *Economic Policy in Socialist Yugoslavia*, Cambridge University Press, Cambridge.

Broeckmeyer, M. J. (1970) *Yugoslav Workers' Self-Management*, Dordrecht, Holland.

Comisso, E. T. (1979) *Workers' Control Under Plan and Market*, Yale University Press, New Haven.

(1980) 'Yugoslavia in the 1970s: Self-Management and Bargaining', *Journal of Comparative Economics*, Vol. 4, pp. 192–208.

Department of Employment Gazette (1976) 'The Self-Managed System in Yugoslavia', March.

Dirlam, J. B. and J. C. Plummer (1973) *An Introduction to the Yugoslav Economy*, Merrill, Columbus, Ohio.

Dmitrijevich, D. and G. Macesich (1973) *Money and Finance in Contemporary Yugoslavia*, Praeger, New York.

Drace, D. (1970) 'The Development of Agriculture 1945–1970', *Yugoslav Survey*.

Estrin, S. and W. J. Bartlett (1982) 'The Effects of Self-Management in Yugoslavia: An Empirical Survey', in Jones and Svejnar (eds.) (1982).

Furubotn, E. and S. Pejovich (1976) 'Tax Policy and Investment Decisions of Yugoslav Firms', *National Tax Journal*, pp. 335–48.

Gorupic, D. and I. Paj (1970) *Workers' Self-Management in Yugoslavia*, Economics Institute, Zagreb.

Granick, D. (1975) *Enterprise Guidance in Eastern Europe*, Princeton University Press, Princeton, New Jersey.

Gregory, M. B. (1973) 'Regional Development in Yugoslavia', *Soviet Studies*, Vol. 25, pp. 213–28.

Hauvonen, J. J. (1970) 'Post-War Developments in Money and Banking in Yugoslavia', *I. M. F. Staff Papers*, Vol. 17, pp. 563–601.

Hoffman, G. H. and F. W. Neal (1962) *Yugoslavia and the New Communism*, Twentieth Century Fund, New York.

Horvat, B. (1969) *An Essay on Yugoslav Society*, International Arts and Sciences Press, White Plains, New York.

(1971a) 'Yugoslav Economic Policy in the Post-War Period', *American Economic Review*, Vol. 61 (supplement), pp. 71–169.

(1977) *The Yugoslav Economic System: The First Labour-Managed Economy in the Making*, International Arts and Sciences Press, White Plains, New York.

Horvat, B., R. Supek and S. Markovic (1976) *Self-Governing Socialism*, Vols. 1 and 2, International Arts and Sciences Press, White Plains, New York.

International Labour Organisation (1962) *Workers' Management in Yugoslavia*, Geneva.

Kavcic, B., V. Rus and A. Tannenbaum (1971) 'Control, Participation and Effectiveness in Four Yugoslav Industrial Organisations', *Administrative Science Quarterly*, Vol. 16, pp. 74–86.

Koloja, J. (1964) *Workers' Councils: The Yugoslav Experience*, Praeger, New York.

Macesich, G. (1964) *Yugoslavia: The Theory and Practice of Development Planning*, University Press of Virginia, Charlottesville.

Mieczkowski, B. (1976) *Personal and Social Consumption in Eastern Europe*, Praeger, New York.

Milenkovitch, D. D. (1971) *Plan and Market in Yugoslav Economic Thought*, Yale University Press, New Haven.

Miovic, P. (1975) *Determinants of Income Differentials in Yugoslav Self-Managed Enterprises*, PhD Dissertation, University of Pennsylvania.

Moore, J. H. (1980) *Growth with Self-Management: Yugoslav Industrialisation, 1952–1975*, Hoover Institution Press, Stanford, California.

Neuberger, E. (1959) 'Yugoslav Investment Auctions', *Journal of Political Economy*, pp. 88–115.

(1970) 'The Yugoslav Visible Hand System: Why Is It No More?', State University of New York at Stony Brook, Department of Economics Working Paper No. 23.

Neuberger, E. and E. James (1973) 'The Yugoslav Self-Managed Firm: A Systematic Approach', in M. Bornstein (ed.) *Plan and Market*, Yale University Press, New Haven.

Obradovic, J. (1978) 'Participation in Enterprise Decision-Making', in Obradovic and Dunn (eds.) (1978).

Obradovic, J. and W. N. Dunn (eds.) (1978) *Workers' Self-Management and Organisational Power in Yugoslavia*. University of Pittsburgh, Center for International Studies.

OECD, *Country Yearbooks on Yugoslavia*, 1970–80.

Pavlowitch, S. (1971) *Yugoslavia*, Praeger, New York.

Pejovich, S. (1966) *The Market Planned Economy of Yugoslavia*, University of Minnesota Press, Minneapolis.

Popov, S. (1970) 'Intersectoral Relations of Personal Incomes', *Yugoslav Survey*.

Popov, S. and M. Jovicic (1971) *Uticaj Licnih Dohodaka na Kretanja Cena*, Institut Ekonomskih Nauka, Belgrade.

Ross-Johnson, A. (1972) *The Transformation of Communist Ideology: The Yugoslav Case 1945–1953*, Cambridge, Massachusetts.

Rus, V. (1978) 'Enterprise Power Structure', in Obradovic and Dunn (eds.) (1978).

Rusinow, D. (1977) *The Yugoslav Experiment 1948–1974*, for the Royal Institute of International Affairs, Hurst, London.

Sacks, S. R. (1972) 'Changes in Industrial Structure in Yugoslavia, 1959–1968', *Journal of Political Economy*, Vol. 80, pp. 561–74.

(1973) *Entry of New Competitors in Yugoslav Market Socialism*, Institute of International Studies, University of California, Berkeley, Research Series No. 19.

(1980) 'Divisionalisation in Large Yugoslav Enterprises', *Journal of Comparative Economics*, Vol. 4, pp. 209–25.

(1982) 'Large Enterprises Under Yugoslav Self-Management', unpublished manuscript.

Sapir, A. (1980a) 'Economic Growth and Factor Substitution: Whatever Happened to the Yugoslav Miracle?', *Economic Journal*, Vol. 90, pp. 294–313.

Schrenk, M., C. Ardalan and N. El Tatawy (1979) *Yugoslavia: Self-Management Socialism and the Challenges of Development*, Johns Hopkins Press, Baltimore.

Sirc, L. (1979) *The Yugoslav Economy Under Self-Management*, Macmillan, London.

Staellerts, R. (1981) 'The Effects of Capital Intensity on Income in Yugoslav Industry', *Economic Analysis and Workers' Management*, Vol. 15, pp. 501–16.

Tornquist, D. (1966) *Look East, Look West*, Macmillan, London.

Tyson, L. D'A. (1977a) 'A Permanent Income Hypothesis for the Yugoslav Firm', *Economica*, Vol. 44, pp. 393–408.

(1977b) 'Liquidity Crises in the Yugoslav Economy: An Alternative to Bankruptcy?', *Soviet Studies*, Vol. 29, pp. 284–95.

(1980) *The Yugoslav Economy and Its Performance in the 1970s*, Institute of International Studies, Berkeley, California.

Vanek, Jan (1972) *The Economics of Workers' Management: A Yugoslav Case Study*, George Allen and Unwin, London.

Vanek, J. (1973) 'The Yugoslav Economy Viewed Through the Theory of Labor-Management', *World Development*, Vol. 1, No. 9.

Vanek, J. and M. Jovicic (1975) 'The Capital Market and Income Distribution in Yugoslavia', *Quarterly Journal of Economics*, Vol. 89, pp. 432–43.

Wachtel, H. M. (1973) *Workers' Management and Wages in Yugoslavia*, Cornell University Press, Ithaca, New York.

Ward, B. (1965) 'The Nationalised Firm in Yugoslavia', *American Economic Review*, Vol. 55 (Papers and Proceedings), pp. 65–75.

Warner, M. (1975) 'Whither Yugoslav Self-Management?', *Industrial Relations Journal*, Vol. 6, pp. 65–72.

Waterson, A. (1962) *Planning in Yugoslavia*, Johns Hopkins Press, Baltimore.

Wedge, M. (1976) 'Strikes in Yugoslavia: Their Causes and Consequences', unpublished mimeo.

World Bank (1975) *Yugoslavia: Development with Decentralisation*, Johns Hopkins University Press, Baltimore.

Zaninovich, M. G. (1968) *The Development of Socialist Yugoslavia*, Johns Hopkins University Press, Baltimore.

Zupanov, J. (1967) 'The Producer and Risk', *Ekonomist*, No. 3.

Index

SOVIET AND EAST EUROPEAN STUDIES

Books in the series

A. Boltho *Foreign Trade Criteria in Socialist Economies*
Sheila Fitzpatrick *The Commissariat of Enlightenment*
P. Wiles, ed. *The Prediction of Communist Economic Performance*
Galia Golan *The Czechoslovak Reform Movement*
Naum Jasny *Soviet Economists of the Twenties*
Asha L. Datar *India's Relations with the USSR and Eastern Europe, 1953–1969*
T. M. Podolski *Socialist Banking and Monetary Control*
Rudolf Bićanić *Economic Policy in Socialist Yugoslavia*
G. Hosking *The Russian Constitutional Experiment: Government and Duma 1907–14*
A. Teichova *An Economic Background to Munich*
J. Ciechanowski *The Warsaw Rising of 1944*
Edward A. Hewett *Foreign Trade Prices in the Council for Mutual Economic Assistance*
Daniel P. Calhoun *The United Front: the TUC and the Russians 1923–28*
Galia Golan *Yom Kippur and After: the Soviet Union and the Middle East Crisis*
Maureen Perrie *The Agrarian Policy of the Russian Socialist-Revolutionary Party from its Origins through the Revolutions of 1905–1907*
Gabriel Gorodetsky *The Precarious Truce: Anglo-Soviet Relations 1924–27*
Paul Vyšný *Neo-Slavism and the Czechs 1898–1914*
James Riordan *Sport in Soviet Society: Development of Sport and Physical Education in Russia and the USSR*
Gregory Walker *Soviet Book Publishing Policy*
Felicity Ann O'Dell *Socialisation through Children's Literature: The Soviet Example*
Stella Alexander *Church and State in Yugoslavia since 1945*
Sheila Fitzpatrick *Education and Social Mobility in the Soviet Union 1921–1934*
T. H. Rigby *Lenin's Government: Sovnarkom 1917–1922*
M. Cave *Computers and Economic Planning: The Soviet Experience*
Jozef M. van Brabant *Socialist Economic Integration: Aspects of Contemporary Economic Problems in Eastern Europe*
R. F. Leslie, ed. *The History of Poland since 1863*
M. R. Myant *Socialism and Democracy in Czechoslovakia, 1945–1948*
Blair A. Ruble *Soviet Trade Unions: Their Development in the 1970s*
Angela Stent *From Embargo to Ostpolitik: The Political Economy of West German–Soviet Relations 1955–1980*
Jean Woodall *The Socialist Corporation and Technocratic Power: The Polish United Workers' Party, Industrial Organisation and Workforce Control, 1958–1980*

William J. Conyngham *The Modernization of Soviet Industrial Management: Socioeconomic Development and the Search for Viability*
Israel Getzler *Kronstadt 1917–1921: The Fate of a Soviet Democracy*
S. A. Smith *Red Petrograd: Revolution in the Factories, 1917–1918*
David A. Dyker *The Process of Investment in the Soviet Union*

DATE DUE